"If Israel should ever fail to protect her own, she would cease to have meaning. We have been forced into aggressive defense and the stakes keep getting higher.

"In the end, we may have to choose between action that might pull down the Temple of Humanity itself rather than surrender even a single member of the family to the executioners.

"Survival in other circumstances is not survival at all. And all of us, whatever our race, won't be worth a damn if we buy our lives at the cost of our conscience."

> Yerucham Amitai, Former Deputy
> Chief, Israeli Air Force.
> From a conversation with
> William Stevenson while flying
> over the Temple of Solomon,
> March 1970

90

MINUTES
AT ENTEBBE

THE FULL INSIDE STORY OF THE SPECTACULAR ISRAELI COUNTER-TERRORISM STRIKE AND THE DARING RESCUE OF 103 HOSTAGES

WILLIAM
STEVENSON

AUTHOR OF *A MAN CALLED INTREPID*

WITH URI DAN

Skyhorse Publishing

To the memory of Yerucham Amitai

Copyright © 1976 by William Stevenson

First Skyhorse Publishing edition 2015

All rights reserved. No part of this book may be reproduced in any manner without the express written consent of the publisher, except in the case of brief excerpts in critical reviews or articles. All inquiries should be addressed to Skyhorse Publishing, 307 West 36th Street, 11th Floor, New York, NY 10018.

Skyhorse Publishing books may be purchased in bulk at special discounts for sales promotion, corporate gifts, fund-raising, or educational purposes. Special editions can also be created to specifications. For details, contact the Special Sales Department, Skyhorse Publishing, 307 West 36th Street, 11th Floor, New York, NY 10018 or info@skyhorsepublishing.com.

Skyhorse® and Skyhorse Publishing® are registered trademarks of Skyhorse Publishing, Inc.®, a Delaware corporation.

Visit our website at www.skyhorsepublishing.com.

10 9 8 7 6 5 4 3

Library of Congress Cataloging-in-Publication Data is available on file.

Cover design by Rain Saukas

Print ISBN: 978-1-62914-442-9
Ebook ISBN: 978-1-62914-849-6

Printed in China

CONTENTS

INTRODUCTION

During the first hour of Sunday, July 4, 1976, a raiding party escaped from the heart of Africa with more than a hundred hostages held by a black dictator. Operation Thunderbolt struck across 2500 miles with airborne commandos in a spectacular 90-minute battle against international terrorism.

In Washington, while Americans began to celebrate the 200th anniversary of declaring independence from British rule, the news came first through the powerful electronic ears of the National Security Agency, which picked up terse radiophone conversations between Israeli troops fighting in Uganda, one of Britain's last colonies to gain independence.

The messages in Hebrew passed between armed jeeps, infantry carriers, four giant Hercules transport planes, two Boeing 707s, and a black Mercedes that appeared to, but did not, belong to President Idi Amin Dada, sometimes known with graveyard humor as Big Daddy. One of the 707s contained the chief of the Israeli air force and an entire battlefield command center, circling five miles high.

Not all of this was immediately evident in Washington. Uganda must have seemed as remote as the moon to the NSA translators; and indeed the African state is better known for its famous Mountains of the Moon than it is for having any significance in world politics. But the reports reaching Secretary of State Henry Kissinger made sense. He had been warned just minutes earlier that an Israeli long-range penetration group of some five hundred soldiers and airmen had made its way down the Red Sea, around Russian-built radar watchdogs, between hostile Arab states, and across part of Africa to swoop along the Rift Valley and into Entebbe.

Israel waited until the last minute to tell the United States about this unprecedented military operation. A small group of men in Jerusalem shouldered the full burden of responsibility. For a whole week they had wrestled with a crisis that should have drawn the support of other governments but did not—a crisis for which there were no ready-made answers, no previous experiences on which to draw, and no perfect solutions.

Israel's ambassadors informed Henry Kissinger and other foreign ministers in order to prevent an alarmed military reaction. They made their disclosures in response to a single coded message transmitted from Jerusalem to the capitals of the world, and delayed so that no foreign government would have time to protest or interfere.

The crisis that Israel faced alone was one that revived bitter memories of other tragedies when Jews had been abandoned to their fate. In reconstructing events leading to those 90 minutes at Entebbe, I was not told by the Israelis that they were haunted by memories of the Holocaust, pogroms, and inquisitions. Not one of the soldiers, airmen, politicians, and statesmen drew an analogy. The facts spoke for themselves. When I sat with Prime Minister Yitzhak Rabin in his Jerusalem office, for example, there was no trace of self-pity in his account of the preceding days of agonizing soul-searching. There was no reproach. When Defense Minister Shimon Peres recalled the desperate moves to win international help, he made no judgments. When the chief of staff, General Mordechai Gur, suddenly buried his head in his arms in a brief betrayal of fatigue, it was merely the gesture of a man expressing relief that Jews can still count on one unfailing protector—the state of Israel.

And this was what Thunderbolt was all about. That Israel does have the most powerful of reasons for its existence. Without Israel the hostages at Entebbe would have died or become pawns in a new kind of guerrilla warfare aimed at destroying the decencies. And the hostages were Jews. And officially, no other government wished to save them by military action.

Thunderbolt marks a turn of the tide, however, in the free world's response to the new techniques of terror. For years we have become conditioned to blackmail and anarchy, so that the hijacking of an Air France airliner on its way from Athens to Paris seemed almost routine. Flight 139 originated in Tel Aviv on the morning of Sunday, June 27. At the time, the men who would spend the rest of the following week in a sleepless battle of wits were going about their business in the most undistinguished way. Some were soldiers with civilian jobs; pilots who were also university students; politicians with a taste for philosophy or archaeology. I know that one man who shot dead an archterrorist at Entebbe was on this Sunday discussing sculpture with an old schoolmate in the artists' colony of Safed.

Flight 139 disappeared for a while from the map and from the minds of most newspaper readers except those with relatives aboard—and except for Israelis, who sensed yet another challenge to their right to exist. Yet Flight 139 was important to those of us who are not Jews but share the same values.

There were a lot of strange aspects to the saga of Flight 139. The terrorists who hijacked it were executing a carefully conceived plan. They were endorsed by the president of the Republic of Uganda—the first time a modern nation and its leader became the protector and spokesman for pirates and political blackmailers. They were nourished by an international terrorist organization whose headquarters were in the neighboring territory of the Soviet Union's strategic ally in Africa, Somalia. They declared war, for all intents and purposes, on Kenya, which has resolutely resisted the influence peddlers from the Soviet bloc and China.

The terrorists were led by a German man and woman whose behavior reminded at least one hostage, himself bearing tattooed numbers from a concentration camp, of Nazis. The name of "The Jackal," an assassin with worldwide connections, arose time and again. The Jackal is not a fictional villain: he is a technician of death employed by revolutionaries of sophisticated backgrounds. Their negotiations with the state of Israel, for example, were conducted with the arrogance of men and women sure of powerful backers. One of their sponsors was Libya, where Flight 139 first landed to refuel: Libya, which has spent part of its enormous oil revenues on guerrilla groups—$50 million to revolutionaries in Lebanon; $100 million to Black September, the terrorist wing of Al Fatah; and millions more to such agents of arson and assassination as the Angels of

Death in Eritrea. The names mean nothing to most of us until too late. The names meant little or nothing to the passengers on Flight 139 whose lives were to be bartered for jailed terrorists, an exchange so common now that we have come to accept it as normal.

In Israel the barter of the innocent for the criminal is still not regarded as moral. The passengers on Flight 139 had to be treated as if they were "soldiers in the front line," I was told by the antiterrorist experts whose hearts bled even as they said it. They were weighing a few lives against the fate of a nation and of a people. Nobody who knows Israel can have any illusions about the pain that is felt at the loss of even a single life in all the years of recurrent warfare. But Israel understands, in a way that the rest of us do not, the dimensions and the awesome future of international terrorism.

Thus the fight to recapture Flight 139's passengers was a battle against the cunning and ruthless ingenuity of those who stand behind such scientific killers as The Jackal. They have learned to bully the democracies. Their defeat at Entebbe, though resounding, is only an interlude. Thunderbolt signified that some men and women have the guts to strike back, and it evoked a response from ordinary people that suggests the public is far ahead of governments in wishing to arm against this new danger. An encouraging feature of the triumph at Entebbe is that it resulted from cooperation between individuals in many other parts of Africa and the Western world.

And perhaps this is what matters. Though statesmen shrank from action and governments turned away, Israel was assisted in many unconventional ways. "The courage of those who fought at Entebbe," a senior Israeli official told me, "was more than matched by the bravery and dedication of our intelligence experts and their friends in many places."

William Stevenson
New York City
July 1976

1
WHERE IS FLIGHT 139?

The woman who walked into the transit lounge at Athens Airport at 6:17 a.m. on Sunday, June 27, 1976, wore a dark denim skirt, light blue blouse, and flat-heeled shoes. Her eyes were slightly bloodshot and her face was marked by acne scars. She looked in her late twenties and stood silent beside a quietly dressed young man who had flown this far with her aboard Singapore Airlines Flight 763 from Bahrain. The pair were ticketed as Mrs. Ortega and Mr. Garcia.

Two young men with Arab passports disembarked from the same Bahrain flight but kept their distance. They too were ticketed to join Air France Flight 139 from Tel Aviv to Paris, due to stop over in Athens at around midday. Their names were given as Fahim al-Satti and Hosni Albou Waiki.

Security was lax at Athens, where a lightning strike of ground staff was sufficiently distracting to persuade airport police not to bother with even rudimentary checks. The timing of the strike was to take on significance later. So was the observation of the one guard who seems to have been awake at Athens Airport that fateful morning. His detailed descriptions of the odd couples would suggest later that the woman was Gabriele Kroche-Tiedemann, a 24-year-old terrorist who helped kidnap oil ministers at the meeting of the Organization of Petroleum Exporting Countries in Vienna in December 1975 and a girlfriend of another German killed more recently when his suitcase bomb exploded in Tel Aviv Airport. Gabriele had lived with Carlos, The Jackal, the world's best-known and most wanted terrorist, and her German companion on this day was a member of the Baader-Meinhof urban guerrillas.

One of the Arabs would be identified as a founder and operational planner of the terrorist Popular Front for the Liberation of Palestine (PFLP).

The four travelers joined Flight 139 without passing

through the metal-detection hoops. Nor was their baggage examined. Inside the Air France airbus they split up. One of the Arabs sat near Moshe Peretz, a 26-year-old medical student from Israel. Peretz, a meticulous young man, had started to scribble a kind of diary on the back of his ticket. As time progressed and scribbling became a dangerous occupation, his notes changed in character. They began as a record which Peretz thought might be fun some day to stick into an album. They finished as frantic bits of Hebrew on airsickness bags, folders, and napkins—entries that trailed into silence exactly one week and three hours later, right back where they started in Tel Aviv.

Sunday, June 27, Athens. 1100 hours.

1210—A few moments after taking off I suddenly hear a terrible scream. My first thought is someone's fainted. I see two persons rush forward. One is a long-haired youth wearing a red shirt, gray trousers, and a beige pullover. The other has a thick mustache, wears long trousers and yellow shirt. They are running toward the first-class compartment.

1212—Frightened and hysterical stewardesses come out of the first-class compartment. With trembling arms, they attempt to calm down the passengers, who begin to show signs of agitation. A minute later, we hear the excited voice of a woman over the plane's internal communications system. Speaking English with a foreign accent she informs us that the plane is under the control of the "Che Guevara Group" and the "Gaza Unit" of the Popular Front for the Liberation of Palestine. When I hear "Che Guevara," that frightens me, because I fear they will not hesitate to blow up the plane in the air. The hysterical voice over the loudspeaker announces that all passengers are to raise their hands above their heads and not move. At the entrance to the first-class compartment there stand two terrorists holding drawn guns and hand grenades without safety pins. They begin a close body search of the passengers. They call the passengers, one after another, and search in all the intimate parts of their bodies. Later their search becomes more superficial. They announce that anyone with a weapon in his possession is to hand it over immediately. A few passengers hand them knives and forks. I too am called, and searched in a superficial manner. The searches last till nearly 1500 hours.

1500—I have no idea where we are flying. Suddenly, out of the windows, we see a coast, arid soil, and one poor landing strip. We guess we approach Benghazi. The plane circles the field ten times before landing. Then the commander of the terrorists—the one in the red shirt—says that we have indeed landed at Benghazi. He says the new "captain" of the plane is, from now on, Bazin el Nubazi, the leader of "Gaza." The plane, he says, will not respond to any message which does not address it as "Haifa." We wait two hours. While we wait, they put a round can, with a fuse sticking out of it, near the left-hand exit of the plane, and a square can on the right. They hold the cans in one hand, and it seems that each one weighs about 200 grams. The one in the yellow shirt says the doors have been booby-trapped with explosives to prevent them being opened. (To tell the truth, the cans do not appear very awe-inspiring.)

1700—One of the women passengers, who reports feeling unwell, is allowed off the plane.

1715—The terrorists have begun collecting passports. They tie them up in a nylon bag. I give them my passport, my army card, my driving license—in fact, all the documents in my possession. They threaten that anyone who does not hand over all his documents faces severe punishment. They speak in English, and one of the stewardesses translates into French. To tell the truth, the atmosphere in the plane is calm.

1800—One of the women passengers faints, and a doctor among the passengers gives her first aid. We are still seated here, looking out of the windows. An arid landscape, four bored soldiers sitting on the runway, a few fire trucks standing nearby.

1915—A cold supper—but not bad. The stewards serve cans of juice, with Arab inscriptions. In the meantime I have seen a blond terrorist and the German woman. She's the sort who gets things together fast. Anyone who wants to go to the toilet lifts a fingers, she shouts an order to go; in one case, when two passengers get up at the same time to go to the toilet, she screams like a veritable animal.

1925—The "captain" (the German) announces that he regrets the upset and discomfort being caused to the passengers, and promises that we will take off as soon as possible.

2135—At long last, in the air. Unbelievable. After 6½ hours on the ground. Our treatment is fairly good. But where are we flying? To Damascus? Baghdad? Beirut? Tel Aviv? or Paris? The passengers conduct a kind of lottery about the destination of our flight. We speak freely to one another, with the unknown factors being our destination and the hijackers' demands.

2300—I awake from a nap. It's very cold. I cover myself with Israeli newspapers.

Flight 139 fell silent soon after leaving Athens. The loss of radio contact stirred little action among the Greek flight controllers. But in Israel the airliner's abrupt silence began a week of tempestuous operations: the week that ran from Sunday, June 27, 1976, to Sunday, July 4; a week now preserved in Israeli intelligence files labeled Thunderbolt and surrounded by unprecedented secrecy.

The sudden disappearance of Flight 139 was registered by a special Israeli intelligence force that has no known parallel. Monitoring the world's airwaves with powerful electronic ears, and by other methods, it watches over travelers for reasons that are unique. It aims to prevent Israel from being isolated and then destroyed. That means the protection of legitimate visitors to and from the Jewish state, and the tracking of killers who wish to turn Israel into a ghetto to be besieged and undermined as if the fortress can then be alienated from the world and destroyed at leisure.

"Flight 139 with a very large number of Israelis aboard has either crashed or been hijacked," ran the first message. "The missing aircraft, an Air France airbus which left Ben-Gurion Airport (near Tel Aviv) shortly before nine this morning . . ."

The message went to the Israeli cabinet, which was halfway through its routine weekly Sunday session. Minister of Transport Gad Yaakobi, a 41-year-old economist, passed it to his prime minister, Yitzhak Rabin. The time was 1:30 p.m., only minutes after Flight 139 failed to transmit after the refueling stop at Athens.

Prime Minister Rabin, a retired general, formerly chief of Israel's military staff, told Yaakobi, who had served as a soldier and finally as a second lieutenant: "If it's hijacked, you take charge of information . . ."

Gad Yaakobi understood in what sense he was now on the firing line. The junior lieutenant was about to learn the burdens of high rank.

More information began streaming in. Thoughts of lunch vanished. "The missing airbus left here with 245 passengers and 12 crew," reported the Ben-Gurion Airport security men already combing their files. "We believe 83 Israelis—but perhaps more because some passengers have citizenship in other countries . . . an unknown number of Arabs are believed to have transferred to Flight 139 from a Singapore flight that landed in Athens shortly before the airbus . . ."

A crisis management team was formed at 3:30 p.m., two hours after the first intelligence report, and 15 minutes before the routine cabinet session broke up. The team consisted of the prime minister and five members of his cabinet. With them was the chief of staff, Mordechai Gur, a formidable general whose paratroop commandos had won him a reputation for swift and unexpected action.

Each member of this crisis task force was supported by specialists: experts on the new international network of terrorists whose attacks on Israel had the same ideological significance as bombings in Ireland; experts on antipiracy tactics; military, political, and diplomatic experts. They drew together swiftly and smoothly. This sort of emergency had happened before, though never on this scale. Nobody yet knew if Flight 139 was a total loss or in the hands of terrorists seeking one melodramatic act of homicide. Or it could be in the grip of a new breed of sophisticated hijackers trained in airline operations and political blackmail.

"I fear the last," Prime Minister Rabin confided to the defense scientific adviser, Dr. Yehezkel Dror. "Face the fact! Our enemies have never had such a catch before—perhaps one hundred Jews who may have relatives of power and influence all over the world, any one of whom might crack under pressure."

The professor had once written a study: "How to Deal with Terrorism Linked with Mad Regimes."

He had no notion how prophetic this was. Nor could Defense Minister Shimon Peres guess that his own arguments in the cabinet earlier that day cast a shadow over coming events, when he replied to criticism of the Westwind, a civilian jet built with Israeli ingenuity but also with Israeli tax money. The Westwind was an investment in Israel's future aircraft industry, said Peres, adding ironically: "Even President Idi Amin of Uganda chose it against the world's best."

That Uganda's dictator had his own Israeli-built Westwind jet was, on Sunday, June 27, an idle joke. So far as anyone knew, the stolen Flight 139 airbus was still in the air but flying southward, instead of northwest toward its scheduled destination, Paris.

Paris was groaning in the worst heat wave in a hundred years. All who could, fled the city. French President Valéry Giscard d'Estaing was flying to join U.S. President Ford at a summit conference in Puerto Rico. With him were key French government ministers. Anyone awaiting Flight 139 at the Charles de Gaulle Airport saw only that beside the landing time of 1335 GMT (1435 Paris time) appeared the single bleak word DELAYED.

"*Attention!*" The voice of a ground-hostess cut through the noise. "*Attention, s'il vous plaît . . .*" Few of the perspiring relatives and friends heard or fully comprehended the brief announcement. "Air France apologizes for the delay in arrival of Flight 139. Those awaiting Flight 139 will please come to the central Air France office."

At precisely the time scheduled for arrival in Paris, the missing airbus was on the final approach to land at Benghazi, Libya. This aroused the worst fears.

It was dusk in Israel when the crisis task force began a grim vigil. By then, certain facts were emerging. The hijackers had prepared for Libya as the opening move in some complicated game. They were experts in the new kind of "war" against Israel waged by the Popular

Front for the Liberation of Palestine (PFLP), whose chief of operations was Dr. Wadi Hadad. Dr. Hadad commanded an international army of fanatics armed with weapons of terror. Israeli intelligence believed he had moved out of strife-torn Lebanon to some more secure base in Africa to train young disciples of violent revolution who might not share his hatred of Zion but did want to share his arsenals and the knowledge of his trained guerrillas. The immediate fear was that this was a repetition of the takeover by Hadad's men of a Belgian airliner that was forced back to Ben-Gurion Airport in May 1972. On that occasion, Israeli commandos disguised as mechanics and ground attendants had recaptured the airliner, killing 2 Arab gunmen, but saving 97 passengers.

If the hijackers were following a careful plan, as indicated by Israel's electronic ears tuned to African and Arab radio traffic, General Gur's commandos would have an unpleasant task ahead. They began moving quietly into position on Ben-Gurion Airport, wearing the white coveralls of mechanics or the casual summer clothes of passengers.

It seemed that Flight 139 would return here, directed by Dr. Hadad's experts in terror and blackmail.

Confrontation with Flight 139's hijackers, if they landed in Israel, would require all the prime minister's powers of self-control. Hitting the hijackers meant the risk of killing innocent passengers. The world would condemn Israel. So Rabin prepared for prolonged negotiations, setting up a command post in the office of El Al's general manager, Mordechai Ben-Ari, who had created a great airline out of his early career moving refugees from Nazi death camps by an underground network of improvised transports.

2

AN AFRICAN DICTATOR
TAKES OVER

From London during Sunday night came the first detailed description of the hijackers. It suggested that two

Germans were in charge; that the terrorists were indeed following a carefully calculated plan; and that Flight 139 would end up somewhere "friendly to the terrorists." These important clues came from a young Englishwoman, Patricia Heyman, age 30, who persuaded her captors to release her at Benghazi because she was in advanced pregnancy and in danger of giving premature birth.

Pat Heyman held a British passport but her home was in Petach Tikva, Israel. She said nothing until a regular Libyan Airlines plane brought her to London. There Scotland Yard took over. In five hours, she passed from the hands of political pirates to specialists in antiterrorist tactics. Whatever the placatory mood of governments, the police of the free world had created their own international underground for the exchange of intelligence.

"Five minutes after departure from Athens, Flight 139 was taken over by a German female, a German male, and what appear to be three Arabs, according to the released hostage," London reported to Israel. "All appear to be armed. Explosives, apparently disguised as cans of dates, were placed at exit doors of aircraft. Benghazi is described as stopover only. Central Africa appears to be final destination."

Three hours after midnight on the second day, Monday, June 28, Israel's defense minister drove wearily back from the airport to his Tel Aviv office on the second floor of military headquarters. Shimon Peres, born in Poland in 1923, had been sent to Palestine at the age of 11 as the child chosen to represent a Jewish family which entertained little hope of joining him in the creation of a nation that would protect Jews from further persecution.

"If Israel means anything," Peres told himself now, "it means Jews can go anywhere as free men without fear. We can't give in to blackmail."

He had just learned that Flight 139 was on the ground at Entebbe Airport in Uganda. He knew something about Uganda and its president, Idi Amin, because for some years Israel had cultivated the dictator and trained his airmen. There was a more ironic reason. Uganda was once touted as the place where Jews could establish their first homeland in 2000 years. Uganda had been the alternative to the Palestine that became Israel.

Peres passed through the security points, disguising his anxiety with brief smiles, already aware of the need to maintain confidence and discourage rumors of disaster. In his office waited General Gur and intelligence advisers, with maps and photographs spread over a long desk.

"It's more than 4000 kilometers," said Gur, answering the defense minister's unspoken question. "We're working on military options, but the distance is enormous and the territory between is hostile."

An intelligence officer broke in. "Terrorists are getting President Amin's support."

"You are sure?"

"Positive. The Voice of Uganda, is broadcasting appeals to revolutionaries, and attacks against France and Israel. The terrorists already have an organization in Uganda. Their operational directors appear to be moving overland from Somalia."

Peres glanced at the maps. British Somalia, no longer British, had become host to the Communist Chinese and then yielded to the superior bribing powers of the Soviet Union. Equipped with Russian arms, "defended" by Russian missiles against unspecified enemies, Somalia was the safe haven for Dr. Hadad's senior specialists in guerrilla warfare on behalf of the PFLP.

The maps told more. Uganda had been British-controlled along with Kenya and Tanganyika. In the wake of decolonization, East Africa passed through storms of unrest. Ethiopia, to the north, had recently overturned the legendary Emperor Haile Selassie and destroyed Britain's traditional influence. French Somaliland was out of French control except for the port of Djibouti. . .

Djibouti? Peres looked up inquiringly.

"It's an option," said Gur. The chief of staff tugged one of his jug-handle ears. "Test French reaction to any possibility of refueling there—"

Nobody had to ask what he meant. If a military operation became necessary—and it could only be if—planes must fly around hostile Arab territories, evade

THE POPULAR FRONT FOR THE LIBERATION OF PALESTINE (PFLP)

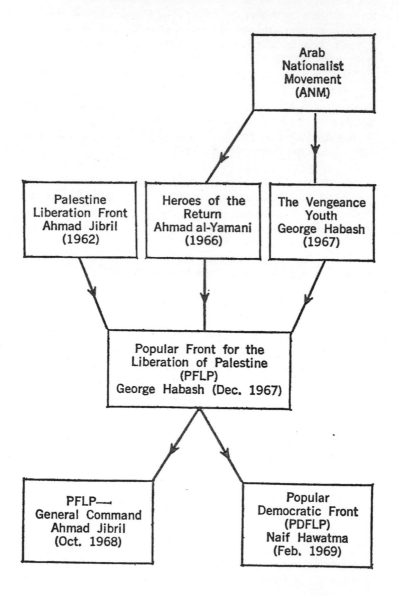

Somalia's Russian detection systems, and complete flights beyond the normal range of Israel's existing military aircraft. Someone picked up the scrambler phone and called for Foreign Minister Yigal Allon. His task would be to sound out the French on the use of Djibouti, with a thousand other unpredictable tasks to follow. General Gur spoke softly into another phone to his paratroop commanders. The special commando units at Ben-Gurion Airport should remain alert and at their positions, although the chances of Flight 139 landing there now were less than 10 percent. "All men of Force X* and Force Y* must stand ready for action elsewhere."

The text of a 2500-word statement from Uganda Radio began to pour into Peres's office. It denounced French occupation of Djibouti, as if the minds of the crisis task force had been divined already. "For Djibouti is only held by France to preserve Israel's sole route to the Far East and Africa," declared Uganda Radio.

This was the language of Dr. Hadad and better-publicized enemies of Israel. The theme was cutting Israel off from the rest of the world: a theory that had once seemed outrageous until the exits were blocked one by one, save those provided by commercial air lanes.

By late Monday, the task force received an astonishingly informed guess of what to expect. Israeli intelligence delivered an analysis of possibilities:

Operation Uganda was a plan devised by 46-year-old Dr. Wadi Hadad, mastermind of the PFLP, a faction operating in apparent independence from Yasir Arafat's Palestinian Liberation Organization, the PLO. Hadad had organized a series of spectacular hijacks designed to strengthen arguments for greater violence rather than the PLO's recent pseudodiplomatic initiatives which emphasized moderation. For Operation Uganda, Hadad stationed himself in Somalia and despatched his hijack team to Athens: a German woman and a German anarchist tentatively identified as Wil-

*Deleted by censors.

fried Böse, known associate of The Jackal, Carlos
Ramirez. The leader of this team could be Fayez Abdul-
Rahim Jaber, born in Hebron in 1930, longtime res-
ident in Cairo, founder of the "Heroes of the Return,"
operational commander of the PLFP's radical wing
linked with leftist-anarchist groups throughout the
world.

The Jackal's running-mate, Jaber, was credited with
direction of the PLFP's political department. That indicated Flight 139 would become an element in political
warfare designed as much to win support for Jaber's
theories of violence as to discredit Israel by forcing the
Jewish state for the first time to kneel before threats.
Jaber organized the attack on a Pan-Am airliner at
Rome in December 1973 when 31 were killed. Jaber's
family, including five brothers, had been under constant
Israeli intelligence surveillance. One brother, Rasmi
Jaber, ran a souvenir shop near Jerusalem, openly
identified with terrorism, and now testified that Fayez
Jaber was "leader of many big operations against
Israel."

Two hours before midnight on Monday, the ominous
speculations began to harden. In a flamboyant display
of jubilation, "Big Daddy" President Amin appeared
before the hijack victims at Entebbe with a bodyguard
of armed and uniformed *Palestinian* guerrillas. Big
Daddy was being projected by Uganda Radio as a
"negotiator" between the hijack team and Israel.

But why only Israel?

An awful truth was reflected in the faces around
Prime Minister Rabin that night. The released hostage,
Patricia Heyman, had spoken to Scotland Yard of "segregation"—of Jews separated from other prisoners aboard
the airbus by the Germans waving pistols. None of the
task force was especially "mystic-minded" (as one described it later), but none could forget that Israel was
born out of the Holocaust in which Jews were told to
step aside in Nazi camps and directed to the gas chambers. "Segregation" was an emotive word. It would be
best if families of the hostages were told nothing of this.

In Uganda, it was now reported by Israeli intelligence, President Amin was parading before the hos-

tages as their protector. Addressed merely as Mr. President by a young Israeli mother, he rebuked her. "I am His Excellency al-Hajji Field Marshal Dr. Idi Amin Dada, holder of the British Victoria Cross, DSO, MC, and appointed by God Almighty to be your savior."

3
TERRORISM AND MAD REGIMES

Word was sent to a shopkeeper in a Tel Aviv suburb. Would he try to get on the telephone to Kampala? Talk to Big Daddy, flatter the African president, remind him of his awesome responsibility as chairman of the Organization of African Unity now on the brink of a summit meeting in Mauritius.

The shopkeeper was Colonel Baruch Bar-Lev, "Borka," former Israeli military mission chief in Uganda. Borka had been an intimate friend of the black dictator. "Keep him talking," was the unofficial request. He began a series of bizarre long-distance phone calls between Israel and Uganda while the task force played desperately for time. There were now, it seemed, some 250 innocent passengers and 12 French airline employees at the tender mercy of Big Daddy, widely regarded as a dangerous buffoon, known to the doctors who had treated him in Jerusalem as a victim of syphilis and entering the final manic stages of that fearful disease, but still an inventive and cunning foe.

Dr. Dror, the chief scientific adviser who wrote the prophetic study on terrorism linked with mad regimes, analyzed a proso-profile of President Amin. These proso-profiles were based on methods of historical research, modernized during the intelligence war against Hitler. A pioneer was Professor Gilbert Highet of Columbia University, a quiet Scot who could re-create the psychological atmosphere of Roman emperors. He had adapted the technique to forecast how leaders of hostile or secret regimes might react to differing sets of circumstances, using limited knowledge concerning their personalities, families, and friends, and current circumstances.

While Dr. Dror worked on Big Daddy, seeking alternative plans for the safe release of the hostages, Uganda Radio made known during the course of Tuesday, June 29, the price of liberation. The hijackers demanded the delivery of 53 convicted terrorists, including 40 supposedly held in Israel, 6 in West Germany, 5 in Kenya, 1 in Switzerland, and another in France.

"We are the only nation with both hostages and convicted terrorists," commented Transport Minister Gad Yaakobi. He had the unenviable task of dealing with a self-styled Committee for Saving the Hostages and another Committee of Relatives, all clamoring for action. The list of hijack victims was not being made public for security reasons, and relatives were contacted but sworn to secrecy. Yaakobi, whose job in the task force required him to keep open channels to Air France and the International Civil Aviation Organization in Montreal, and to speak for the government during the crisis, was unhappy with the early signs of Israel's isolation. Words of condolence did not alter the fact that the French seemed unwilling to take firm action, while ICAO, being an agency of the United Nations, already reflected the UN's submission to the dictates of Uganda's fellow third-world nations, all hostile to Israel. Only 73 of the 134 members of ICAO were parties to the main Hague convention that covered the agreements making it easier to extradite and prosecute hijackers and penalize countries that accommodate them. Yaakobi, once an executive of the General Federation of Jewish Labour—Histadrut—had become increasingly disenchanted with third-world governments that embraced socialist theories but practiced dictatorship.

Yaakobi cherished a photograph of himself with David Ben-Gurion and kept it in his modest home in a Tel Aviv suburb. He consulted Ben-Gurion's writings on such historical matters as the way Thucydides portrayed the factors in a nation's survival. "The condition of the fields, the morale, the strength of the walls and the wisdom of tactics. . . . Here was our supreme test. How could Israel yield to demands from Uganda and continue to pretend to be the nation with Ben-Gurion's moral strength?"

Another and most disturbing counterpressure on the

government was being exerted by families of the victims, and this was growing. They wanted to negotiate. Yaakobi faced fresh pleas to make a deal when the hijackers followed their demand for the release of jailed terrorists with a threat to kill the hostages and blow up the airbus if there was no Israeli response by 2:00 p.m., Israel time, on the morrow—Thursday.

"Israel is the target," Yaakobi said wearily when he joined another session of the task force. The tight-knit group moved wherever the prime minister happened to be when consulations were necessary. All were acutely conscious of the need to behave democratically, and a cabinet meeting was scheduled for Thursday, before the terrorists' deadline.

4

THE OPTIONS

Then came the sudden freeing of 47 passengers by the hijackers. This action helped unite Israel in an unexpected way, because it gave the first link that Jews were the target, their lives to be the subject of bazaar-style haggling with Israel. The nation had been badly divided since the Yom Kippur War of 1973. There was a sense of unease, manifest in public places and in parliament: irritability, recrimination, uncertainty about how to deal with enemies who switched from soft words to sudden gusts of hate. When 47 passengers were released and arrived in Paris late on the night of Wednesday June 30, they gave warning of the real danger. At first it had seemed that President Amin was truly mediating. But the freed hostages told a different story to French intelligence. This, passed to Jerusalem, strengthened the belief that Uganda was hand in glove with terrorist chief Dr. Hadad. The secret intelligence was fed into Jerusalem's military-political computers, now locked onto what would become known as Track B . . . the military option.

Track A was the diplomatic option of negotiation. It was necessary for several reasons to keep on this track, not the least being public concern in Israel. What was known publicly, however, about the release of the 47 hostages had a unifying effect on the nation. From one end of the country to the other, with the speed of the bush telegraph, ran the news that an old woman, marked visibly for life by a Nazi concentration camp number on her arm, had been negligently released among the lucky 47, perhaps because her passport gave no sign of her Jewishness. She was quoted: "I felt myself back 32 years when I heard the German orders, saw the waving guns, and imagined again the shuffling lines of prisoners and the harsh cry: *'Jews to the right,'* and I wondered, so what good is Israel if this can happen today?"

At a base in the desert near Beersheba, where Abraham once watered his flock, crossroads for centuries of camel trading, some 20 miles from the Mideast's largest nuclear research center, the story of the old woman distracted the pilots and paratroopers in vast underground hangars. Deep under camouflaged runways was a war room that duplicated the primary operations center close to Defense Minister Peres's office in Tel Aviv. On duplicate plots, the tracks of Israel's enemies were pursued as a matter of routine from Baghdad to Libya. Here, condensed and laid out with electronic precision, the picture of a land under siege was continuously updated. Radar dots were the spoor of Russian warships and Russian or East European aircraft shuttling across the Mediterranean. Ground intelligence recorded the movements of terrorists.

Here the commander of the Special Air and Commando Service, Brigadier General Dan Shomron, continually adapted his tactics in coordinating raids against terrorist bases beyond Israel's borders.

Dan Shomron's mind was on Track B. He was accustomed to producing action plans that were aborted for political or diplomatic reasons. He knew that Track A, the option to negotiate an exchange, was in the cards. He did not like it. This was not the prejudice of a senior paratroop officer, though Dan Shomron in his 39 years never had much time for compromise. Shomron simply believed there was a military solution to the problem of extracting one or two hundred hostages out of the heart of equatorial Africa.

He had learned a lesson from the Yom Kippur War, prolonged beyond Israeli expectations because of political errors, lack of preparation, failure to exploit the talent for speed and surprise of his and other special forces. "The Russians were given time to judge the progress of balance," he concluded. "When the balance shifted in Israel's favor, the Soviet Union threatened large-scale military intervention and practically ordered Henry Kissinger to report to the Kremlin, where the United States approved the cessation of hostilities just as the tide was turned in our favor." Others spoke of a stopwatch war in which the hands moved slowly when the Arabs felt they had time to strike and bleed Israel. When the Kremlin saw Israel move into the ascendency, the hour hand spun swiftly. Thus Israel must always lose, for the world would never let her win. And that being so, thought Brigadier General Shomron, there was little point in paying attention to world opinion.

So he continued to work on Track B. With him, producing one ingenious plan after another, were Israelis of every rank. The plans were screened. Only the practical schemes went up to the task force under Prime Minister Rabin. The man most likely to have to execute a military plan, Shomron, must pretend in public to be standing idle. That was how he found himself, on the evening of Tuesday, June 29, translated from the heat of the desert arguments to the garden of a private home in Ramat Gan, a pleasant suburb of Tel Aviv, twirling whiskey in his glass.

"What about your paratroops? Can't you take over Entebbe Airport?"

The question came from a guest at the wedding of the daughter of an ex-paratroop colonel. This was anything but a war room; but the garden was full of paratroopers, past and present. Chief of Staff Mordechai Gur was in one corner. Beside him stood the Head of the Mossad—Israel's Central Security and Intelligence Institute, an anonymous figure and a mystery to the foreign visitor. Assistant Defense Minister Yisrael Tal circulated among the groups on the lawn. Major General (Reserve) Ariel Sharon was pumping the hand of bearded Brigadier Danny Mat.

Despite the festivities, talk always came back to the fate of the hostages in Uganda. What will the government do? Use force? Bomb Lebanon or some other target where such retaliation had taken effect before? Or were they going to capitulate and release those on the list received that same day from Wadi Hadad?

The best known among the prisoners in Israeli hands were these:

•Archbishop Hilarion Capucci, head of the Greek Catholic community in east Jerusalem. In 1974 he was sentenced to 12 years' imprisonment on the charge of gunrunning (in his car, which enjoyed diplomatic immunity). He operated in the service of Al Fatah.

•Kozo Okamoto, member of the Japanese Red Army terrorist organization. In July 1972 he was sentenced to life imprisonment for committing mass murder at Ben-Gurion Airport, Lod, in a bloody incident in which 24 persons were massacred and dozens were wounded. He operated in the service of the PFLP.

•Fatma Barnawi, a black African Muslim from east Jerusalem, who was convicted of laying a demolition charge in Jerusalem's Zion cinema in 1968. She operated in the service of Al Fatah.

•William George Nasser. Arrested in east Jerusalem in 1968, he was sentenced to life imprisonment for numerous acts of sabotage, as well as the murder of a Druze watchman in the Jerusalem corridor. He operrated in the service of Al Fatah.

•Muzna Kamel Nikola, a nurse by profession, who spent a number of years in London, and returned to Israel on a mission for Al Fatah, for the purpose of espionage and recruitment of additional members.

•Kamel Namri, of Jerusalem. His mother is Jewish; by profession he is an engineer. In 1968, he was sentenced to life imprisonment for acts of sabotage. He operated in the service of Al Fatah.

•Samir Darwish, of Acre, was arrested before the Six Day War. He planned the escape of two security detainees from Ramleh prison and was a member of the organization headed by Jabril, the leading terrorist in Uganda.

Initiatives taken by Defense Minister Peres were reported to Prime Minister Rabin as the need arose. Just prior to Thunderbolt, however, the misconception took root among units of the armed forces that the political rifts that had been widely publicized between the two men continued within the crisis task force dealing with Flight 139.

This impression arose largely from the way Rabin entrusted Peres with handling the day-to-day demands and proposals for military action.

The paratroopers held one opinion, voiced heatedly: "Whatever the cost, we must go to Entebbe. If we give in, it will be a curse for generations. Next time they take a plane, they'll demand our leaders, or withdrawal from the West Bank . . ." Brigadier General Shomron, in civilian clothes, shrugged: "Come on boys, what do you want of my life? Depends on me? If the government wants—we can reach anywhere . . ."

Shomron was the antithesis of a guerrilla. Tall and well-built, with curly hair and blue eyes, he was born in Kibbutz Degania in 1937. ("We belong to the founding fathers. Both my father and mother were at one time or another 'kibbutz secretary,' and now my brother has the honor.") He enlisted in the army as a paratrooper and participated in retaliation actions against terrorists before the Sinai War of 1956. In the Six Day War he commanded a force of jeeps armored and carrying recoilless guns—the first forward element to reach Al-Qantara on the Suez Canal. He was mentioned in dispatches. He was a paratroop battalion commander, and then transferred to armor. In the Yom Kippur War he commanded a standing army brigade in Sinai, first in the containment battles against the Egyptian breakthrough, then across the Suez Canal. He and his force reached Adabiyeh on the Gulf of Suez to close the ring of encirclement around the Egyptian 3d Army. After the war Dan "returned home" to the paratroops —as senior paratroop and infantry officer, a title revealing very little about the special Air and Commando Service.

To understand Shomron's operational mind, consider his past operations and missions. Before the Six Day War, he was sent to IDF Staff and Command College. "From the moment the war started, it was clear to me that reaching the Suez Canal would mean the end of the war," he said later.

He fought his way through an Egyptian commando battalion. When he reached the waterline he considered the war over—but that night he was sent to attack an Egyptian force at Firdan Bridge while under constant enemy air attack himself. The next morning he watched trucks bring Egyptain soldiers from the direction of Cairo to the west bank of the canal, the first preparation for the War of Attrition that would follow a year later.

At noon on Yom Kippur, 1973, Shomron was preparing to take his armored brigade toward the Suez Canal. All the indications were that war would begin at 6:00 p.m., and his brigade, alternating with another, was responsible for the Suez line. While his preparations were under way, Egyptian aircraft dropped bombs on the brigade laager, killing ten of his men. His first thought had been: "Madmen. They might hit us."

Shomron said later: "My big trauma after the Yom Kippur War was when I went home on my first short furlough. I had the feeling of a serious alienation. It was afternoon when I arrived in Tel Aviv. I found a city going about its daily life as always. I went home and showered. Then the phone rang. There was disturbing news. I was to report to the airport and fly back south. When we took off, and I saw the lights of Tel Aviv—as though nothing had happened—I suddenly felt that my men and I were going to our private war. Then I remembered the sentence often heard among officers and soldiers of the line: 'We fight on the front, that life can go on as always back home.' But I put it differently: 'I don't want everything to be as usual on the home front. I don't think it should be that way. This is total war, and should involve all the nation in Israel. Everyone must contribute whatever he can.' I know that this troubled others and not only me. I saw the expression on the faces of soldiers coming back from furlough. They didn't have to tell me anything. I knew what they were thinking and feeling.

"Home in days like these should be like the front line. People who can't work for one reason or another should go to help the moshavim and kibbutzim whose men have gone to the line. This is not some utopian vision. It can be done, and should be—not by volunteering, but in organized and planned fashion."

Prime Minister Rabin took a different view. He wanted to preserve the air of calm routine. He briefed a full cabinet that afternoon and got what he requested: continuation of authority for the crisis task force to act as it saw fit. "Assignment of responsibilities had been made," Rabin said later. "Each operational team was making its separate assessment—what moves we could expect from the French Foreign Ministry, what line other governments were taking with regard to the hijack demands."

5
"WHERE THE HELL IS UGANDA?"

From the moment they presented their demands, the terrorists' conditions included the release of five of their comrades-in-arms imprisoned in Kenya.

Five months before the hijacking, according to British sources, Ugandan President Idi Amin provided three Palestinian terrorists with Soviet antiaircraft missiles with which they almost succeeded in shooting down an El Al plane about to land at Nairobi Airport on January 18, 1976. Before they had time to fire the missiles they were apprehended by Kenyan security agents. Their car was found to contain machine guns, hand grenades, and pistols. All these weapons had been smuggled from Uganda with the knowledge of President Amin. Two of the three men had taken part in the bazooka attack on an El Al airliner which took off from Orly Airport in Paris in January 1975. In December of that year, the three reached Nairobi on visitors' visas issued by the British embassy in Beirut.

On January 21 two sympathizers—a man and a woman, both German-speaking—arrived in Nairobi to learn what had happened to their three terrorist colleagues. They were arrested and interrogated. When they were searched, the woman's stomach was found to bear instructions, written in invisible ink. The instructions ordered the terrorists to try and carry out the attack on an El Al plane. Kenya's President Jomo Kenyatta secretly agreed to make the five detained terrorists available for Israeli interrogation, and this was done on February 3. Now the hijackers threatened that Kenya would be subject to reprisal actions "all over the world" if it did not release the five terrorists.

While the terrorists were presenting their conditions for the release of hostages, Moshe Peretz continued to write his journal of events.

Monday, June 28. 0035—We expect to land at any moment—after all, three hours have passed. Where are we flying to?

0040—I request permission to go to the toilet. I raise my hand, and the terrorist in the red shirt waves his gun to indicate that I can go. Near the toilet I meet one of the stewards busy in the rear kitchen. He tells me that we are flying south.

0315—After a short nap I wake up. The commander announces that we are landing at Entebbe, and orders us to close the window blinds.

0600—I open the blind slightly and see daylight. I can make out that we are parked on a runway beside a gigantic lake. Many soldiers are lying on high grass surrounding the runway. I address the yellow-shirted terrorist in Arabic and he tells me that we are going to stay here for a long time. He tells me that he was born in Haifa.

0620—The "captain" (The German leader of the terrorists) politely offers his thanks to the passengers for the great patience they have displayed, and announces that negotiations are going on with the Uganda authorities. Idi Amin is due to arrive personally to announce his decision . . .

0800—The "captain" announces there is nothing to

worry about, everything is being handled properly. He will explain later the circumstances of taking over the plane. He wishes us a good breakfast and jokes, saying this will be the first breakfast of our lives eaten in Uganda. It is a single roll, nothing else.

0900—The rear door of the plane is wide open . . . A rope made by the terrorists from the stewards' neckties is all that is between us and outside where I see the large figure of Idi Amin negotiating with the guerrillas.

0915—The "captain" announces the main danger is past. He asks us to remember that he and his companions are not a group of cruel murderers.

0935—The "captain" explains the hijack was undertaken by the Popular Front for the Liberation of Palestine . . . He is not planning the mass murder of the passengers but aims only to attract public opinion.

1205—The "captain" announces we are all to leave the plane in buses.

1210—The decision has been altered; it is now decided that we shall travel by other means.

1215—One by one we get off the plane. Three terrorists stand at the exit, and we clamber down the gangplank. Several passengers, convinced that the whole affair is over, wave goodbye to the terrorists. We enter the airport's old terminal—a huge room, dirty and dusty. We sit down on armchairs while the Ugandans bring in additional chairs. Our hand luggage is with us, and several passengers ask when their suitcases will be brought.

1415—We eat lunch at the Entebbe Airport building. Ugandan servants bring in pots overflowing with rice and hot curry. I am afraid to touch the meat (it might be from giraffes) or water—so I eat it dry. Ugandan paratroopers surround the airport building, their guns cocked. It is still not clear how long we shall remain under house arrest like this. Flying time from Uganda to Paris is about nine hours—so that if we fly off now we shall arrive at night. We have been photographed a number of times for Ugandan television. We are waiting for the "king" of Uganda, who may arrive at any moment.

1720—Idi Amin appears, with a green beret and Israeli paratroopers' wings. Received with applause by the passengers, he declares: "Some of you know me, some of you don't. For those who don't—I am Field Marshal Dr. Idi Amin Dada." He tells us that it is thanks to him that the passengers were permitted to disembark from the plane and to remain in Uganda. He announces further that the hijackers' demands have been rejected in their entirety by Israel, while the other states have accepted them. After his statement he is applauded again.

1935—Supper. The menu: meat, potatoes, green beans, and dwarf bananas. The passengers and crew get involved in a long debate about how the terrorists managed to get on board the plane.

2035—The Ugandan doctor gives each passenger two antimalaria pills.

2245—People decide to get a bit of sleep at long last. Everybody lies down on the filthy floor; it's hot as hell, and there is a veritable symphony of snores. People shout at one another to keep quiet; it's like a summer camp of the Gadna [Israeli military cadets].

Tuesday, June 29. 0730—After breakfast, some of the people hear a radio report that Israel is refusing to negotiate with the terrorists, who are threatening to blow up the plane if their demands are not met. The passengers' faces show signs of anxiety. The morning passes without any special incident. The terrorists continue to keep us under guard, sitting beside the door; afterward, they permit women and children to play on the patch of lawn at the front of the terminal. The Ugandan paratroopers are ordered to move back 50 yards from the building.

1355—I have proposed that a separate section be reserved for the snorers, to prevent a repetition of last night's experiences. The fact that I write about such things only stresses further the contrast between the tranquility here and the tension being experienced by our relatives abroad. Here there is no talk of threats against the passengers' lives, blowing up the plane, or any ultimatum. I hope the family informs the hospital of the reason for my absence from work.

1530—The terrorists read out a list of their demands—including the release of 53 detainees, 40 of them in Israel—by noon on July 1, 1976. In view of

Israel's almost certain refusal, I wonder what the options are? Either the terrorists carry out their threat to murder the hostages, which seems less probable; or a compromise, which seems most probable—by which a small number of detainees are released, or all the passengers, with the exception of the Israelis, are released on Thursday.

1910—The terrorists separate us from the others: a most dramatic scene. Every person who possesses an Israeli passport is called upon to leave the central hall and move to an adjoining room. The women begin to cry. The feeling is like an execution. The terrorists begin to burrow through the hand luggage. They find two albums of the Yom Kippur War and show great delight in leafing through them before the Israelis. We go out to the neighboring room. Across the door, in the middle, they have laid a plank, and the narrow space remaining is divided again, so that we are forced to bend and squeeze to get through to the other room. People with dual nationality are also ordered into there. In the meantime they have confiscated cameras and personal belongings.

2000—We are in a small room, part of which is filled with cardboard boxes. The terrorists warn us that they are full of explosives and if touched will go off. At first, we are frightened, but in time the fear wears off and people hang their shirts over the boxes. While we are getting organized one of the hostages goes up to a terrorist and asks for a cushion for his baby. The terrorist strikes him violently with the butt of his revolver. Our second night in Uganda.

Wednesday, June 30. 1130—Idi Amin arrives by helicopter. In the central hall he is welcomed by applause. When he enters our hall, he is received coolly, but when he says "Shalom" in Hebrew, he is rewarded with clapping. All he can promise us are blankets and pillows. He also informs us that the terrorists have no grudge against us, but only against the fascist Israeli government—and if the latter does not agree to the guerrillas' demands, it does not care about the fate of its citizens. One of us, Ilan, tells him that by being here there is nothing we can do, and we would be able to help more if we were returned safely to Israel, where we could repeat the terrorists' statements. Someone else criticizes Amin for not taking steps to overpower the guerrillas and release the detainees. Amin says that if he were to do so, the whole building would be blown up by the terrorists. From a conversation with one of the terrorists, I discover that their demands for the release of convicts have not yet been accepted, and that they do not intend to kill us. At times it is possible to talk to them calmly. Most of the time they walk among us with their guns hanging over their shoulders, but the ones outside have their guns cocked. In the meantime, over half the non-Israeli passengers have been released. Our fate will be decided in the course of the next 24 hours.

1400—Lunch.

1500—Rest.

1700—People are playing cards, reading books, or arguing about the various options open to the terrorists.

6

THE TERRORISTS' ULTIMATUM

"The various options open to the terrorists." Thus Moshe Peretz closed his diary on Wednesday.

Let another diarist take up the tale at this point: a government spokesman in Israel.

It is Wednesday, June 30, and we scurry between Jerusalem and Tel Aviv, trying to maintain an outward air of calm.

In the morning the government convenes and hears a report on developments. Immediately after the cabinet session, the team of ministers meets to hear an up-to-date report from each ministry. It is clear to the ministers that there is close cooperation between President Idi Amin and his army and the hijackers. The Foreign Ministry is busy that same day in considerable diplomatic effort to bring pressures to bear on Uganda. The ministry calls on heads of state from different continents to get to Amin and persuade him to discontinue his cooperation with the terrorists. Ambassador

Chaim Herzog is in Israel (at a Congress of Jewish Organizations), and he is summoned to apply pressure to UN Secretary-General Kurt Waldheim. Religious bodies are approaching the pope. The French government is trying its luck with African governments and heads of state.

The Security and Foreign Affairs Committee of the Knesset convenes at 2:30 p.m. The prime minister and director general of the Foreign Ministry report on the diplomatic activity. Israel is not asking UN intervention (as differentiated from a personal approach to Waldheim with the intent of his putting pressure on Amin), in order not to relieve France of responsibility for the passengers. The German position on the release of the Baader-Meinhof prisoners is troubling Jerusalem. Israel knows of the German reluctance to respond to demands, and accordingly there is an assessment that the matter of prisoners not in Israeli hands is considerably hardening the government's situation. The free world is showing sympathy: not one of the Western countries with nationals among the hostages is suggesting capitulation to the hijackers' demands. Meanwhile the government is beginning to feel the pressure from families of the hostages—for whom the Transport Ministry has opened a special bureau.

The ministerial team convenes in the prime minister's office at 9:00 p.m. They hear a brief summary describing the prisoners whose release is requested by the terrorists, and offer preliminary suggestions on Israel's attitude in the event of a decision to negotiate with the hijackers. These proposals are brought up with a background of feeling that pressures on Amin are making no headway, and that the deadline of the ultimatum is drawing near.

Night: the transport minister and the director general of the prime minister's office, Amos Aran, meet with families of the hostages, and clarify to them that the government is sensitive to the timetable that the hijackers have dictated, and that the main interest is in saving the lives of the passengers. The families are excited and demand abandonment of every other consideration as long as the hostages come home safe.

Bar-Lev holds a number of conversations with the

African president, in the style of: "Mr. President, God has sent you. The hand of history has decreed that you shall carry out God's purpose and release the hostages. You know what they write about you in the world. You know what a bad name they have given you. Now is your chance to prove to the world how great a man you are. You, brave soldier, you will get the Nobel peace prize. The whole world will see who is the true Idi Amin. You must rescue the hostages to prove that the bad things written about you are lies."

Another tack went: "Mr. President, Uganda is your country. It isn't possible that you shouldn't be the one to make decisions on what happens there. Nobody will lift a hand in Uganda without your agreement. You must intervene to rescue the hostages."

President Amin replied: "The release of hostages doesn't depend on me. Your government must release the terrorists that they have asked for. The hijackers are tough . . ."

Thursday, July 1: at 7:45 a.m. the ministerial task force meets in the prime minister's office in Tel Aviv. They report on activity in their areas of jurisdiction. The diplomatic field must be worked to its utmost. The team decides to inform the hijackers of Israel's willingness in principle to open negotiations. The ministers are guided by the assumption that the deadline is close (at noon the same day), that the attempts to persuade Amin have failed, and that the hostages are in tangible danger. All the members of the team agree to recommend to the cabinet to open negotiations—both in order to extend the deadline, and because there may be no other alternative but to negotiate. At this moment the team is fully aware that negotiations must proceed cautiously, because they will involve a whole complex of subjects.

At 8:30 a.m. the cabinet convenes and decides unanimously to accept the conclusion of the team, presented by Minister Galili, that the task force should be empowered to negotiate with the hijackers, while expressing willingness to release terrorists. After the meeting a number of ministers are of the opinion that the significance of the decision is both tactical and in principle. There is a willingness to respond to a part of the demands, and—at the same time—it is a move to gain time.

While the cabinet meeting is in progress the security and foreign affairs committee convenes. Rabin is delayed at the cabinet session, and in place of him appear Amos Aran, Shlomo Avineri, and the prime minister's adviser on intelligence affairs, Rehavam Zeevi. The committee endorses the government decision, though a number of its members (Yigal Horowitz, Esther Herlitz, Mordechai Ben Porat, Yehuda Ben Meir, Eitan Livni) spoke among themselves afterward in terms of reservation about the decision.

The government's decision is reported to Ambassador Gazit in Paris. Yigal Allon clarifies its significance: Israel will discuss with the hijackers the release of terrorists in her prisons against the release of the hostages. In other words, Israel seeks to avoid a situation in which she must apply to other countries (Switzerland and Germany) for the release of their prisoners. In the same spirit, the foreign minister passes on the decision to a number of world personalities.

While the government and the security and foreign affairs committee are holding their meetings under the impression that they must hasten to pass on Israel's decision before expiry of the ultimatum, Colonel Bar-Lev hears from Idi Amin that he would do well to listen to an important announcement on Radio Kampala at 1:00 p.m. A similar message comes from France. What does it mean? Israel doesn't know. At 1:00 p.m. Radio Uganda announces the hijackers' decision to extend the ultimatum to Sunday. They have extended the ultimatum without reference to the government decision.

At 1:30 p.m. the ministerial team convenes for a discussion of the new developments. They reach the conclusion that the problem has become purely Israeli: with the second release of hostages, all hostages have been released except Israelis and those who hold dual nationality. At this meeting there is a proposal to send Moshe Dayan to Entebbe to negotiate, in parallel with the negotiation through Ambassador Gazit in Paris.

At 11:00 p.m. the team again meets to discuss the tactics of negotiation. The administrative personnel suggest checking first the logistic side of a trade. Where will it take place? What planes will transport the terrorists from prison in Israel? How will the swap be carried out? The team instructs Gazit and Zeevi to open negotiations on these questions. It is agreed that until there are satisfactory answers on these points there will be no discussion of the number of terrorists to be released or of their names. A joint Israeli-French negotiation team is proposed. In Paris this is conveyed and the French foreign minister agrees. Israel suggests that the released terrorists be flown by El Al to French territory as the hostages are brought to the same place.

It seemed, that Thursday, a victory for Track A. Or as many Israelis saw it, a surrender to terrorist blackmail. A black mood settled upon the nation, despite a bulletin that the two chief rabbis had delivered opinions favoring negotiation.

7

TRACK A: SURRENDER?

"Thursday was critical," Prime Minister Rabin said later. "I had to report that we had no military option that could be applied before the Thursday deadline set by the terrorists."

Relatives of the hostages broke into the prime minister's compound as that deadline neared, demanding the release of the jailed terrorists named by President Amin's companions as the price for the return alive of the hijacked victims in Uganda.

"I could not resist the demand to negotiate," said the prime minister. "Military operations depended upon accurate intelligence and proof, by way of full dress rehearsals, that a commando strike could be conducted with success."

His military commanders continued to work around the clock on the Track B option. They knew President Amin was to fly to the summit conference of African states, completing his term as chairman of the OAU. If the proso-profiles on President Amin and the sus-

pected terrorist chiefs were accurate, there was hope
for an extension of the hijackers' deadline. With time,
Dan Shomron's tactical squads might hammer out a
scheme with air force cooperation. Already Israeli specialists dressed in business suits were flying down to
Nairobi, 4½ hours away by Israel's state airline, El Al,
which stopped at the Kenyan capital on its route to
Johannesburg. Certain of Israel's intelligence agents
were driving into Uganda from Kenya, following the
long road through the spectacular Rift Valley, a five-
hour drive if the cars did not overheat and border police
gave no trouble.

Some of this intelligence effort had come from Yerucham Amitai, a senior officer of the Israeli air force
during the earlier War of Attrition. Deputy Commander
Amitai had trained Uganda's pilots during the honeymoon with President Amin until the dictator demanded
that Israel supply him with supersonic jet fighters.

"When I told President Amin the fighters were too
complicated and costly," Amitai said, "he misunder-
stood and flew into a rage. I meant of course that
Uganda's air defenses were best built on more modest
aircraft. He thought I meant Ugandans were not good
enough to fly sophisticated jets. 'We can do anything,'
President Amin ranted. 'We shall put our men on the
moon. We shall get Migs from Russia and bomb my
greatest enemy, Julius Nyerere in Tanganyika.' "

When relations between Uganda and Israel were
broken, the Russians moved in. They had been on the
sidelines while Amitai was with the Israeli air force
mission. "If I had Ugandan pilots in the air in my
trainers," Amitai had recalled, "and a Russian got into
the Entebbe Airport circuit, I'd keep my boys circling
and force the Russian to remain in second place until
he began to plead to get down. But these were pin-
pricks. I knew Russian control was inevitable and that
one day we'd have to reckon with enemies hiding behind Uganda's mad president. We couldn't play that
game. We couldn't give Uganda all its toys at the whim
of a self-appointed field marshal, grand admiral, and
super air chief! The Russians would, and did—including
the Migs."

Planning for the inevitable clash, Amitai and other

Israelis kept meticulous records. They knew what Communist arms Big Daddy was getting, and how these were used to train Palestinian and other terrorists. They watched professional terrorists move into key Ugandan posts. More than three hundred Palestinians were appointed to civil service jobs vacated by Asians who were expelled as remnants of British colonial rule.

Israel built the new additions to Entebbe Airport during Amitai's service. The men on Track B had already built models of the Entebbe runways and buildings when word came from Uganda that President Amin's departure for the African summit talks coincided with the deadline extension of three days. To the paratroopers and commandos of the Special Air Service there was the sense of gears being shifted, of a nation delicately shifting balance from submission to action.

"Once you yield to blackmail," Amitai had once said, "there's no end to it. There will be more demands and more demands. The West is being blackmailed and we keep yielding to each challenge. It has to stop."

The decision to stop was taken almost subconsciously. Yerucham Amitai, a great airman, survivor of Warsaw, a godly man, was not able to share the moment. He was killed in a crash some time after 1972, when Uganda dismissed all Israeli military, diplomatic, and technical aid missions.

He possessed immense resolve. He would never have softened after that dreadful word *selekzia,* the selection of Jews, appeared in Thursday's headlines.

Selekzia was the word repeated now as the hijackers released another 101 hostages from Uganda. All who remained in terrorist hands were Jews—plus the Air France crew whose captain refused to leave and persuaded his French colleagues that they too must remain to witness where the selection process might lead.

Some notion was conveyed by a 62-year-old woman among the released hostages whose name was transmitted to Jerusalem as Julie Oiserant. She told interrogators:

During the stopover in Athens I noticed two young Arabs boarding the plane with cans of stuffed dates, which seemed odd. One was red-haired and later I learned he wore a wig. They were followed into the plane by a German couple. The woman was about 28; she wore blue stockings, a dark blue skirt, and a light blue blouse. Her hair was dark, of a strange color. Later I discovered that she too was wearing a wig. The man, who looked slightly older, accompanied her to the first-class section.

After Athens, suddenly, I noticed the steward talking with one of the Arabs and raising his arms in surrender. He drew back, his face showing fear. From that, I comprehended that the Arab was aiming a gun at him. I couldn't believe my eyes. I thought that I was dreaming.

I saw the entire cabin crew—stewards and stewardesses—raise their arms above their heads, and then lie down, face downwards. One of the stewardesses was close to my seat. She lay on the floor with her hands on the back of her neck.

In the first-class section the two Germans raced toward the pilot's-cabin I was too far away to see what was happening there, but the first-class passengers told us about it later.

Everything happened at a dizzy speed. The German woman came to the tourist section where we were sitting and began shouting in German. I did not understand her words, but several times I heard her shout: "Che Guevara." After that, one of the stewards, who spoke English, was ordered to translate. We were told that we were being hijacked in the name of "Arab and world revolution." We were forbidden to move— any unnecessary movement would lead to shooting.

We were told that the hijackers were renaming the plane *Arafat*. The German woman added that, in place of Air France, we were to use the name *Arafat*. A short, bearded man, about five feet three, who spoke French with a heavy Yiddish accent, tried to resist. The hijackers knocked him to the floor and beat him severely—the German woman doing most of the punching. We froze in our seats. The head steward told us there was nothing to worry about. We should not be frightened. But he himself was shaking like a leaf. Surprisingly, we became relaxed. Mothers continued to look after their children, other passengers sat in silence, and there were even those who went on reading papers or books.

None of us knew where the plane was heading; all we knew was that we were flying to some other place. When I went to the toilet—after requesting permission, and escorted by the German woman—I saw the Arabs and the German speaking into the plane's radio transmitter.

One of the hijackers' first acts was to confiscate our passports and other documents in our possession. They noted down every item. After that the stewards passed along the gangway, distributing drinks and biscuits, as though nothing had happened.

Benghazi—where we landed that afternoon—was nothing more than a geographical name for us. The chief steward called out, "Benghazi!" and that was how we knew where we were. We knew—my neighbors and I—that our "visit" to an Arab country dedicated to destroy Israel was not good news. This was certainly not a safe haven for us. An hour passed, and another hour, and we sat there in silence, heavy with foreboding.

When the plane took off we sensed relief. Someone said we were flying south. The rest remained silent. They didn't speak: the hijackers did not permit conversations. The German woman was especially strict, she walked along the gangway, one hand scratching her hair—or, to be precise, the wig she was wearing— while the other held a grenade. She barked at us to be silent, over and over.

I heard crew members whispering that the gang knew where we were going from the start, that the chief pilot was shown a chart with the different places marked. Still I could not guess where.

We landed at a time when it was very dark—the darkest hour, perhaps 3:30 a.m. Then a steward told us we were in Uganda. Uganda? Nobody near me knew where this Uganda was, or anything else about it. And then somebody whispered that this was the country of Idi Amin. Now we knew where we were.

I must confess I was frightened. For me Amin resembled Hitler. He had boasted how much he admired

Hitler. First the German woman was screaming out orders and casting terrifying glances—and now: the country of Idi Amin. During those moments I fancied that I had entered a terrible nightmare world—the world of the concentration camps of World War II.

We sat in the plane for several hours, waiting; no one knew why. From our seats we could see the airport building, the terminal, and a number of Ugandan policemen and soldiers running toward the plane. After that, powerful searchlights were switched on, illuminating the plane like daylight.

We waited there till 10:00 a.m. Then the door of the plane was opened and we were permitted to descend, one after another. We were taken to the central lounge, from where we could see Lake Victoria. I never dreamed I would see the lake.

A few minutes later, a helicopter circled above us. Idi Amin arrived, together with his son, who is about seven or eight years old. Father and son wore identical uniforms, with identical decorations and medals.

Idi Amin entered the lounge, laughing and shaking hands all round. "Welcome, welcome to Uganda!" he said over and over again.

Idi Amin said that he would try to make sure that our stay in Uganda would be as comfortable as possible. Numerous African women entered the lounge, carrying armchairs. I think there were enough armchairs for all of us—250 or more. After that breakfast was served: tea, bananas, bread and butter, eggs, and even potatoes. Idi Amin launched upon a long speech, encouraged by our applause. The Palestinians are entitled to state of their own, he said: the Zionists and the imperialists are depriving the Palestinians of a state. He told of his recent visit to Damascus, and to its Jewish community; he assured us that the Jews of Damascus were treated well. "Don't worry about them," he said, "the Syrians are looking after them and supplying all their needs."

He was followed by a doctor and a nurse. They asked each of us whether we were ill, or in need of medical attention. The doctor looked like an Arab, and several people said he was a Palestinian. The few examinations made were hurried and superficial. One of the passengers—Solomon Rubin—suffers from a heart ailment; for him, the doctor prescribed a few aspirin tablets.

Throughout the night we were guarded by two of the hijackers, who were armed with submachine guns. I noticed that the Germans—the man and the cruel woman—did not sit down for one moment. They stood throughout their turn of guard duty. The German was still carrying the submachine gun, which had previously been strapped to his back, underneath his jacket. That was how he brought the gun onto the plane at Athens.

All the hijackers were well armed and determined to complete the operation they had begun. The German carried a submachine gun; each of the others carried a pistol in one hand and a hand grenade in the other. It appeared that relations between the terrorists and the Ugandans were excellent. Before we went to sleep, we were warned that anyone trying to "cross the lines" would be shot dead.

The Ugandan soldiers were stationed at least 20 yards away from us. We had the impression that the Ugandans were helping the hijackers to keep us prisoners.

After we were brought to Entebbe the hijackers received reinforcements. Two men who looked like Palestinians joined our captors. Someone said they were members of the local PLO office in the capital, Kampala. In any case, the armed terrorists, together with the Ugandan army—which surrounded us and seemed to be cooperating with the hijackers—precluded any attempt at resistance.

Idi Amin came to visit us again. He said that he was doing everything in his power to bring about—by means of negotiations—the release of some of us: in other words, elderly people, invalids, mothers, and small children. Afterward he claimed that the hijackers had offered to release 40 persons, but he succeeded in persuading them to release 48.

Throughout the time we were in the lounge in Entebbe we did not once see the French ambassador or anyone else, except for our captors, Idi Amin, his bodyguards, and the African women.

Tuesday was sad and tragic. In the evening, just

before supper, the German hijacker entered, holding a list. He began to read out names. After four or five, it became clear that they were all Israeli names. Those whose names were called took their suitcases and possessions and moved to another room. Many of the 83 were crying as they went to the second room. Many of us who remained where we were felt miserable. It was a terrible scene—that thick German accent and the *selekzia*.

The 83 went. A few minutes later Amin entered the outer room to meet them. We couldn't hear everything he said—only fragments reached our ears. Several times we heard him say the Hebrew word "Shalom." When he concluded, the Israelis clapped. It was an awful night, even though I myself and many others knew that we would soon be released.

Yesterday, Wednesday, we knew it was all over. Idi Amin visited us again. We, the lucky ones who were about to be released, were preparing our departure. Idi Amin shook hands with each one. He wished us a good journey, and assured us that he was our friend.

A French nun, whose name was on the list of those to be liberated, protested. She wanted to stay behind, and give her place up to someone else—an elderly person, or an invalid. Another person—a Frenchwoman, about 55 years old—made a similar offer; but it soon was clear that the list was fixed and unchangeable.

We were taken in a bus to the French consulate, where the ambassador awaited us. That was the first time we saw him. We shook hands, we were given orange juice, and then we drove to the new airport, where we boarded the plane. It was all over. After a flight of nine hours, we reached Paris. For us the adventure was over.

For us—and for us alone. None of us who have returned knows what will happen now, or what will be the fate of those who remained. It's clear that the hijackers seem determined, that over two hundred hostages are still captives in their hands, and that they are capable of anything.

Moshe Peretz, the Israeli medical student, was recording Thursday's events at Entebbe:

0800—The routine timetable: breakfast, washing clothes, the children on the lawn, house arrest.

1200—Amin appears in battle dress, together with his son, and informs us that so far negotiations have failed, because of the obstinacy of the Israeli government. He announces that he is negotiating with the government through the offices of his good friend Colonel Bar-Lev, and that he has gained an extension of the ultimatum to 11:00 a.m. on Sunday. There is an air of depression among the Israeli group. People are quiet and sad; they don't talk much with one another—they've withdrawn within themselves. The children continue to play.

1400—A second group of Frenchmen leaves. Those remaining are the Israelis, 20 young Frenchmen, and the crew. In the meantime the terrorists have invented a new form of entertainment: they read out the names of the Israelis and each one who is called lifts his finger. The terrorist takes a long look at his face and makes some mysterious mark by his name. Are these marks the signs for life or death? It's horrifying. One boy, about 16 years old, apparently slow in raising his hand, was rewarded by one of the Arabs with a sharp slap, accompanied by terrifying shouts. Rumors are going around about tortures which four of the passengers have undergone. It's reported that the hijackers have subjected them to electric shocks and threats of murder. Four persons were, indeed, taken to a neighboring room. One of the men was beaten severely, and one of the women was treated to threats.

1600—We are brought back to the central lounge. We feel united, together with the Frenchmen and the crew. A good feeling (under the circumstances).

1800—We've just received tidings which have made us all jump for joy. It has been made known that the Israeli government has accepted the terrorists' conditions in their entirety! What joy! Everyone is hugging and kissing one another, as though they had just been "born anew." The news came from the French captain of the plane. However, a few of the hostages say the decision leaves them with a strange taste in their mouths. True, they are included among those to be released, but the fact that all the terrorists' demands have been accepted means giving them further opportunities to operate against civil aviation.

2000—We organize sleeping arrangements and make preparations for tomorrow's flight home.

8

SHIFT TO TRACK B: ATTACK

While the hostages and their families were rejoicing and indulging in wishful thinking a feeling of depression spread through Israel: the heavy sense of surrender and of helplessness. The cabinet felt the same way. Some ministers contended that surrender—in the face of the *selekzia* the only option open to them—would inflict a further blow at the government's position. Israel's antiterrorist campaign would peter out.

The cabinet's decision to surrender was genuine, and no mere ruse. Nevertheless, as is his way, Prime Minister Yitzhak Rabin was trying to gain time. Hours. Days.

A combined intelligence operation by Friday, July 2, began the shift to Track B, the military option.

Police and military specialists in terrorism fed information to Israel from several Western capitals, disregarding the timid views of politicians and the official policies of governments. An underground network created itself out of the challenge of the tyrant and his terrorist allies in Uganda. President Amin was a puppet of his so-called State Research Department, organized by Soviet Russian advisers and staffed by highly trained protégés of the Palestinian guerrilla agencies. State Research Department was the cover name for a secret police so powerful that Big Daddy, despite his self-proclaimed titles of operatic splendor, performed a stage role. This much was made clear by the collection of intelligence from many sources.

From West Germany came information on Wilfried

Böse, tentatively identified as the German who declared himself captain of the hijacked airbus.

From Canada came a flood of material collected by Guy Toupin, coordinator of security for the 1976 Olympic Games in Montreal. Toupin had worked for more than a year with the police of a dozen countries in preparation for the Olympics. He recalled only too vividly the massacre of Israeli athletes during the 1972 Olympic Games in Munich. That had been the work of Palestinian guerrillas, and Toupin pointed out that that Uganda's President had cabled the United Nations his joy and approval of the slayings, adding his praise of Hitler for killing 6 million Jews. Was it not probable that the mastermind behind the Olympic massacre of 1972 sheltered in Uganda?

The speed and efficiency of "Captain" Wilfried Böse in taking over the airbus was confirmed by information smuggled out of Uganda by the Air France crew. Captain Michel Bacos, the slim gray-haired skipper of the airbus, insisted that in no circumstances would he or the plane's other crew members leave Uganda without all passengers; when the two batches of hostages were released, he sent with them a detailed report of events between Athens-Benghazi-Entebbe. "It was a dangerous action, dangerous to his own safety," commented an Israeli minister later. "But it characterized all his actions. Captain Bacos even swept the floors and made the beds of sick passengers, advising them what to say and how to behave so that none of the terrorists nor Amin would be provoked. Most important, though, was this intelligence that the hijacking was calculated and executed by experts whose leaders were now gathered in Uganda."

Shimon Peres, the Polish-born defense minister who had learned to fly during 25 years of public service in Israel, understood and admired what Captain Bacos was trying to do. Peres was the architect of good French-Israeli relations in the 1950s that led to the acquisition of the French Mirage jet fighters. The Mirage was modified by research scientists who were mobilized by Peres while he served in defense under David Ben-Gurion, then both prime minister and minister of defense, and this new Israeli version made the Mirage one of the world's most envied fighters.

In his Tel Aviv office Peres dealt with a constant stream of soldiers and airmen. From the first day of crisis he was convinced that surrender was the greater risk.

"What use is it to speak of freedom if people are afraid to make sacrifices for it?" he demanded of Chief of Staff Mordechai Gur.

There was no need for Gur to reply. His mind had been on Track B all along, though he could offer no realistic military option before the first terrorist deadline. All week he had encouraged ideas from his men. By Friday the more outrageous schemes had been eliminated. Attention focused on the single rescue plan that seemed to offer the least danger to life.

The great rescue depended on these considerations, laid out coolly by Peres:

1. President Amin was enjoying the tremendous publicity and the terrorists encouraged him to bathe in the light of world attention. There was no possibility of arguing Amin into cooperating with Israel, but there was every indication that he and the terrorists wished to prolong their act. Therefore, Gur should try to put together a precise operation on the basis that there was time for a full dress rehearsal.

2. Six terrorist leaders were known to have driven from Somalia to Kampala, preferring surface transport to avoid detection. President Amin had spoken of "the number one" standing beside him during one of the bizarre phone exchanges with shopkeeper and ex-military adviser Bar-Lev in Israel. This might be Dr. Hadad, whose chief concern must be to milk the situation for its propaganda value within the Palestinian guerrilla movements as well as outside.

3. President Amin would use the conference of the OAU to make a grand entrance, then rush back to watch the countdown to Sunday's new deadline.

4. There was reason to fear that the execution of hostages would begin Sunday, one by one at long intervals, to demonstrate the gravity of the terrorist threats.

5. The Uganda State Research Department would

control any lunatic urge on President Amin's part until Sunday. Then the secret police might see some advantage to displaying brutality.

The great rescue should aim for Saturday night, therefore, no less than six hours before the dawn of Sunday, July 4, when the executions might begin.

A report, was leaked to the public from the scene of the Olympic Games in Canada. The Jackal was in Montreal. Other circumstantial details were released to persuade terrorist organizations that the identity of Wilfried Böse had not been guessed; that the presence of terrorist leaders in Somalia and Uganda was not suspected; and that Israel felt itself alone in dealing with a dangerous and unknown situation.

The Jackal, known also as Carlos, identified as Ilich Ramirez Sanchez, was trained in the tradition of the assassin sent by the Soviet Union to kill Stalin's personal enemy, Trotsky. There was a slim chance of catching him in Entebbe, and on July 2 The Jackal's file was hastily assembled from intelligence drawn from Europe and the Americas. He was connected with the killing of two Paris police officers, the kidnapping of delegates to the Vienna conference of the Organization of Petroleum Exporting Countries (OPEC), and other acts of violence. His companion and technical adviser was, of course, the German now watching over the hostages at Entebbe.

"It would be useful to take the hijackers alive," commented an intelligence officer, reading The Jackal's file.

Defense Minister Peres shook his head doubtfully. "The priority is the rescue of the hostages. However—"

A scheme to send General Moshe Dayan to Uganda pierced the screen designed to filter out the crazier proposals. "It reached the task force because someone saw Dayan as the man to get the terrorist leaders, another saw him back in the role he performed long ago with Nasser of Egypt, and yet another thought it would flatter President Amin." Prime Minister Rabin commented later, "I saw nothing but humiliation and the loss of Dayan."

Dayan, the soldier with the black eye patch who seemed to symbolize Israel to the world outside, was considered first as a possible answer to the question: Can we get Hadad or any other senior terrorist alive?

There was a faint chance, because "Big Daddy" Amin was introducing Dayan's name repeatedly in the telephone conversations between himself and "Borka" Bar-Lev. At one stage Dayan was asked to phone the African dictator. His reply: "If he wants to talk, make it face to face."

That was the way the idea grew. The chief of staff had told all units that the channels of communication to the top were wide open: "We'll give any plan a chance."

Dayan, since he was military commander of Jerusalem more than a quarter century ago, had developed a reputation for dealing diplomatically with his enemies when he was not taking them by surprise on the battlefield.

Prime Minister Rabin's greatest fear was that if Dayan got wind of the plan to send him into the hostage camp, his love of danger and action would make him virtually unstoppable. A dashing rescue mission might suit his temperament, but it would encourage Israel's foreign critics to accuse her of reckless military impulses.

"Still I had to analyze the proposal and prepare to argue against it," said Rabin. "Every scheme that reached the task force became the subject of attack and defense, as if we had all the time in the world for devil's advocates and the adversary system.

"If Dayan went, he was likely to be killed. If he dazzled Amin instead, the president would maneuver him into the same act of humiliation as the British general sent by the queen, who was obliged to kneel publicly as the price of saving lives during another of Amin's adventures."

Plans were laid for getting an emissary to Entebbe nonetheless. The time was not wasted. The flight details could serve as well for a commando raid. And as it happened, Dayan knew all about the scheme and was packed to go. But he knew that more was at stake than his life. Uganda's secret police would turn over such a prize to the terrorists, and Dayan had just studied the declaration from Lebanon that confirmed the eagerness of the PFLP to keep world attention: "Flight 139 was taken in order to remind the world of our intention to expel Zionists so that we may replace Israel with a 'socialist democracy.' The Air France plane is the price of French military intervention in Lebanon designed to divert attention from our cause."

This was the political arm speaking for the guerrillas in Uganda, and Dayan had no intention of walking into a trap. Instead, doing his best not to seem an interfering old soldier who should stick to his archaeological digging into the past, he suggested that identikits and profiles of PFLP guerrilla chiefs be shared out among leaders of commando groups earmarked for any military action. This had been done. "In that case, if you want my opinion," said Dayan, "I'm 150 percent in favor of military action." And as new information reached Israel through the French Direction de la Surveillance du Territoire (DST), Scotland Yard, the CIA and FBI, the security branch of the Royal Canadian Mounted Police (RCMP), and more was smuggled out of Uganda by released hostages and Israel's informants within "Big Daddy" Amin's government, commando groups were given photographs and identikit details to memorize. They were to proceed on the basis that action would be required.

There were still those praying for the capture alive of those like The Jackal who knew the supporters of the new terrorist agencies, and where they functioned, and how. The biggest prize would be Dr. Wadi Hadad, identified as the author of the Entebbe demands to Jerusalem. Hadad had been described by Israeli intelligence as "being outlawed, behaves like a 19th-century Russian anarchist who derives almost mystical satisfaction from knowing—with others of his organization —that he is cut off from the rest of the world and thus obeys rules and standards of his (and their) own making."

9

DR. HADAD: PLANNER OF TERROR

Fresh facts hardened the conviction of Defense Minister Peres that military action must be taken.

"If Israel gives way," he said during the critical hours between Thursday and Friday, "I fear a tremendous catastrophe for this country. And when we discuss the lives of the hostages and the danger to their lives, I want you to know I regard them as if they were Israeli soldiers in a war."

He spoke in measured tones under the portrait of David Ben-Gurion, and the soldiers listening said later it was as if they were in the presence of that "stubborn, rebellious, tempestuous spirit," as Peres himself had described it when Ben-Gurion died in the aftermath of the Yom Kippur War. "His was the spirit of the Jewish people," Peres had said then. And for the young commanders streaming through the defense minister's office with operational plans that ranged from kidnapping President Amin to more sedate methods of releasing the hostages, it seemed that here was someone who would remove the bitter taste of that last conflict and erase the memory of dangerous hesitations and near-fatal delays in the response to the sudden massive attacks that had almost overwhelmed Israel only three years before.

For the soldiers saw time running out fast. Commanders like Dan Shomron recognized that the campaigns against Israel had shifted to worldwide terrorism in the hope that the nation might become an outlaw— pushed outside by a new law of the jungle in which other free nations feared for their own survival and put their safety above all moral considerations.

The soldiers had no fear of striking into the heart of Africa. Airmen reported no problems in landing by night on a blacked-out airfield under heavy and hostile guard. The navy had ships equipped to provide electronic protection.

But world opinion? The casualties in a rescue mission might be very high. Peres had experts making estimates now on the basis of alternate plans and variants. What the world refused to believe was that terrorism was war, conducted without declarations, aimed at the structure of traditional societies built painfully by trial and error.

Peres and the rest of the task force knew fairly accurately who their real enemies were in Uganda. A report laid before Peres was explicit. A terrorist headquarters had been set up in Somalia, which had joined the Arab League against Israel three years earlier. Uganda was the first country that extended a helping hand to hijackers, and success would encourage neighboring Somalia and others. Out of Somalia had come Dr. Wadi Hadad.

Dr. Hadad was as shadowy a figure as The Jackal, and the time was approaching when Israel's intelligence agencies would have to disclose how much they knew about him.

On July 11, 1970, Dr. Wadi Hadad was saved from death by a miracle. The fact that he survived was to influence the course of Palestinian terrorism throughout the world. The story was summarized by the Lebanese Security Service:

A rocket attack on Dr. Hadad's home on July 11 is entirely similar to the bombardment of the Palestine Liberation Organization offices in September 1969.

This time the target was the home of one of the senior men responsible for the Popular Front for the Liberation of Palestine, headed by Dr. George Habash —the home of Dr. Wadi Elias Hadad, a 40-year-old Palestinian. He is considered to be the number two man in the PFLP and a founder of the Arab Nationalist Movement.

The Arab freedom fighter Leila Khaled, who took part in the hijacking of a TWA plane to Damascus in August 1969, was a guest in Dr. Hadad's house at the time of the bombardment, but was unharmed.

At 0214 hours a loud explosion was heard in Dr. Hadad's house, which is on the third floor on the

Katarji Building in Almala District—Muhi Aldin Al-
hayat Street.

Six Katyusha rockets of Soviet make were launched
from an apartment on the fifth floor of a building which
faces the Katarji Building. The rockets were launched
from a distance of approximately one hundred meters;
three of them penetrated the salon and bedroom of
Dr. Hadad's apartment. Two rockets did not work because of technical malfunction. Fire broke out in Dr.
Hadad's apartment. Doors and windows in the apartment, and of cars parked in the street, were damaged.

Dr. Hadad was slightly injured. His wife, Samia
Hadad, and his son Hagi (eight years old) suffered
burns and were taken for treatment to the American
University Hospital.

In the apartment from which the rockets were fired
was a standard wardrobe, a simple bed, and some
cheap furniture. Surgical gloves were also found in the
apartment. The assumption is that the criminal used
them to assemble the rockets without leaving fingerprints.

A man representing himself as Ahmad Batzrat, holding an Iranian passport, arrived in Beirut three months
ago and rented the apartment from which the rockets
were fired. He bought modest furniture and drove a
beige Volkswagen. The suspect had written an English
sentence by the launching assembly: "Made by Fatah,
1970."

Dr. Hadad manages considerable activity in the
PFLP and devotes himself completely to the cause;
he no longer practices medicine. He is a graduate of the
American University, and is very close to Dr. Habash.
He is always on the move, and never stays anywhere
permanently.

The information department of the PFLP has published a communiqué on the incident in which they accuse the Israeli enemy and American intelligence circles
and agents of the assassination attempt. Dr. Hadad is
quoted as saying that the bombardment of his home was
the work of Zionist and American organizations.

The suspect Ahmad Batzrat is a dark-skinned young
man in his thirties, thin with a mustache, and wears
black glasses; he represented himself as not having a

command of Arabic, and avoided meeting people.
The investigation is trying to establish how the assassin succeeded in discovering the home of Dr. Wadi Hadad and how he knew that Leila Khaled was there at night, particularly since Dr. Hadad had been in France and only returned to Beirut two days before.

The investigation revealed that the terrorist came from Europe, and that he traveled by Lufthansa and Air France, as evidenced by the labels on his valises that remained in the rented apartment.

The two valises that were found had false bottoms and sides. The assumption is that the assassin used them to get the rockets through Beirut Airport.

It became clear that Ahmad Batzrat was the chief agent among a number who were assigned to bombard Dr. Wadi Hadad's home and kill him, and that he did not act alone in carrying out this mission, which required the work of more than one man. He was apparently chosen to be the overt operative of the gang.

Yasir Arafat condemned this act and said that this criminal operation was a link in a chain of conspiracy woven by the counterrevolution in order to eliminate Palestinian resistance. Arafat added that this team was preceded by many others, and especially by the firing of rockets at the Palestine Liberation Organization offices in Beirut, and the attempt to assassinate Haled Yasrami, also in Beirut.

The agent could have brought the rockets through Beirut Airport, or across the frontier, or by buying them on the local black market. In each case, the agent would need a local base, an inside net which would carry out each mission, observation posts, planning, renting of an apartment, and preparation of the equipment. The agent is the expert who comes when everything is ready, aims the rockets at the target, sets the time mechanism, and leaves.

It is almost certain that there is a network depending on a few hired local agents. Uncovering these, of course, calls for an intelligence and police effort at a high scientific level, but first there is a need for deterrent force.

It is clear that the man called Ahmad Rauf came from West Germany and returned there, as did Ahmad

Batzrat, whose papers left in the apartment are West German documents; the airports of West Germany share some of the responsibility, as do the German security mechanisms who for the second time running have allowed fake passports to pass through their airports going and coming.

The great diligence with which the conspirators covered their tracks suggests that the proofs left behind are planted evidence. The implication is that the rockets were not brought from abroad but procured in Lebanon. The evidence to prove the contrary was deliberately fabricated.

Hadad has not hesitated to use aircraft hijacking as a means to finance his terror activities. The classic example of this was the hijacking to Aden of a Lufthansa plane in February 1972, which netted a ransom payment of $5 million for its release.

Intelligence reported that "all strings lead to Dr. Wadi Hadad, who up till now has served as operations officer of the Popular Front for the Liberation of Palestine."

At first West German security thought that gangsters were involved in the hijacking of the Jumbo; or, because the operation was so professionally executed, that it was a "brilliant tactic of the Israeli Shin Beth," with the intention of discrediting the Palestinians.

A review of Hadad's career, and the burdens placed on Israel when Flight 139 was pirated to Uganda, provoked an outburst from the transport minister, Gad Yaakobi, whose ministry dealt with the security of travelers. During the crisis he was disturbed by evidence that other nations preferred to shy from taking precautions and collaborating in the frustration of terrorism. Too many governments were afraid of offending Arab, African, and Asian sensibilities. "Yet nobody hijacks aircraft to Communist countries," Yaakobi observed dryly.

"With Flight 139 we paid the bill and took the whole responsibility," he said. "Israel suffered from the neglect of others from start to finish."

Because Israel felt it was fighting international terrorism alone, and because of the feeling that many

Western governments choose for political reasons to play down the formidable nature of aerial pirates, Israel on Friday, July 2, made available further information on Dr. Wadi Hadad. It was a preparatory move to disarm those who would criticize Israel if the rescue mission to Entebbe failed.

Dr. Hadad's followers run the splinter PFLP, which hijacked Flight 139. They seek to extend terror against Israel beyond the frontiers of the Middle East through tight cooperation with non-Arab underground organizations. . . .

The members of this faction engage in very little ideological propaganda or information diffusion. They concentrate on showpiece actions. Numerically they are very few, and their advantage lies in administrative capabilities, in their operational experience, and in utilization of international contacts.

Wadi Hadad, 46, is Greek Orthodox. He was apparently born in Safad, but spent his youth in Jerusalem. His father, Elias Nasralla, was one of the most famous Arab teachers in Palestine at the end of the Ottoman Empire and during the British mandate.

Hadad, the son, studied medicine in Beirut's American University together with Dr. George Habash. The two of them started the Arab Nationalist Movement, an organization that set up a chain of branches throughout the Arab world and established links with President Nasser.

With the founding of the PFLP at the end of 1967, Hadad quickly became the main operations figure. In 1968 he devised the hijacking of an El Al airliner to Algeria—the first in a chain of hijackings. He discovered and encouraged Leila Khaled (who was careful not to mention him in her memoirs).

Dr. Hadad began his underground activity in 1963 in Jordan, when he opened (with his friend George Habash) an eye clinic in Amman which served as a cover for the Arab Nationalist Movement.

In the clinic was a small press where they printed handbills in which medicines dispensed to needy Palestinians were wrapped. After the Six Day War the

Arab Nationalist Movement became the PFLP, led by Habash with Hadad as his operations officer.

When the PFLP headquarters transferred to Beirut, Dr. Hadad's apartment not far from the main al-Hamra Street became the operational center of the organization. Ie was here that Hadad met with his operatives and planned the first strikes of the PFLP outside Israel.

Dr. Hadad is the man who thought of transferring the terror war beyond the frontiers of Israel. The first operation was an attempt to hit David Ben-Gurion during a transit stop in Denmark. Afterward he began to plan aircraft hijackings. Under his guiding hand, an El Al plane was taken to Algeria and a TWA aircraft to Damascus (with Leila Khaled in command of the hijackers); Hadad's planning is also evident in the operation—the biggest and most sophisticated to date—of hijacking simultaneously three aircraft.

Dr. Hadad is a handsome man who includes women, some of them his mistresses, in all his operations. Thus it was with Muna Saudi, a beautiful painter, who took part in his first operation in Denmark. Thus it was with Leila Khaled, and again with Leila's successor, the beautiful Iraqi Katie Thomas, who led the hijacking of a Japanese Jumbo, and was killed when a grenade exploded in the plane.

Hadad rarely appears in public. He has almost never been photographed, and is most cautious in his movements and travels.

Lufthansa and the German authorities gave in to Hadad's extortion, so this terrorist had ample means to finance more terrorism.

In July 1973, Hadad's men, again commanded by a woman, hijacked a JAL airliner and demanded $15 million ransom; the plane was demolished on the runway of Benghazi Airport.

On April 12, 1976, Dr. Wadi Hadad began preparing a new wave of terror, and advocated terror against Israel throughout the world.

And so it can be said today that it is doubtful whether there is any other Palestinian so expert in terror and with such serious links with international terror organizations. For years he has served as nerve center for Palestinian links with German terrorists, South Americans, Irish, Japanese, Scandinavians, and many others who are prepared to share in sabotage and murder.

Only Wadi Hadad would be capable, in present circumstances, of organizing a group apparently including foreigners to carry out the Flight 139 hijack. Hadad has friends and helpers not only among terror operatives. Muammar al-Qaddafi in Libya could be included in the list, as could Idi Amin in Uganda and leaders of the regimes of South Yemen and Iraq.

In Japan, Hadad recruited the members of the Japanese Red Army, from which Kozo Okamoto and his comrades appeared on the international terror scene for the first time to carry out the massacre at Lod Airport in May 1972.

The list—in the last five years—is long and staggering. But not all Dr. Hadad's attempts and plans work out successfully. He also has failures. His strikes are sometimes foiled. A man like Hadad does not give up. If he fails, he immediately appears elsewhere with another plan. And the terror balance sheet is in his favor.

Hadad's movements are kept a secret—and from time to time he appears in odd parts of the world: Southeast Asia, Europe, South America, the oil emirates, and, of course, his favorite countries where he receives support—Iraq, Libya, Uganda, Somalia, and South Yemen.

Hadad is the supplier for various operations. Palestinian and other, of documentation, funds, weapons, and explosives. His hand has shaken those of The Jackal, of Baader-Meinhof, and of the Japanese Red Army.

Before Hadad started planning and executing the Air France hijacking to Uganda, he failed in a terror attempt at Ben-Gurion Airport in Israel. He sent a German, Bernard Hausman, as a "walking bomb." Hausman came to Israel from Vienna in May 1976, not suspecting that his Palestinian friends had installed in his bags a device that would explode upon opening. He succeeded in passing negligent security at Vienna, and in putting his two booby-trapped suitcases on an Austrian Airline plane.

He was suspected the moment he got off the plane in Israel, and was asked to open his luggage. A woman security officer watched over him. Hausman confidently opened one of the cases, and a loud explosion reverberated around the terminal. He and the security officer were killed. A miracle had prevented a tragedy at the terminal—one that might have equaled that inflicted by Hadad's Japanese messengers four years earlier.

The Israeli and German authorities investigated Hausman's past, and found a model example of how German anarchists are recruited into Hadad's service. Had he not been killed at Lod Airport, Hausman would have celebrated his 26th birthday four weeks later.

Hausman was trained in a camp of George Habash's PFLP. He was classified among the terrorists who might be identified with The Jackal.

In similar fashion Dr. Hadad has recruited Japanese, South Americans, Frenchmen, Scandinavians, and other Germans for his "Terror International." That is also how he put together the team to hijack Flight 139. The German woman in the team that took the passengers from Athens to Uganda was a close friend of Hausman. She was not told that Hausman was tricked and sent to Israel as a walking bomb, but that "the Israelis murdered your friend Hausman."

She set out to revenge him, and this perhaps is the way to explain her crazed behavior throughout this week.

These were some of the details included in an intelligence digest that helped to justify the extreme measure code-named Thunderbolt, a continuation of the war between the terrorists and Israel.

10

INTELLIGENCE FILTERS IN

Thunderbolt would prove an operation unprecedented in history. But military aspects aside, it was also a unique test of democracy under siege. Prime Minister

Rabin had tried the peaceful option of Track A and now felt morally justified in switching to Track B. But he needed the cabinet's unanimous vote. All through the crises, a meticulous record was kept of every conference, every task force session, every military consultation. No one was more sensitive to this need than Rabin, the soldier who paraphrased de Tocqueville: "A democracy can only pursue firm action in foreign policy with great difficulty and slow resolve. It lies at the mercy of a dictator. If it surrenders the democratic process in order to survive, it loses the moral reasons for fighting."

Rabin was determined that Israel must move democratically. All through Friday he had argued this quietly with the commanders.

Later, it would be said that Thunderbolt was agreed upon as a practical military operation on Friday. The prime minister knew otherwise. Only on Saturday morning was it possible to say the raiders had the smallest chance of success.

That chance was taken then because intelligence from Uganda reported that the execution of the first hostages was being prepared for next morning.

"President Amin flew to Mauritius for Friday and Saturday," reported Rabin. "We gambled that nothing would happen while he played to the grandstand of the Organization of African Unity. It gave time to bring all the processes—political, military, diplomatic, and intelligence—to their logical conclusion. By Sunday, however, we could expect a new demonstration of his mania for killing."

There were no perfect answers to a problem set by madmen and fanatics. There were only choices. And each choice invited disaster. "Thunderbolt will either prove a spectacular success or a terrible catastrophe for Israel," said Rabin.

This kind of dilemma was indicated Friday night to Professor Zbigniew Brzezinski, one of the chief foreign policy advisers to U.S. presidential candidate Jimmy Carter, who dined with the chief of Israeli intelligence. The host was Defense Minister Peres, who talked quietly in Polish to Brzezinski, who like Peres is Polish-born.

The defense minister, like every other task force minister, was keeping up a front of "business as usual." On this night when Thunderbolt's dress rehearsal took place in the desert—a rehearsal whose outcome would decide if the hostages in Entebbe were doomed—he was not unhappy to have the bonus of a guest who might one day replace Henry Kissinger.

Brzezinski, a 48-year-old professor in international affairs at Columbia University, where many U.S. policymakers have emerged, examined the problem with the analytical approach of a Jesuit. He was a Catholic sensitive to the Jewish dilemma. Nothing he said that night bore upon Thunderbolt or influenced the machinery behind Track A, now virtually abandoned, or Track B, still unsettled but approaching an inevitable rendezvous with the reality of the pending executions in Uganda. But he came away with a clear picture of how Israelis can keep secrets and yet convey information. What was said at dinner became meaningful only when Professor Brzezinski phoned his New York home early Sunday and heard of the Entebbe raid. Then his discussion on ways to handle international terrorism acquired new meaning. Brzezinski had been talking about U.S. fears that the biggest danger to humanity in the next decade would be the improved technology available to small suicidal teams of fanatics. The anarchist's smoking bomb, that cartoonist's delight of the last century, would soon appear as an equally small nuclear device. Defense Minister Peres had spoken optimistically of how countermeasures might improve if the nations collaborated in inventing new responses to each new threat.

"An amazing performance," remarked Daniel Patrick Moynihan, the most outspoken of U.S. ambassadors to the United Nations. For Moynihan, too, by happy coincidence was in Israel and shared a meal with a member of the task force on Friday: Foreign Minister Allon. "He conversed long after coffeepots were empty, relaxed and seemingly without a care in the world. If his intention was to help prevent any leak of what was really being planned, he succeeded with me."

Was there a deliberate plan to deceive the world and the hijackers while Thunderbolt got underway?

"No, because of the dangerous delay in releasing the aerial armada carrying the raiders. They were airborne but still not ordered to go in case negotiations might succeed. Every wasted minute consumed tons of precious fuel and raised the risk of unpredictable changes in the Entebbe situation. That should be sufficient reply," in Daniel Moynihan's view.

A closer examination of last-minute procedures confirms this. The task force pursuing both Tracks A and B was practicing a technique of crisis management. The general staff, being a military body, concentrated on Track B. In Israel there is nothing to keep enlisted men, corporals, or brigadiers from going over the heads of their superiors. A system of communications, perhaps only possible in a family-type environment, allows ideas to flow to the top; "but God help the ambitious border guard who wastes the chief of staff's time with requests for ice cream and refrigerators" is the unofficial warning. For days fairly practical schemes had gone forward. Some that looked promising were broken into component parts and each part assigned to an intelligence team working within a sealed department.

Each intelligence research and planning cell, as they were called, had no means of knowing why it was required to determine, for example, the specific movements of President Amin. One IRP cell worked on Big Daddy's normal working routine. Another examined only the methods of transport available to him. In retrospect, it was easy to report, after hearing gossip from such cells after Thunderbolt was completed, that a dummy of Big Daddy in his black 1973 Mercedes was taken by the raiders and landed ahead of the commandos as a means of deceiving Entebbe guards. (There was such a scheme, discarded in the end as risky.)

As Big Daddy was the subject of intensive scrutiny, so were the terrorists. Deputy air force commander Yerucham Amitai's very full reports on Big Daddy's interest in aviation led to the mobilization of pilots who had served as instructors to the Ugandan air force. Their studies included an account of President Amin's demand for Japanese-style kamikaze pilots, for Phantoms to bomb President Nyerere of Tanzania, "the whore who spreads vile sexual diseases all over Africa," and for a tiny airplane just big enough for his small nine-year-old son to fly—"but no higher than the trees, and very slow."

The massive six-foot-four, 280-pound ex-British army sergeant had expressed a desire to memorialize Hitler and reprint the spurious *Protocols of the Elders of Zion.* The Russian ambassador protested against a monument to the Führer, but there is no record that he complained of the lies about Zion. An Israeli political study emphasized that buffoon though Amin might look to non-African eyes, he had capitalized cleverly on tribal divisions, destroying the backbone of the progressive Baganda by massacring 50,000 to 120,-000 of the followers of King Freddie of Buganda, who was forced to jump over his palace wall to a brief freedom that ended violently. Mixing bully-boy tactics with bursts of generosity, he kept the more educated Baganda in useful bureaucratic and commercial jobs.

At the beginning of the week Big Daddy seemed a harmless joke. Nobody in the task force had given him much thought before Flight 139's disappearance. Now he was a joke no longer, despite the Monty Python-style conversations that were launched by Borka Bar-Lev, working from his self-contained cell, unaware of why he was making ludicrous phone calls beyond the obvious need to make some unofficial contact. Personalities all over the world had been asked to seek help in Uganda to save the hostages. Bar-Lev felt he was part of an international effort that included British diplomats and Kenyan newsmen when, in the back of his shop, he lifted the receiver and asked the international exchange to get him Kampala 2241, the office of President Idi Amin.

"This is your friend Bar-Lev speaking."*

"Who?" said Amin.

"Bar-Lev . . . B as in 'bomb' . . ." and Bar-Lev spelled out his name to his old friend. Radio Uganda shortly afterward announced proudly, "Colonel Bar-Lev, an old friend of his honor the president of Uganda, has made contact in the name of the government of

---

*See transcripts of three of five telephone conversations between Bar-Lev and Amin, p. 209.

Israel. His honor the president asked him to convey to the Israeli government his request and demand that Israel should carry out the will of the hijackers. Colonel Bar-Lev will call back his excellency the moment he receives the answer from his government."

On Friday, July 2, Radio Uganda announced that Colonel Bar-Lev had spoken again with Amin. The radio station praised the Israeli officer and recommended that Prime Minister Rabin promote him to general. "Bar-Lev has done more for the hostages than the prime minister himself."

Jerusalem announced officially that it knew nothing of these telephone conversations, but secretly the government was ready to make use of Bar-Lev. He had close contacts with Amin and knew him better than others. In 1973 Amin ordered all Israelis to leave Uganda in angry reaction to the recall of Colonel Bar-Lev, then chief of the Israeli military mission in Uganda. Amin's relations with Bar-Lev while the former was Ugandan commander in chief (Amin visited Israel at this time) were so close that when President Milton Obote of Uganda, was forced into exile, he alleged that Israel was involved in Amin's coup against him.

Bar-Lev said during the Flight 139 crisis that he knew of Amin's plan to depose Obote. As far back as 1970 it had been decided to end the activities of foreign experts in Uganda. Bar-Lev persuaded Amin to sign a three-year agreement for military training and rewarded Amin for this assistance later.

According to Bar-Lev the voracious Idi Amin Dada —field marshal, honorary doctor of philosophy, president for life—was in fact no cannibal but almost a vegetarian. Bar-Lev, reporting all he knew to Israel's intelligence analysts, had this to say:

Amin is allowed nothing but vegetable salads and chicken. He likes whiskey, brandy, and other drinks; but the doctors have forbidden him alcohol, so he drinks large amounts of tea. Maybe it reminds him of the British army's NAAFI tea. When I returned to Israel, I felt there would be no difficulty in finding a job. I could direct any lunatic asylum. Amin's behavior during this crisis betrays most of the traits in Amin's complex character.

Amin is from a lesser northern tribe. He has never read a book in his life. The hijacking is the most historic opportunity for him. The whole world is writing about Uganda and about Amin, its president. Important governments negotiate with him, diplomatic messages go back and forth. He visits the hostages every day, in a different uniform each time. He comes with his small son Sharon (named after Israel's Sharon Hotel where Amin once stayed). He is applauded by the hostages and he orders them food and drink, blankets and sheets. He has only shown anger once—when one of the Jewish hostages omitted one of the titles which must be used when addressing the field marshal-doctor-president.

Idi Amin Dada's mother loved the Bible. In her will she ordered her son to honor the Jewish people. In his childhood he had no religion until convinced he was a Muslim. When he visited Israel I took him to the Omar Mosque in Jerusalem, whereupon Amin proclaimed, "Now I'm a hajji [Muslim pilgrim]," a word included in his name now. When told that to gain that title he had to undertake a pilgrimage to Mecca, he asked, "What is Mecca?"

When he was a strong 14-year-old, the British inducted Amin into the East African Rifles. He did not know English and learned numbers and letters from signs in the British barracks. He attended school for two years. During World War II he fought with his battalion in Burma and attained the rank of sergeant major. There is no doubt he has the gift of leadership; his control of his soldiers—most of them from the northern tribes—comes largely from his tall stature, his great physical strength, his mastery of English, and his Führerlike rhetoric.

But behind the hero stands the invalid. He often has sharp pains in his legs and arms. When pain attacks he goes wild. In Israel, when he underwent treatment in the Tel Hashomer hospital following his visit to Sinai after the Six Day War, he was full of praise for the Israeli army. But when the pains grew, he began to shout: "You are bad people. I saw what you did to the

Egyptian army. I want to fly home immediately and tell Obote about it." When he was told there was no plane that day he said angrily: "I'll walk to Athens, and take a plane to Uganda from there." Later Amin used to get tablets from his Israeli doctors through me.

Amin acts upon visions which no one dares disbelieve. One morning he woke up and announced that Uganda should manufacture cars adapted to Uganda's harsh climate (his country has one of the best climates in the world). On another morning he was about to conquer Kenya and Tanzania to give his country an outlet to the sea, yet he knows his army cannot carry out any exercise lasting more than two hours. The units simply disintegrate.

After the British left, Sergeant Amin became a captain. When President Obote clashed with King Freddie of Buganda, Amin's jeeps with their recoilless guns— supplied by the Israeli army—opened fire on the king's palace and turned the tide in Obote's favor. Amin was promoted to deputy commander in chief, and then commander in chief. When he reached this rank he took great care that all other officers should be at least two ranks inferior to him. He only appointed brigadiers after promoting himself to field marshal.

Amin is haunted by paranoia. He keeps a special jeep reconnaissance unit as his personal bodyguard. This unit enabled Amin to survive when Obote decided to arrest him. This led to the coup which brought Amin to power.

Amin has an uncanny, animal sense of impending danger. Like many megalomaniacs, he has a devilish way of escaping death.

During the last year before the coup his position was weakened as commander in chief and senior officers urged then President Obote to arrest him. Amin flew to visit the Egyptian minister of defense. He received a telegram ordering him back to Kampala immediately. Amin notified the president that he was not returning but, instead, going to Mecca to attain the status of hajji.

On his return from Mecca he was met by his faithful jeep unit, which escorted him to parliament. Uganda's numerous Muslims now received Amin as a holy man, preventing his arrest. He has often participated in Muslim religious ceremonies, and he has a special announcer read verses from the Koran over Uganda Television every evening.

Amin loves movies. His palace contains a collection of about thirty or forty films about World War II, which he sees over and over again. He never could learn to operate a simple projector, and it was one of my duties to project kamikaze-style films for him.

When Amin went to the Soviet Union he took a camera I gave him. Amin took many pictures but on his return, when the films were developed, they were all blank.

Amin loves women; any woman he likes becomes his wife. His wives live around his palace. He is reputed to have 18 children.

Nothing can weaken his position, his pride, or his self-love more than a defeat at Entebbe. This is why it must be supposed President Amin will turn more dangerous than ever before.

The answer to the question whether Big Daddy Amin was collaborating with the hijackers came early Friday. Intelligence from Uganda, supplied by special agents and through the released hostages, established the Ugandan army's part in the fate of Flight 139. Amin's credibility as a mediator was proved baseless for those few persons among the Israeli leadership who still hoped that he could be influenced by past connections or by his phone conversations with the little Tel Aviv shopkeeper. Amin permitted additional terrorists who were present in Uganda or in neighboring Somalia to reinforce the hijackers. An Israeli reconnaissance plane reported a special flight from Libya that, "to judge by radio traffic, brought a special advisory team." Six additional armed men joined the terror group at the old terminal building in Entebbe where they conducted talks with Amin.

Most of the passengers in the second batch of hostages released from Entebbe possessed French citizenship and this reinforced an Israeli view that Uganda and PFLP propaganda attacking "French military imperialism" was taking second place to a new drive to exploit the plight of the Jews.

One of the released captives, Murray Schwartz, an American television producer, boarded the plane at the stopover in Athens. He related that, after the plane landed in Entebbe, the hijackers were joined by several persons who looked like Arabs.

Two released Flight 139 passengers alleged that everything had been prepared in Entebbe to receive the hijacked plane. They believed that the Ugandan authorities had prior information about the hijacking. The systematic segregation of Jews reflected a modification of terrorist plans.

Jean Choquette, from Montreal, Canada, got the impression that Idi Amin is "very sympathetic toward the hijackers." According to Choquette—and the other released hostages—their captors had not treated them badly. "Aside, of course, from the psychological pressure they applied." Choquette also related that the hijackers were joined by several additional persons, with guns. He also reported that a box had been brought to the plane at Entebbe—it contained, said the hijackers, dynamite to blow up the plane "whenever necessary."

Reports from Paris related how the Israelis looked while the released hostages left for the evacuation planes. The men waved their arms goodbye and the women held handkerchiefs to their eyes and held their children up.

President Amin seemed to be responding to the pressures of the terrorist PFLP political strategists rather than to Western diplomats or eccentric approaches like that of Bar-Lev. An Israeli Phantom was detailed to shadow Big Daddy's private jet on the flight to Mauritius for the African summit conference. Events during his two days' absence from Uganda were reported hourly by informants working through a Kampala-Nairobi-Jerusalem route. The watch on Big Daddy was maintained by round-the-clock air missions, backed up by a Reshef (Flame)-class Israeli missile ship, dispatched to a station off the East African coast on the previous Tuesday. The naval vessel carried, in place of a new advanced version of the Gabriel sea-to-sea missile, electronic gear necessary to handle all communications. The task force had decided it could not rely on foreign help in these preparations, for fear of leaks that would tip off the terrorists.

"We were haunted in the final hours by fear of hitting Entebbe to find the hostages gone," said a commander of the 35th Airborne Brigade, which was standing by. "Naturally we thought we might conduct a raid, as early as Tuesday. We remembered how American rescue missions struck into North Vietnam only to find nothing in place of the prisoners they hoped to release.

"This was a major problem in gathering intelligence and in conducting variations of a raid on Entebbe: this danger of arriving to find the hostages gone. None of us, reading the briefs on Amin, had illusions about his cunning and ruthlessness."

This was why Bar-Lev's dialogue with Big Daddy was vital. It kept alive some hope that he would not move the hostages.

During these preparations, the young medical student Moshe Peretz continued to keep his diary of a hostage.

Friday, July 2. 0600—Rising after a night of sleeplessness. Everybody's possessions are packed, and we await notification when we move off.

0700—Idi Amin comes in, with a wide-brimmed hat, accompanied by a beautiful wife in a green dress and the son Gamal Abdel Nasser Jwami. He shocks us by telling us that Israel has not accepted the hijackers' demands, and that our position was very grave, for the building is surrounded by TNT and would be blown up if the terrorists' demands were not met. He announces that he is setting out for Mauritius where he will discuss our situation. He will return this evening or tomorrow morning. He also advises us to send a letter to be published in the press and radio asking Israel to accept the terrorists' demands.

0800—Stormy debates between those who favor writing the letter and those opposed. Most of the family men, and the crew members, except for the [Air France] captain, are in favor. Others are against it. What will happen? I don't care. The ebb and flow of feelings is breaking people, and bringing them to the threshold of collapse. It hurts to think of the family at home.

1100—We continue the daily routine. Jean-Jacques

Maimoni, 19 years old, exudes good spirits. He brings everyone tea and coffee, gives out food, and makes sure no one is left without his portion, and that no one is deprived. He demands nothing for himself. The women are doing their laundry, hanging it on lines. A boring lunch and a nap.

2030—A letter is given to the Palestinians expressing thanks to Amin for his fair attitude and encouraging Israel to release the captives. The letter was written by a number of Israelis. The terrorists are satisfied with its contents, for it does not appear to have been written under pressure. It is Saturday; fellows are making up parodies of the editorials dealing with the situation. How a religious paper might describe it, or a sports journal. Somebody says we should not feel so bad; after all, Herzl did once propose to establish a Jewish state in Uganda. We sang Shabbat songs, quietly, because those outside were nervy, especially in the evening.

The possibility of intercepting President Amin's personal jet and forcing it down where Israeli agents might grab him was considered. Since Israel built the plane, its technical specifications were known—so well indeed that an earlier proposal had been put forward to tamper with the fuel tanks at Entebbe, causing the pilot to make an emergency landing at Nairobi.

11

AMIN: THE PLO PUPPET

A visitor from Nairobi on Wednesday, June 30, was of inestimable help. A confidant of President Jomo Kenyatta, he was a highly intelligent Kikuyu who had been put in editorial control of Kenya's *Daily Nation,* a newspaper established in 1961 as part of a chain financed by the Aga Khan in the hope of exercising a moderate influence on East Africa as it approached *Uhuru*—independence from British colonialism. There had been a *Daily Nation* of Uganda and a *Daily Nation* of Tanganyika working in concert. But Britain's withdrawal saw the collapse of an embryo East African federation and the countries and the newspapers separated. The Englishman who had edited the papers was replaced by Africans, and in Kenya this was now George Githii.

Githii reached Israel from Teheran as a guest of the Israeli government. There was no publicity. There was no specific role he was expected to play. He knew a great deal about Uganda under Amin, however, and about communications—which are the essence of a newspaper's life.

Those who talked with George Githii were enclosed in a small intelligence cell. They had no more concept of why he was important than another group knew why it was studying President Amin's attachment to the Palestinian cause. It was this secret alliance between Uganda and the PLO that offended and finally frightened some of Kenya's leaders.

Amin's support for the Palestinians began long before Flight 139 landed in Entebbe. Three hundred commandos from the Palestinian terrorist organizations protected the president. These Palestinians were trained in Libya, as were six sturdy muscular women, armed with revolvers, members of Amin's own tribe, who joined them.

The building which used to serve Israel in Kampala had been placed at the disposal of the Palestine Liberation Organization, the Palestinian flag hoisted to the top of the flagpole which once displayed the Star of David.

Since Libyan President Muammar al-Qaddafi promised Amin tens of millions of dollars in economic assistance (a promise never kept) Amin had permitted the PLO to build training camps in his territory, invited a PLO delegation to the Organization of African Unity (OAU) summit conference held in Kampala on July 28, 1975, and went so far as to permit Palestinian terrorists to train on his Russian Mig jets.

"The harder the training, the easier the mission," Amin assured the Al Fatah terrorists who learned to fly the Migs. In October 1975 Radio Uganda described the "rigorous training" undertaken by the squadron of "Palestinian and Ugandan suicide fliers" in southern Uganda. Civil aircraft were warned not to approach the training area till further notice.

The standard of the Palestinian pilots' operational performance—and possibly, that of their Ugandan instructors—could be deduced from reports of accidents. During 1975–76 reports were published of planes crashing in which Arab student-pilots were killed. A Palestinian pilot, born in Hebron, who was killed when his plane crashed in Uganda on October 29, 1975, was not untypical. His code name was George; his real name, Yusuf Bragit. He joined Al Fatah in 1967 and was appointed to command the Palestinian volunteers' squadron after training in China and Algeria during 1968–70. While he was on a training flight, his plane collided with two other planes piloted by Ugandans and Palestinians in northern Uganda. A Ugandan delegation—headed by Amin Maka, President Amin's personal representative, and Ahmed Daudi, representing the Ugandan air force—escorted George's coffin to Damascus, and from there to Amman. Amin seized the opportunity to send a message of condolence to Yasir Arafat, "in his own name and in the name of the soldiers of the Ugandan army."

It was not ideological reasons that persuaded Amin to aid the Palestinian cause. In April 1976 Amin sent a message to the Arab League requesting urgent economic aid. The Arab League honored him with a cold official reply, stating only that his request had been circulated among governments of the league. In his fury Amin criticized the Arab states and, according to the Nairobi *Daily Nation,* proclaimed that all Uganda's problems "stem from my firm support for the Palestinians."

Two months earlier an official PLO statement published in Beirut confirmed that Uganda was training Palestinian fliers. In return, "the PLO is extending military assistance to Uganda." The statement did not reveal what this assistance was. The truth is concealed in the enthusiastic words of Amin's thanks to Arafat: "This assistance has contributed to strengthening Uganda's capacity, and her ability to take part in the liberation of Palestine and of South Africa from Zionism and racism." He entertained the Palestinian pilots in his palace and announced that Yasir Arafat had placed them under his command; "and as your commander, I have the authority to send you on missions connected with Palestine, and Arab or African problems. As long as you are here, consider yourselves as though you were in your own country, among your brethren who serve in the Ugandan air force. It is your duty to prepare here for your principal task in Palestine.

"However, you are not the only ones who must prepare to fight the enemy—but all the states which wish to liberate Palestine, among which, of course, is Uganda," Amin concluded. His words were given prominence in the PLO organ *Falastin a-Thura,* published in Beirut.

Why did the terrorists need Amin's services in training their pilots? The answer was supplied not long ago by one of the terrorist commanders, "Abu Jara," when he offered public praise to the Ugandan president: "You, general, have done things for the Palestinians which their Arab brethren in other Arab states have refused to do. We need an air force."

How did Field Marshal Idi Amin arrive at such a violent hatred of Israel, if Israel helped him to take power? He even owed his life to an Israeli officer, Ze'ev ("Zonik") Shaham.

It happened in 1965. Zonik was head of the Israeli military mission in Kampala, while Amin was deputy commander in chief of the Ugandan army. In the course of his duties Amin frequently inspected the units under his command; a Dakota, acquired from the Israeli air force and flown by an Israeli pilot, was placed at his disposal. One day Amin took off for a routine inspection of one of the units of the West Nile tribe. While the plane was slowly making its way to its destination, Zonik in Kampala learned that officers of the West Nile unit had resolved to assassinate Amin. The officers were waiting for their distinguished visitor on the runway, intending to open fire at Amin when he stood in the exit. Zonik ordered the Israeli pilot of the Dakota to turn back and the mutinous officers waited in vain.

Amin thanked Zonik warmly. So did President Milton Obote, inviting the head of the Israeli military delegation to his office to praise him. Years later, when Amin had deposed Obote, Zonik wondered how the former president would have behaved at the time of the assassination attempt had he known the fate that awaited him.

The first links with leaders and parties in Uganda were established by Asher Naïm, of the Israeli Foreign Ministry, from his post in Kenya. With quiet persistence, avoiding the attentions of British security and the considerable forces of regular troops and operational intelligence units deployed in the war against the Mau Mau, Naïm established contact with Dr. Obote, who was to become the first president of Uganda after its independence.

Shortly after Uganda became independent, Shimon Peres, then director general of the Israeli Defense Ministry, came to Uganda on a visit. His hosts asked him to help establish their army and air force. Peres gave his consent and in April 1963 then Foreign Minister Golda Meir signed an agreement for assistance and cooperation with Kampala.

Colonel Shaham arrived in Uganda as head of the delegation of the Israeli army and defense ministry that followed the agreement. A superficial inspection showed him there was much to do. The Ugandan army consisted of one infantry battalion, numbering 700 to 800 men. The commander of the battalion was British, as were the officers, senior and junior. The infantry battalion excelled, above all, in parade-ground drill. It was a largely ceremonial battalion, which served for festive parades. To Zonik and the Israeli officers who accompanied him, this was a comic opera battalion that should be converted into an effective fighting force.

They began on a small scale, training only one company in an attempt to convert it into a combat rifle unit. Ugandan soldiers were sent to train in the Israeli army's central officers' school, and in the air force pilots' school. The Israeli officers' success in training the infantry company induced President Obote to ask the Israeli delegation to undertake the training of the Ugandan special police. Using Fouga-Magistas and Dakotas sent from Israel, Israeli air force instructors established the Ugandan air force, starting from the ground up, even establishing a technical school. On Uganda's second independence day, six Fuga-Magista jets flew past in an aerial display, pleasing Israeli observers, who were in those days still convinced that only British colonial rule prevented Africans from developing an independent, responsible, and powerful fighting capability. Idi Amin cultivated special relations with the Israeli group in Kampala, perhaps because these fellows from Tel Aviv treated him as an equal. He visited Israel often and each time returned full of admiration. His praise for Israeli diligence knew no bounds. When the first jet trainers reached Uganda, broken down into sections for shipment by sea and land, he was astounded to see how the Israelis converted these "bits of metal" into jet planes. He volunteered to fly in the first flight of the first assembled Fuga-Magista and returned excited as never before. Later he acquired a rare award from the Israelis: paratrooper's wings, which he continued to wear with unconcealed pride even on his July 2 flight to Mauritius.

Relations were so close that one day Amin presented to Colonel Shaham, who was acting as Israeli military attaché in Kampala, a request that Israel should help sell an enormous quantity of gold stolen from the Congo. Amin told Zonik that Israel must carry out his request. The Israeli government turned down Amin's offer to share in the booty, but bankers arranged for disposal of the gold without feeling any compulsion to look into the source.

When Israel turned down Amin's demand to help attack neighboring Tanzania, he grew furious. Israel's foreign ministry in Jerusalem still believed that deterioration in the relationships between the two countries would not go so far as a complete severance of ties. But President Amin—ever more unstable, rash, and impulsive in his decisions—soon smashed this last illusion. In February 1972, in a festive statement issued by Amin and Libyan ruler Muammar al-Qaddafi, the two men undertook to support the struggle of the Arab peoples against Zionism and imperialism, for the liberation of all the occupied Arab lands, for restoration of

Palestinian rights, and for the Palestinians' return to their lands.

In March 1972, during the last days of Israel's official presence in Uganda, the Israeli ambassador sat waiting for the verdict of the unpredictable president. He tried to learn Amin's intentions from a senior member of Uganda's Foreign Ministry, who was of the opinion that Amin had no real intention to break off relations. Twenty-four hours later notification was received of the severance of relations.

Dozens of Israeli families were forced to leave Uganda in the middle of the night from Entebbe Airport. They were the early victims of the monster they, like Frankenstein, had created. It was not only the Israelis who miscalculated. The British in their zeal to decolonize had earmarked Amin as one of many African leaders who could be supported, flying in the face of experienced white settlers and Western observers not struck dumb by the fashionable refusal in the 1960s to say that "the emperor has no clothes."

12
THE GENERAL STAFF EXAMINES TRACK B

Shimon Peres, in addition to being defense minister, possessed an intimate, firsthand knowledge of Uganda and President Amin. He could see the strongest arguments against any high-flown action against Amin or involving harm to Ugandan armed forces.

His special knowledge and close identification with Israel's military evolution since early days made him the natural confidant of military commanders impatient with the slow processes of Parliament. He had worked closely with antiterrorist experts too, and by Friday had arrived at certain conclusions with regard to the jailed terrorists whose deliverance to Uganda was demanded as part of the price for releasing the hostages.

Peres's initiatives were reported to Prime Minister Rabin as the need arose. Here is the defense ministry's summary of how the general staff operated in those days.

The general staff followed the developments from the first moment of the Air France hijacking. But at the beginning of the week no one thought it would be necessary to go to Entebbe. The defense minister consulted the chief of staff, Mordechai Gur, who consulted his generals, while the government gave priority to diplomatic activity.

During the first night, while the aircraft was on its way to Uganda, the task force watched the flight path constantly. The hijackers told Cairo control tower their destination was Amman. When the plane landed in Uganda and was obviously going to stay there, the general staff began operational planning.

As the diplomatic process moved toward stalemate and the government's dilemma grew, the desire to use the military option strengthened—to the extent that, when the terrorists' conditions were published, a senior defense ministry official said: "The end will be that the military echelon will save the political echelon, just as they did in the Six Day War and the Yom Kippur War." Prime Minister Rabin gave a sharp reply: "I am awaiting a firm, clearly feasible military proposal. I am not interested in your philosophy of war. I want facts not theory."

On Tuesday at noon, 48 hours after the hijacking, the chief of staff was called to an urgent meeting in Jerusalem. He sensed that the army was about to be asked for action, and radioed for commando units to be put on alert that evening. Gur was asked if he thought a military operation could be mounted, and answered: "Such a possibility exists." When he returned to his Tel Aviv office, Gur ordered planning teams be set up in the general staff that evening to prepare the operational proposals coming in from the field. He was encouraged by what could be called "the pressure from below," from Brigadier General Dan Shomron and the Golani Brigade's infantrymen, tough men who deal with terrorists across the border every day. These were men who would have to go on the mission. They were typical Israeli soldiers, steeped in a philosophy as old as the struggle for Israel.

"Know what you fight for and love what you know" is a quotation handed down to them from the early

Jewish resistance movement, which got it from Orde Wingate, who got it from Oliver Cromwell. Wingate was a British guerrilla warfare expert in World War II, with a biblical sense of the Jewish cause matched by a lack of orthodoxy. Wingate gave his name to the first quasi-military training camp. The renegade Englishman organized special night squads among Jewish settlers in prewar Palestine to strike at Arab killers. His influence was described in the Flight 139 crisis by a former Israeli air force chief, Ezer Weizman: "I chanced to meet one of the most colorful characters to figure in the long annals of our wars, [who] came on the recommendation of my Uncle Chaim [a founder of modern Israel] . . . He looked much more like a missionary than an officer of the British Empire, and he would spend hours talking about the Bible. I suppose it was his link to the land of Israel and the Jewish people—a mystical, very personal link."*

What they would be fighting for in Entebbe was clear to the general staff—it was the right of every Israeli to travel without fear, and ultimately the right of citizens everywhere to make free decisions about where they lived and how they lived. The issue at Entebbe was how to defeat enemies of this freedom of choice, and whether the hostages should be regarded as soldiers in such a fight.

On Wednesday the chief of staff summoned several officers to present their plans to him. On the face of it these seemed feasible. On analysis—or as the jargon has it, "when they were attacked" in argument—each was revealed to have at least one weak point. Here and there were ideas that were more imaginative than pragmatic, and the chief of staff treated them as unrealistic. "These plans don't promise mimimum chances for the lives of the hostages, and so I cannot recommend them." The officers departed disappointed, some with long faces, but they quickly recovered as the intelligence data streamed in, and made new plans. They worked day and night in the general staff and in the headquarters of senior paratroop officer Dan Shomron.

On Eagles' Wings (Jerusalem, 1976).

Air-strike forces were always ready with contingency plans. There were plans to seize oil wells and plans to take over well-defended airfields in hostile countries in the event of all-out war. The essence was to capture a strategic point from which the surrounding enemy could be dominated. Some plans called for paratroops to be dropped from the air; others for night landings (by helicopter) of commandos trained to infiltrate guarded bases. All demanded speed and surprise. The realities of Middle Eastern instability and the threats against Israel demanded these preparations and this kind of training. The men and women instructed in these contingency plans were pursuing peaceful civilian occupations; they had learned to separate in their private thoughts the daily routine and the prospect of sudden danger. A large medical corps, for example, consisted of doctors trained to fight alongside airborne commandos. In the use of this versatile force the general staff had the grave responsibility of making precise plans based on precise intelligence. The defenses surrounding a target had to be known in detail.

There was not enough intelligence at this stage. What antiaircraft defenses existed at Entebbe? Where were the guards positioned? There were two Ugandan battalions known to be guarding the airport. The chief of staff explained: "The problem is to preserve the safety of the hostages. We are taking a risk for our own soldiers in advance. We have to have a specific answer on the Ugandan positions at Entebbe Airport."

On Thursday Shomron felt the situation at the airport had become clear. The marathon discussions accelerated. The chief of staff was encouraged by the fact that Defense Minister Peres was pushing the army to act at Entebbe. Brigadier General Shomron appeared that day before Gur, head of operations branch Yekutiel Adam, and air force chief Benny Peled to propose a new plan.

"Believe me," said Shomron, "from the moment that we will be on the ground in Entebbe, we can carry it out easily. We have done things a thousand times more complicated." Dan was the youngster in this group of planners. All were Independence War veterans. He was the only one born in the state of Israel.

He knew that these generals looked on him as the child of their old age.

But Shomron got what he wanted: qualified approval of the plan to land combined forces at Entebbe under his command with special units to be directed by Yonni Netanyahu. There were three provisions: a dry run must be carried out during Friday night to convince General Gur that aircraft could be landed in pitch darkness on a strange airfield under heavy guard; there must be some foolproof way to get the hostages safely out of Entebbe and home; and the whole operation must be based on complete, tested intelligence.

"Everything depends on reliable intelligence," Gur warned.

13

THE INVISIBLES

On-the-spot intelligence began to reach Dan Shomron's final planning team before and during the Friday night rehearsal. Uganda's defenses were based on a relatively large number of armored troop carriers (267), unknown quantities of missiles, howitzers, and mortars, and at least 50 combat aircraft including 30 Mig-17s and Mig-21s based at Entebbe. Out of 21,000 fully trained, well-armed Ugandan soldiers, about half were thought to be stationed between Entebbe and the capital at Kampala, 21 miles away. The airport was guarded by an outer ring of good Ugandan troops equipped with Russian-built weapons, including tanks.

More details of Entebbe's defenses were offered in the final hours by a highly specialized group which had flown to Nairobi on El Al Flight LY 535 on Wednesday. Out of this team of 50 "businessmen," a few set up headquarters in the private home of an Israeli trader whose house promised peace and seclusion. From here, discreet contacts were made with Lionel Byrn Davies, chief of Nairobi police, and a colorful ex-British Special Air Services commander, Bruce McKenzie.

A powerful figure on the Kenyan political scene for three decades, Bruce McKenzie had survived the Mau

Mau insurrection as a white farmer and befriended the leader of it, Jomo Kenyatta. Big, burly, bewhiskered, and bluffly contemptuous of whites who refused to recognize Kenyatta's leadership in the 1960s, McKenzie had become minister of agriculture until replaced by a Kikuyu of Kenyatta's tribe. He continued to serve in the capacity of friendly adviser to President Kenyatta, who respected McKenzie's soldierly frankness. At 85, Kenyatta himself was a benign but unpredictable ruler whose one-party government blended the traditional tribal system of following strong leaders and the trappings of Westminster-style democracy. His political wishes were enforced by the euphemistically named General Service Unit (GSU), which took care that parliamentary debate never went beyond a mild discussion of Kenyatta's policies.

The crucial question was: Would Kenya permit the rescue planes to refuel at Nairobi? This was the only airfield in relatively friendly hands. The giant Hercules with full loads could help themselves to Uganda's fuel, at a pinch. But they would never make it back to Israel without taking aboard fuel somewhere during the operation. A proposal to refuel in the air had been rejected as too dangerous because of the combination of circumstances: the flight must be conducted at night for the sake of surprise; the route lay within range of hostile aircraft; and it would be too easy for an enemy to stage-manage an accident during the delicate refueling procedure.

The commander of Kenyatta's GSU strong-arm units, Geoffrey Karithii, was able to give assurances that his president would turn a blind eye if the GSU and Nairobi airport police isolated the rescue force during a stopover—provided this phase of the operation was conducted as a routine matter under cover of El Al charters. Charles Njojo, Kenya's attorney general, offered a legal opinion that so long as the laws governing international civil aviation were observed (at least in the eyes of Kenya's airport authority), facilities could not be refused.

Black African agents hired by Israel's Mossad reinforced the last-minute reports on Entebbe's defenses and conditions. The rescue pilots needed to know the

serviceability of runways, the location of fuel tanks
(should there be time to draw from them), and the
degree of alertness in the control towers—one of which
took care of Uganda's fighter squadrons based on the
old part of the airfield. Some of this information came
from casual questioning of commercial airline pilots.
Some came from observers on Lake Victoria. Techni-
cians of the East African Directorate of Civil Aviation
were familiar with the customary modifications that
take place daily in routine, providing details to El Al
officials without understanding the significance of their
questions.

The changing habits of the hijackers were crucial.
A new figure was reported to be on the scene. He
seemed to be the terrorists' commander and traveled
from and to Entebbe airport in a car driven by Ugandan soldiers. Word filtered back that the hostages
called him Groucho Marx because of his drooping
black mustache and slouching gait. The German woman
was identified as Gabriele Kroche-Tiedemann, 24, a
member of the team that kidnapped OPEC members at
Vienna, and a known associate of Carlos, The Jackal.

On the whole, Entebbe's defenses seemed vulnerable
to a swift attack. A cautionary report that two Uganda
Migs might dive-bomb the hostages was discounted.
The numbers on the Migs were given as 903 and 905
—known to be earmarked for training, they seemed
more likely part of the daylight routine of student pilots. Nervous hostages would be unfamiliar with the
"circuits-and-bumps" cycle of landings and takeoffs
that are the lot of trainee pilots. Rather more worrisome
was the mood of the terrorists and the control they
seemed to have over Ugandan troops.

A host of "invisibles" had been consulted, often without their knowing. The invisibles were knowledgeable
observers, given the nickname because they were unconsciously serving Israel intelligence. Among them
was the chief editor of the *Daily Nation* of Kenya,
George Githii, another close friend and adviser to President Kenyatta. He left Israel early on Saturday, July
3, for Nairobi after informal talks that would bear
fruit. Ahead of him sped messages to the El Al airline

manager in Nairobi requiring him to have large sums of money ready. Without being asked, and out of personal curiosity, El Al's man measured off the distance from Nairobi to Entebbe—380 miles.

An extraordinary Israeli was learning the distance to Entebbe the hard way. He landed there in his private aircraft at such a critical moment that his Tel Aviv office began to receive cryptic requests to bring him home. He was Abie Nathan, the so-called Peace Pilot whose crusades in a one-man search for alternatives to each of Israel's wars had earned him some grudging admiration, though his earlier "mercy" flights had caused embarrassment. There was always a risk that Israel's enemies might see him as evidence of weakening military resolve. The risk this time was that he would be caught in the crossfire of Thunderbolt. He flew into Entebbe shortly after President Amin took off for Mauritius.

"I had a bad feeling when Ugandan soldiers surrounded me," he reported later. "They took me for interrogation in the new terminal building, away from where the hostages were held. Then Amin's chief aide came and agreed that I might speak through him with one of the hijackers.

"The hijacker was concealed behind a screen. I spoke through Amin's man. I saw that the president, while in Mauritius, was relaying decisions to his Ugandan aide. The hijackers took instruction from him, and from the senior officers sent to join the terrorist group that originally took Flight 139. They told me there was no room to bargain."

Abie Nathan flew back to Nairobi. His attorney, Arieh Marinsky, was phoning frantically from Tel Aviv. "Do not fly back to Uganda," he told Nathan sharply. "You understand? Your doctors here are worried about your liver."

"My liver?" Nathan demanded. "There's nothing wrong with my liver."

"You remember the doctors said tropical fruit is bad for it," Marinsky said with fierce emphasis. "And the altitude—"

"But here in Nairobi it is more than six thousand feet," argued Nathan. "In Entebbe, it's almost half as high."

"Then it's on your own head," sighed his attorney. "If you get sick, don't blame me."

Abie Nathan finally understood and spent Saturday disclosing the details he had observed on Entebbe's airfield. His most significant observation was that he felt certain the Ugandans, if not the terrorists, would begin executing Jews the following day in keeping with the Sunday deadline. He thought this because President Amin seemed the ultimate authority and Amin would feel his prestige was at stake if Israel wheedled more concessions.

Other details were being extracted in Paris from an American doctor under hypnosis. A team of Israeli intelligence specialists had reached France and were concentrating on the released hostages. Many could not consciously remember vital details like the location of doors in the old terminal building or where exactly the hostages were held, or whether the long French windows in the building opened, in or out. Hypnotists skilled in debriefing soldiers and captured terrorists worked, with their consent, on those suffering the normal amnesia following shock.

Under hypnosis the American doctor revealed a great deal that he had been unable to recall while consciously trying to help the interrogators. They were working against time and it was Friday before they were sure the released hostage had seen and heard enough to reconstruct not only the physical scene but the psychological atmosphere among Ugandans and terrorists at Entebbe. They reported to the task force by heavily encoded messages radioed from the Israeli embassy in Paris: "Earlier analysis of President Amin needs to be modified. His tendency has been to prolong negotiations for publicity reasons. But he is also anxious to please his 'comrades' of the PLO and the PFLP. They are becoming trigger-happy. On the basis of evidence set forth below, it seems likely that Amin will agree to begin 'propaganda executions' on Sunday, July 4, at dawn."

This assumption was supported by the Paris team's findings. It was not intended to be alarmist. The team knew it would be weighed against a mass of other, perhaps contradictory, evidence. It was read in the prime minister's office as pointing to the same conclusions indicated by Abie Nathan and by George Githii from Kenya, speaking unofficially for President Kenyatta. The rising probability of executions put new pressure on Prime Minister Rabin. He had hoped until then that the earlier assessment was correct: President Amin would prolong the palaver to keep himself in the spotlight.

"If we are talking about a nation that does not submit to demogogues," Rabin was to say later, "then as prime minister I had to make a final decision based on consensus."

Rabin did most of his lonely agonizing in the provisional office of the prime minister in Tel Aviv. This is a small red-tiled building which, ironically, has housed first the German Order of Templars and then, during World War II, German civilians suspected of Nazi espionage by the British. Then it became British military headquarters in the tragic postwar period before Israel was born, when a Jewish underground army (which included most of the older men involved in the Flight 139 crisis) fought the British. Later it was David Ben-Gurion's provisional government quarters before the birth of Israel.

Inside a long room bare of ornament except full-length portraits of the founders of Israel—Theodor Herzl and Chaim Weizmann—Rabin wrestled with his conscience between sessions with his full cabinet. He would have preferred to be in the first plane landing at Entebbe, he said when he came to review the final fateful hours before the decision on Thunderbolt . . . GO!

He talked with opposition leader Menachem Begin, which seemed strange to those unfamiliar with Israel's checkered history. During the Palestine mandate, Begin was the most wanted man by British security forces after the assassination of Abraham Stern of the Stern Gang. Begin had been the elusive leader of the underground guerrilla organization of Irgun Zvai Leumi and to this day is identified with the "hawks" and thought to be critical of Rabin's hesitations. But the bitter political battles of previous weeks were forgotten in this unifying reaction to danger.

Rabin himself had been a commando at the age of 18 in the guerrilla forces fighting underground during the British blockage of Palestine against Jewish immigration. Yet oddly enough, he began as a saboteur under British direction against the Nazis in World War II. His life since that boyhood experience has been involved in warfare of an unconventional kind; yet he is by inclination a farmer and embodies contradictory characteristics in the Israeli civilian-soldier: a tough recognition of the need always to fight to preserve his Jewishness, and in the thick of fighting a kind of gentleness which is a consequence of an underlying philosophical approach to life and death.

Rabin took British Staff College training after the birth of Israel. He understood the role of the air force in subduing enemy airfields on the first day of the 1967 Six Day War. "Once these were made unserviceable," said Rabin (then chief of general staff), "the burden fell upon our desert units to crush the Arab invaders."

Rabin the humanist was visibly upset when relatives of Flight 139's Jewish passengers stormed his office. Rabin the soldier calculated the risk of the unprecedented raid in view. It could jeopardize a large number of hostages' lives because there was to be no needless killing of Ugandans defending the target. Rabin the logician recalled that there were precedents for a prisoner exchange. He recalled them bitterly in one of the heated cabinet discussions: "In 1968 we released Palestinians in secret negotiations leading to a silent exchange for Israelis on an El Al plane hijacked to Algeria. In 1969 there was another silent exchange of Syrian airmen and other prisoners of war to get back two Israeli hijack hostages after they were held ninety-eight days in Damascus.

"Finally, we returned more than a hundred saboteurs and spies after the Yom Kippur War to get back the bodies of a few Israeli soldiers killed in that conflict."

But the relatives of Flight 139's passengers only demanded: "Do you want to wait until people are dead before you make an exchange?"

And Rabin the humanist said later: "I have to live with my conscience for the rest of my life. I adopt with Flight 139 the principle by which I stick until something changes the situation. And that principle is that as the situation existed until Friday, and even until I could be convinced on Saturday that dress rehearsals were faultless enough to meet prescribed requirements, some sort of exchange must be made."

The prime minister, standing rocklike against accusations of nervous delay, distinguished three forms of reaction to the terrorist methods of blackmail:

One, reaction to terrorists operating on our territory. Then it is better to fight than to give in, though sometimes our commandos attack and in doing so (as in the case of an Israeli school held by terrorists in which more than a score of children died in the operation)* innocent lives are lost. In such a case, within our frontiers, we must fight.

Two, reaction to the taking of hostages onto friendly foreign territory where the government policy is hostile to terrorists. This was the case in South Africa and we dealt with it because we had support from the authorities there. So there was no moral dilemma.

Three, reaction to the capture and removal of hostages to territory friendly to terrorists. This is the Flight 139 case where I know our forces have the capability to conduct a long-range battle but I cannot justify the loss of a hundred innocent lives or even of one.

I want no rescue operation with soldiers holding one-way tickets.

I want proof that the first plane into Entebbe can land safely and get back. A catastrophe will be the most tremendous victory for our enemies.

Until this last minute, there is nothing to tip the scales away from Thursday's decision to negotiate.

Begin, the grizzled ex-Irgun guerrilla, agreed. He had been taken into the counsels of the cabinet and accepted its Thursday decision to negotiate. Then, on Friday evening, Rabin completed his review of the latest intelligence from Entebbe and told his political adversary and former comrade-in-arms: "I think we can

---

*The tragedy at Maalot in May 1974 was that when commandos stormed a school, hoping to free 100 children held hostage by PFLP Arab infiltrators, 22 children perished in the crossfire before the guerrillas could be overpowered.

do it. What remains is to have General Gur attend a rehearsal of Thunderbolt and then if he is satisfied, we'll ask for full cabinet approval."

14
THE NIGHT OF THE DRY RUN

Only a handful of the men and women destined for Thunderbolt knew they were rehearsing the real thing on Friday. The rehearsal was divided into sections. Each team performed mock combat assaults during the day, as far as possible independent of the others. Combat-trained doctors were already familiar with airborne surgery and were not required to participate. Most of them were quarantined that afternoon. One returned to his hospital to deal with an emergency and was seen by a colleague stowing away special webbing designed like an ammunition belt to carry basic drugs and surgical instruments. This, and the sudden absence of other doctors, soon became known, and the hospital was one of the very few places where outsiders guessed a rescue mission was in prospect.

Otherwise security was nearly watertight. Airmen told to go into quarantine, however, protested. "I want to spend my last night in my own bed" was the typical lament. Since three times as many fliers had been earmarked as would go on the operation, and they were unlikely to spill information because they are the first victims of leaked secrets, the quarantine was lifted. Pilots had suffered brutal torture and mutilation when shot down over hostile territory in the past. All were concerned for the protection of their wives and children from vengeful terrorist attacks on their homes. This made the pilots the most tight-lipped group in the country.

General Gur had to be convinced that the C-130 Hercules, known to the Israeli air force (IAF) as the Hippo, could fly with a full load into the unknown and return without mishap after delivering a commando strike with half-track infantry carriers, recoilless-rifle jeeps, and rocket-armed troops in the course of a

5000-mile round trip without external navigational aids. He doubted that a group of aircraft could pack an adequate punch without being detected on the way in. He questioned if any large combat aircraft could sneak onto guarded runways some 3800 feet above sea level without alerting the defenders.

Suppose, he wanted to know, one of the aircraft smashes its landing gear, damages an engine, or gets hit by a stray grenade. Suppose nothing worse than that a vulture is sucked into an engine. The Hercules armada, in the proposed operation, was being kept down to the minimum of four. If one was damaged or delayed at Entebbe, how would the crew and commandos get away?

"No problem," IAF chief Benny Peled assured him. "I'll be flying overhead. We'll have reserves within call. And you haven't seen what our Hippos can do when pushed. Come on."

Gur went through one of the most hair-raising experiences of his long life as a fighting man. For nearly three hours he sat on the huge flight deck while the four-engine Hercules was put through tests that would try a thoroughbred jet fighter. Designed for an enormous range of workhorse jobs, the Lockheed C-130 had made trial deliveries of 92 fully armed troops 2000 miles from home. In one test the transport had dropped onto beaten-earth strips to unload howitzers, trucks, and troops, then boarded 74 stretcher cases in a total elapsed time on the ground of 33 minutes.

Benny Peled, who had been flying since boyhood, knew these things were possible from experience. General Gur knew it from reports. But he had yet to feel the immense power and flexibility of this huge machine.

That night the chief of staff's Hercules flew in and out of the desert and between mountains in what seemed to him total darkness. In jump-takeoffs, with the four turboprops at full power and the pilot standing on the brakes, the 70-ton transport climbed more like a helicopter. Landing on the invisible desert, it seemed to drop out of the sky.

These were deadly serious tests. Several times Gur found himself gripping crossbraces, fighting sudden acceleration or deceleration. Once he burst out: "Where

the hell are we going?" Peled gave him a comradely
punch in the shoulder. "To Entebbe, we hope."

The Hercules was put through these paces because
Entebbe would demand a swift, near-silent arrival, the
minimum use of runways, and the shortest and steep-
est possible getaways. The pilots were prepared to land
on packed earth if the runways should be knocked
out by forewarned Ugandans, and they were ready to
lift the hostages almost vertically out of what might
become a battlefield. The Hercules was ideal for these
tasks; but while it could do astonishing things, it carried red warnings on the panels too. The plane was
built for slow-speed flight, and rolling it too quickly
into a fast getaway could buckle the highly flexible wings.

In the kind of short takeoff needed at Entebbe,
the acceleration would be breathtaking. The captain in
such an operation keeps his left hand on the nose steering wheel and his right hand on the throttles. He keeps
the two outboard engines at half power and the inners
at full power while his copilot juggles frantically to
keep the wings level by using the ailerons. The reason
is that the tremendous power generated by the four
turboprops becomes dangerous if one engine fails during the critical run-up to 90 miles an hour. Below that
speed there is not enough rudder control to counteract
the terrific drag on the side with the failed engine.
"Flying the ailerons" is an unusual technique, required
because the fat low-pressure tires and narrow landing
gear are not enough to prevent, at worst, one wing
digging down too far until the Hercules "roller-skates"
sideways.

General Gur was shown the quirks and the qualities.
But the demonstration was done in the blackness of
night. A stranger on the flight deck, surrounded by
picture windows that give a greenhouse effect in sunlight, has the nightmare sensation of being flung
through a void. The fact is, of course, that the four-
man crew have electronic aids that give a picture of
conditions outside the aircraft. Even knowing this, General Gur must have shared the sense of disaster that is
normal when the Hercules is dumped into a small landing space in a kind of controlled crash. The speed goes
down until the big machine seems to rock with every

puff of air. Controls are sluggish because of the low airspeed. When the throttles are chopped the plane slams into the ground and the great wings curve down as if about to snap off. Several times Gur was treated to a short-field landing that felt more like a falling elevator. The distance eaten up during landing was never more than 700 feet, which would perch the Hercules on the outer edge of Entebbe Airport and hopefully beyond earshot of the terrorists.

During the night he talked with soldiers who had flown in the Hercules. They were all confident that if the planes put them into Entebbe they could complete their tasks within an hour.

"Make it 55 minutes," said Gur. The teams rehearsed their individual missions again, this time using a cannibilized Hercules and pouring down the ramp and spreading out in simulated attacks on the Ugandan guards, the radar station, the control tower, and most important of all, the old terminal building. In rehearsal it was decided that the hostages could be released within 75 seconds of the rescue commando knocking out the terrorist guards.

Still Gur was not satisfied. He studied scale models of Entebbe, with the latest intelligence applied to show where armor and guards might be found. A full-scale model of the hostages' "prison" was gone through yet again by the small team of marksmen and commandos whose sole task would be to free the passengers and speed them into the Hercules equipped to yank them out of Entebbe with rocket takeoff gear if necessary.

"What impressed me," Gur said later, "was that nobody felt there was anything impossible in the plan. They had conducted combat operations in which at one time or another a feature of the Entebbe raid had occurred. They had fought and trained to the degree that the business was almost routine. They did not underestimate the difficulties and dangers. They approached them with the precision and confidence of surgical teams in an operating theater. The surgeon knows everything he possibly can beforehand, but he is prepared for something unexpected once the operation begins. He always has a set of alternatives in mind. And so it was with these men."

The chief of staff spoke to them of the thinking behind the operation, the need to avoid bloodshed as much as possible; but above all he spoke of the moral justice of Thunderbolt and its importance in demonstrating once more that the Jewish people need never fear persecution or feel naked and unarmed in facing their enemies.

There was one bright spot in the surrounding sense of isolation. The British, with terrorists leaving a trail of blood and bombs from London to northern Ireland, were offering the fullest cooperation within limits set by the fact that British citizens were still living in Uganda. They had a secret defense alliance with Kenya, negotiated by an earlier Conservative government, that allowed the Royal Air Force and airborne commandos to make use of Nairobi and other Kenyan airfields.

They had one further contribution—not a welcome one, but certainly necessary as the task force weighed the odds. With Thunderbolt in rehearsal, an estimate was made of the probable casualties. The largest number of raiders and hostages in danger of being killed was thought to be 30 to 35. Was this acceptable?

A late report from British sources in East Africa warned that, for reasons ranging from President Amin's return from the African summit to the growing unease among some of the PLO strategists in Kampala, the risk had increased considerably that execution of hostages would begin early on Sunday morning. If Thunderbolt was to be launched, the time frame was reduced drastically. The equation was now simple. Risk losing 35 Israelis by taking action, or face the possibility of 105 dead by the sin of omission.

15

THE HIPPOS ASSEMBLE

The women and men involved in Thunderbolt were warned to move to their bases in civilian clothes, to travel by bus or private vans and cars, to hitch rides rather than utilize military or government vehicles; for this was the Jewish Sabbath, and in Israel any military operation is likely to signal itself by the interruption of family life or religious devotions.

"Secrecy, speed, and surprise" were the key words employed the previous night by Thunderbolt's commander, Brigadier General Dan Shomron. It was ironic that a threat to secrecy came from Israel's tendency to become one large family on Saturdays, when everyone gossips and the elders interrogate the young: "Where did you go? What did you see?" If the answers are "Out" and "Nothing," the elders know something is up. And on this particular holiday there was only one possibility in every mind.

So Saturday seemed a normal, hot summer day: the beaches crowded, roads cluttered with traffic. The chosen few, the commandos selected from the Golani Brigade, the paratroops of the 35th Airborne, the hand-picked members of the counterguerrilla force, and the young air force girls who would tend the wounded in the air, the motley stream trickled unobtrusively from the kibbutzim, from Tel Aviv, and from Jerusalem toward the secret assembly points.

At one air base in the desert engineers of the Solel Boneh construction company were kept in isolation. They had produced for the dress rehearsal a replica of Entebbe, using blueprints from which they had built new sections of the airport during Israel's honeymoon with Uganda. The replica was modified by intelligence from Paris and the debriefing of released hostages, and from photographs taken by Israeli reconnaissance jets or retrieved from U.S. satellites. The engineers had been detained by unexpectedly lavish hospitality from the base commander and later by polite suggestions that they should remain on base to rest from their exertions. If they guessed why, they did not say. There is an invisible line between the family life of Israel and the business of defending it. An air base conveys the feeling best.

This base, scarcely visible, lay in a great depression ringed by tall trees and haunted by the ghosts of Super-hornets, large helicopters past their prime and now broken down to provide training for airborne commandos. Behind the husks were jump towers and tightropes. Between thick ranks of eucalyptus trees were old aircraft from previous wars, preserved as monuments.

The machines that mattered now were the giant, low-profile Hippos. It is astonishingly difficult to spot one of these troop-carrying aircraft on the ground. The fact that the Lockheed C-130 Hercules is regarded affectionately as the "hippopotamus" by IAF pilots is curious: the hardest animal to see on the shores of Lake Victoria is the lumbering hippo heaving itself onto the shore of Entebbe.

But Thunderbolt was full of such coincidences and surprises. Take the matter of President Amin's Mercedes. Years earlier, his future foreign minister (who had been offered a choice of ambassadorships), during a 24-hour marathon drinking session kept asking himself where he would like to be posted. Like Amin, he was fascinated by cars and planes. He judged foreign posts solely by the type of limousine he could buy duty-free . . . London and a Rolls-Royce? Paris and the new Citroën? Washington and a Lincoln? Or Bonn and a Mercedes?

He chose Bonn. He recommended that President Amin get a Mercedes. By then, foreign governments were competing unashamedly for the favors of the black dictators who leaped into power behind the receding colonial tide. Amin had a choice of half-a-dozen bribes and chose a Mercedes. (Israel had nothing to offer in this line until someone thought of providing another kind of toy: the IAF's Fouga-Magista jet trainer.)

On Saturday, July 3, Amin's black Mercedes, or one exactly like it, stood behind the closed door of a large hangar. All Israel had been scoured during the final days of Flight 139's hijacking by specialists in deception operations. They found a Mercedes fitting the description supplied by the Mossad intelligence teams, but it was white. Getting it sprayed black presented a security problem. Who wants an expensive limousine converted overnight on a whim? Nobody in Israel has that kind of money. So the borrowers of the Mercedes painted it themselves.

A burly paratrooper was made up to resemble President Amin by "Reu'ma," a girl in the air force reserve who normally worked for a Tel Aviv television company. Now she worked from photographs of Big Daddy in the back of the cavernous hangar concealing the Mercedes. How and if the fake president and his Mercedes would be used had to be left to fate. What began as a joke had found its way into the final scheme.

At another base, a makeup artist worked on the men commanded by Lieutenant Colonel Yehonatan "Yonni" Netanyahu, whose commandos were to lead the attack. They were expert marksmen, trained as snipers and drilled continuously in the terrible art of killing guerrillas. Yonni was the U.S.-born leader of this grim unit, the son of a distinguished Jewish historian and himself a graduate student of philosophy from Harvard University. The men called him by an old Hebrew phrase that translates as "The man of sword and Bible." He had a passion for the land of Israel. On operations into terrorist ground, he led. On exercises, he made the landscape come alive.

"Yonni knew each corner of Israel in biblical terms," said a comrade. "Wherever we were, he would relate that place to some event in Jewish history."

Yonni discussed Uganda with his unit. Half-a-dozen were made up meticulously as Ugandan soldiers. They were nervous boys of 20 or thereabouts, "nervous in the sense that we had no concept of Africa," said one later. "We were accustomed to night raids, to fighting in unfamiliar conditions. But this was something else. We were trained to be dropped anywhere in the Middle East, to attack an oil well or take over an airfield from Arab control. None of us had considered 'Darkest Africa.' "

Another in Yonni's unit ("Rafael" is his nom de guerre) explained: "Nerves were strung taut. Yet those of us who could not take part in the operation fell back with tears in our eyes—tears of frustration. The nervous tension prepares you. To be left out is tragic."

The last-minute separation of those who would board the Thunderbolt planes and those who must wait had been anticipated. It reflected the precise adjustments to the operation that continued until the last moment, each adjustment a reaction to some new piece of intelligence.

Some intelligence was beamed back from the skies over Uganda where IAF planes relieved each other in patrols that watched the weather, the movement of Ugandan aircraft, and President Amin. Amin was due to fly back to Entebbe from Mauritius. The final changes in Thunderbolt would depend on when he returned.

Other intelligence continued to stream in from abroad. In Paris, the task force's special adviser on counterterror, Major General Rehavam Zeevi, had been busy since his arrival on Tuesday with negotiations and debriefings. He telephoned Prime Minister Rabin at 2:30 p.m., one hour before Thunderbolt began, to report another hitch in the bargaining. "There's some breakdown," he said, referring to the awkward channel to the terrorist leaders in Entebbe.

"Keep trying," replied Rabin.

Zeevi returned to the frustrating task, still believing that a deal was being made with the terrorists. Unconsciously he had disclosed to the task force that the terrorists were unable to respond to a revised plan for an exchange of prisoners. They could not respond because Amin had not returned. Thus, an hour before action, one more small piece was fitted into the mosaic.

In Nairobi, the El Al manager was advised to prepare to refuel "some extra charter flights—maybe two planes or so." He knew now why he had been instructed to draw out cash from his emergency reserve. It would be cash on the barrelhead. Where the charters were going he was not encouraged to guess.

Refueling was still a big question mark. Prime Minister Rabin had focused on this weak link from the start. The Hercules transports and the Boeing 707s would be operating at extreme range. The 707s could refuel at Nairobi without attracting comment. The Hercules, plainly geared for a military action, could not land on the way to Entebbe, nor could they be refueled in the air without attracting the attention of hostile radar. One Hercules was being loaded now with pallets of fuel to be pumped into the other three Hercules at Entebbe. That meant taking along special fuel pumps. It also meant a tremendous risk for the pilot and crew.

In the early hours of Saturday, still struggling with

the political and diplomatic implications of Thunderbolt, and still unable to give the final approval, the prime minister again questioned General Gur, IAF commander Benny Peled, and his intelligence advisers. Was there an alternative to hauling the spare fuel such a distance?

By then the news from Nairobi was encouraging enough for Rabin's advisers to suggest that Thunderbolt rely on refueling in Kenya. As a backup, a fifth Hercules with the fuel on board would fly ahead and wait at a Kenyan air force base near Mombasa. The standby air tanker, though, must be used only in a grave emergency. If the rescue mission was forced to land at an African military base there would be violent repercussions, and Kenya would be charged with aiding and abetting a military assault on Uganda. Nairobi, on the other hand, was a commercial airline base and since the raiders would be flying under civil registration, it would be difficult for anyone to raise serious objections.

The time limits were also set now, dictated by the imminence of some violent action against the hostages and the lack of busy commercial air traffic on the air lanes from the Mideast through Nairobi to South Africa. It was known, for example, that Entebbe Airport would not be disturbed by commercial air traffic from midday Saturday until a British Airways VC-10 refueled there at the scheduled time of 2:30 a.m. on Sunday on its way from London to Mauritius. This, incidentally, set the outside limit for the departure of the Thunderbolt planes. They should be well away from the scene before the British airliner entered the circuit.

There was never any question of which aircraft would be used in the mission. The Hercules in the C-130E and C-130H configurations had been in IAF service since 1971. They had undergone considerable Israeli modification since the first batch of 16 had arrived. On a long-range penetration mission of this kind, one machine acting as pathfinder would be crammed with electronic gear that virtually acted as long-range eyes and ears. The planes, though heavy and clumsy in appearance, had the handling qualities of fighters. Their pilots were trained to put them through a range of aerobatics, to fly them on two engines, and to land with three engines dead.

The Hercules pilot nonetheless misses the glamour that surrounds IAF jet fighter pilots. One whose nom de guerre for the rescue mission was "Ariel" described later how he felt:

A little earlier I was sitting on a yacht. In the peaceful atmosphere of a summer evening, I never imagined that within hours I would be called to fly 20 tons of fuel to Kenya—to fly a bomb ready to explode through a moment of carelessness or blow up if hit by a chance Ugandan shell.

On the yacht there was a festive meal with lots of booze. Some of Tel Aviv's beauties adorned the deck. They had little interest in the fate of the hostages, contenting themselves with sighs of "Poor things" and hurried to change the subject.

The men argued about the hijacking. Most criticized the government for inaction. Suddenly, everyone turned to me and asked: "You people in the air force —can't you do anything? Can't you bomb Entebbe?"

I felt at a disadvantage in this intoxicating atmosphere. I replied: "What do you want of me? I'm just a transport pilot. If they tell me to fly to Entebbe—I fly to Entebbe."

Ever since the days of the Dakotas and Stratocruisers, we transport pilots are like stepsons in the air force. We don't reap the glory of fighter pilots who engage Migs in combat and attack missile batteries. We are the truck drivers.

In our squadron the atmosphere is somewhat civilian. The men are veterans, with many hours of flying time on other planes. Work is routine and predictable. Members of the crew come aboard in casual clothes, carrying large bags like messengers.

In the Hippopotamus, the big Hercules, the captain sits with a second pilot. Behind our chairs is the flight engineer. At the back of the cockpit sits the fourth member of the crew—the navigator. The navigational system of this plane, unlike that in the air force's other transport planes, is built with great sophistication. The

Hercules can fly in conditions of no visibility and any weather—from the north pole to the equator. We have yet to go to the north pole.

On the large instrument panels which stretch in front to both sides and up to the ceiling, are the most sophisticated navigational aids, including very precise radar. These aids are a revolution in the navigation systems and instruments of military air transport.

The high-tailed Hippo has four turbojet engines. At the height of their power they sound muffled—an important advantage in the Entebbe raid. The machine takes off very rapidly from short runways. It is fitted with rockets for a quick getaway.

The atmosphere among us Hercules pilots is pioneering. The large number of crew members creates a cheerful and friendly spirit. There is special significance in controlling a four-engined plane. You are in charge of a giant.

The Hercules transports stood in line at the far end of a long runway at another base. Canvas-covered trucks and command cars edged up to their gaping cargo ramps. Somewhere on nearby runways an occasional interceptor landed or took off—a Phantom or maybe a Skyhawk. Most of the base personnel had gone to stretch out in their rooms. A few were still in the mess. Young pilots chatted in the bar.

Few noticed young soldiers jump out of helicopters and move to offload equipment and stow it in the depths of the aircraft: boxes of grenades, bazooka rockets, radiophones, and the trappings of war.

Two jeeps, with 106-millimeter recoilless guns installed, were swallowed up in the belly of a Hercules. Heavy machine guns joined the arsenal. A half-track crawled into another of the planes. Everything passed quickly. No raised voices. Expressionless faces. There was the special smell of the unknown before battle.

Field security officers made sure that no stranger came near. The team of senior officers was very small; the commander of the base and his operations officer, Brigadier General Dan Shomron, Lieutenant Colonel Yehonatan "Yonni" Netanyahu.

If Thunderbolt had been kept carefully secret at the political level, it was nothing compared with the wall of silence erected within the army and air force. The whispers travel in Israel as swiftly as gossip on the Arab grapevine or, as Shomron said, "the beat of the African tom-tom." Security officers burned every piece of paper to do with the mission once it had served its purpose.

Last orders were given at an assembly base where all eyes focused on a gigantic sketch of Entebbe Airport. Yonni analyzed for his men each detail of their sectors, paying particular attention to the old terminal building where the hostages were being held.

The problem, Yonni explained, was "to reach the hostages at high speed, and eliminate the hijackers. It's a matter of seconds between success and a massacre."

A young officer commented: "It reminds me of the Sabena rescue at Lod. There was a problem about sorting out hijackers from passengers. Most passengers were saved because the whole thing took seconds."

"That's why you have identikits on the terrorists," Yonni replied. "You've had time to memorize. Still, keep going over details during the flight. The bastards mustn't be allowed to fire a single shot. A single grenade could mean disaster."

The atmosphere was relaxed. Yonni's soldiers, some of whom looked like children, spoke of Entebbe as if it were Petach Tikvah just outside Tel Aviv—as if it were "Anatevka," Shalom Aleichem's little township in *Fiddler on the Roof*. Briefings had made it seem so familiar. They seemed to forget this was a journey into the heart of Africa. The only Africa they knew was the front line across the Suez Canal in the Yom Kippur War. "Well," shrugged a paratrooper, "the distance is the pilots' problem."

They talked of the hostages. There would be murderous crossfire. How to warn the hostages to fall flat on the floor? By loudspeaker? Or simply burst in and shout?

Yonni chose his best marksmen. The first shots at the terrorists must be fatal. Prisoners? "It would be nice to capture the leader, Jaber," said Yonni. "But they're killers. There won't be second chances."

They planned how to get the passengers to the planes. How many stretchers? What about old people and children? Would they have to be carried?

The sessions at the general staff, with the participation of the air force commander, General Benny Peled, and the head of operations branch, Major General Yekutiel Adam, were almost scientific: precise planning of the flight plan to Entebbe and back, a detailed timetable of anticipated maximum stay at Entebbe, examination of alternatives in case of complications or unexpected hitches somewhere in Africa, far from home. Mission Commander Dan Shomron, who had worked almost 24 hours every day of the week, was coordinating the different formations—Yonni's unit to see to the hostages, Force 629 to neutralize the Ugandans, a Special Air Service detachment to destroy Idi Amin's Russian jets, men to protect the planes, the communications experts, medicos, and a team of intelligence technologists for a small independent mission. One thing was abundantly clear: if anything happened to the planes, Thunderbolt's force might be trapped in Entebbe in a worse position than the hostages. For this reason there would be special air support held in reserve.

Peres had called the operation "the farthest in range, the shortest in time, and the boldest in its imagination." Chief of Staff Mordechai Gur called it a "calculated risk" in the war on terrorism. To which Peres made a final amendment: "A relative risk—we are dealing with relative dangers and we have no ideal solutions."

The planners knew enough about what to expect to stress "neutralizing" the Ugandans rather than harming them—if they did not open fire first. After all, the officers and men of the Ugandan army had once been students of Israel's military mission. As Peres put it, "The Ugandan nation is not responsible for the actions of Idi Amin—who isn't really responsible for them himself."

On his way from the top-level briefing, Dan Shomron glanced at a cartoon from an English paper pinned on a bulletin board. It showed Idi Amin asking Adolf Hitler: "Perhaps you could advise me on how to build a command bunker like the one you had in Berlin?"

During the last hours when military and task force approval had been obtained and the final decision depended upon the full session of the cabinet, 280 paratroops gathered in a hangar beside a row of half-tracks and jeeps armed with recoilless guns. Special Service commander Major General Shomron waited until the huge hangar doors had been wheeled shut, then jumped onto the step of an armed command jeep.

"What you are required to do is important for the state of Israel," he said, voice hoarse from the hours and days of argument. "I know you will each do your duty. Good luck. Thank you."

The pilots regarded their passengers with some dismay. Some men stripped to the waist as soon as they walked into the bellies of the Hercules. Others wore crumpled coveralls. They were joined by civilians dressed untidily as if for a day digging in their gardens.

"I never saw such a mob," commented a pilot later. "They looked ruffians, the lot of them. After we were airborne, they slumped under half-tracks or wriggled into spaces between containers and jeeps and went to sleep!"

This pilot had so many flying hours in his military logbook that it would have been reasonable to suppose that he was ready for any surprise. He knew some of the civilians were doctors. He guessed others were technical experts on secret secondary missions. He said: "When I looked at the commandos' faces I was reassured. But anyone who saw them walking onto the base would have dismissed them as men recruited from street urchins and schoolboy gangs. That, of course, was how they wanted to look."

The air conditioning inside his Hercules failed to fight off the considerable heat. Soldiers sat packed like sardines around the equipment. Some perched on a jeep, others squeezed in at the side of a half-track. The crew climbed the short ladder to their control cabin. There were pitying glances for the handful of men in Ugandan uniform squashed inside the black

Mercedes, their blackened faces streaked with perspiration. The government had convened in full session at 2:00 p.m. Yitzhak Rabin, looking anxious, explained, possibly confessed, that if the operation did not succeed —and if there would be demonstrations—he as prime minister would bear responsibility. With a heavy heart he announced that he approved the plan. Throughout, Rabin behaved as on the eve of the Six Day War: a long waiting period of calculation up to the last moment of decision. But in 1967 Rabin was chief of staff and wanted government approval. Now he was himself the authority of last resort. Without his agreement the planes would not leave for their destination.

The discussion went on. The prime minister said he did not want to limit the time each minister could speak, so the decision wouldn't be rushed through under the pressure of time—a fact that added to the fateful atmosphere of the discussion, as each of the ministers wanted to speak on this "historic occasion," thereby, of course, delaying the time of the final decision.

But the democratic delay served a purpose too, reducing the time to an absolute minimum during which Thunderbolt might be betrayed by the slip of a tongue.

16

THUNDERBOLT: GO!

Thunderbolt got off the ground literally 15 minutes *before* final cabinet approval. The largest airborne commando raid ever to strike at long distance was on its way, the commanders under orders to turn back if the crisis task force failed to convince all government ministers that the operation must proceed. The word *"Zanék!"* meaning "Jump!" or, in the jargon of another war, "Scramble!" was flashed to all pilots at 3:30 p.m. It was the Jewish Sabbath, Saturday, July 3, and two of the ministers who represented strictly religious sections of Israel had walked all the way to the cabinet

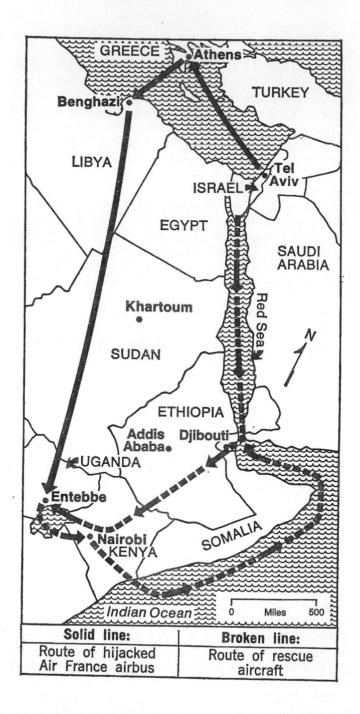

Solid line:	Broken line:
Route of hijacked Air France airbus	Route of rescue aircraft

session, obeying scruples against the use of transport. Since the meeting was in Tel Aviv and one of the ministers lived in Jerusalem, Transport Minister Yaakobi thoughtfully warned his colleague the previous day to spend the night away from home. The second, Zevoloun Hammer, the minister of welfare, walked for 90 minutes from his own quarters in a Tel Aviv suburb, politely rejecting a chauffeur-driven car sent to pick him up by Prime Minister Rabin.

"We'll run out of gas while those idiots continue arguing," complained a pilot, heading toward the Red Sea with commandos getting blackface "facials" from a makeup expert snatched that afternoon from a Tel Aviv theater.

"They talk, we sweat, and Big Daddy eats his first hostage," muttered a paratrooper, huge and uncomfortable in the white starched coveralls of an East African Airlines mechanic.

"They reckon on 30 dead and 50 wounded," said one of 23 doctors and 10 medical specialists in the Boeing 707 converted into a flying hospital. "They've figured the odds. Why the hell can't they just tell us . . . GO!"

"If the government takes much longer to make up its mind," said an airborne radar operator, "the Russians will scramble their Migs . . . and they won't be Migs flown by Ugandans."

The natural edginess of men and women in this remarkable aerial armada would echo through the aftermath. Fighting men, trained for action, were impatient with the slow processes of democracy in an artificial peace. Huge aircraft and fighter escorts were moving toward their target with no firm order to attack while "old men" were "mumbling in their beards."

In the final political discussions on Saturday, the chief of staff opened: "This time I'm presenting a plan for execution." He quoted Dan Shomron, the commander of the operation: "From my point of view, if I succeed in landing the first plane safely, the operation will succeed."

The atmosphere was tense. Many of those who spoke confidently were still feeling uncertain. The hands of the clock would not stand still. The flight to Entebbe takes seven hours. If the plan were to be approved it must be done within minutes.

In theory it was possible to recall the planes at any time before landing at Entebbe. This was taken into account in case some sudden development endangered the operation. Idi Amin was scheduled to cut short his visit to the African summit conference in Mauritius that night and return to Entebbe. Suppose the men of the commando and Idi Amin landed at the same moment, face to face, at the airport?

Intelligence stressed that no more than 10 terrorists were guarding the hostages, with 80 to 100 Ugandan soldiers nearby. There was considerable anxiety over a revival of the fear that the aircraft and the building where the hostages were held were mined for demolition.

Ahead of the Thunderbolt armada flew a Boeing 707 wearing the colors of El Al and a civil registration number, and carrying the IAF commander, Benny Peled, a veteran pilot whose logbook included every warplane in Israel's history, and the deputy chief of the general staff, Yekutiel Adam. They followed the international air lane down the Red Sea, turning south to cross Ethiopia and letting down just west of Lake Naivasha for the landing at Nairobi Airport.

So far so good. Nobody had challenged them. There was no reason why anyone should. The 707 was a commercial airliner in its present garb. If anyone looked inside, they would see businessmen in civilian suits and a rather unusual quantity of cargo where half the seats should have been. The cargo was an entire air-command center, the flying version of Benny Peled's headquarters in Tel Aviv. The air force chief was listed on the manifest as Sidney Cohen, a South African furrier. The plane taxied to the maximum security area of Nairobi Airport where El Al planes customarily receive the protection of Kenyan police. The commander of the airport police, Lionel Davies, was one of the few Kenyan officials who knew why these unusually strict precautions were needed.

A second 707 followed the same procedure. Its IAF markings, too, were painted over and El Al's livery substituted. Inside were some of the doctors and nurses assigned to care for the yet-to-be-wounded.

Tankers refueled both planes without attracting attention. El Al's Nairobi manager had ensured the disinterest of Kenyan ground crews. A routine telex went back to Tel Aviv—but the recipients were far from routine. El Al's boss, Mordecai Ben-Ari, flashed a copy to the general staff. Ben Ari had been glued to his office throughout the week and this was the climax of sleepless days and nights not unlike the years when he directed Jewish refugees in borrowed trucks and planes through the ruins of Hitler's Europe.

With both 707s safely in Kenya, the Thunderbolt fleet of four Hercules and fighter escorts could be properly unleashed. The small armada had been ordered into the air shortly after 3:30 p.m. and was passing over Sharm al-Sheikh at the southernmost tip of Israel when the final word GO! reached the pilots. From that moment military radio fell silent. All four Hercules were camouflaged by civil registration numbers and followed the same commercial route. Pilots followed normal civil aviation procedures. They could hardly disguise the high-tailed profile of the Hippos from inquisitive eyes. But on radar, the Hippo looked like any other blob.

The troop transports kept a loose formation, remaining in comfortable radarscope view of the leader. They followed well-established skyways, but soon after leaving Israeli airspace they reduced altitude. Before turning inland they spotted naval vessels of Russian origin but apparently under Arab command. The vessels were thought to be electronic surveillance ships and the fleet of high-tailed Hippos descended to sea level.

"There were times when we flew them like combat planes," reported an airman. "We did everything but dogfight. We made sudden sharp turns to dodge the Russian-built radar pickets on sea and land, then had to climb fast to get over the mountains."

They ran into "tremendous storms" and rode through them because of the need to conserve fuel. "We had nowhere to land if we got engine trouble," said a navigator. "Addis Ababa is closed after dark to all aircraft and anyway the place is dangerous—you never know what group of Ethiopians happens to be on top, and what military units are sitting trigger-happy at the airport. And finding your way there in pitch darkness between mountain peaks is an invitation to disaster."

Aboard the pathfinder, the crew concentrated on finding a path through these alien skies. A tremendous bullet-shaped radome ahead of the flight deck shielded a spherical dish swinging through a 360-degree circle and projecting two powerful beams of energy. The first pencil beam reflected off specific targets like ships, mountains, and aircraft, returning the information to the Hercules crew. The second beam swept a wide area in constant lookout for a variety of objects. Together they provided the Hercules with an all-seeing eye that kept track of land, vessels, thunderstorms, and rainfall. An electronic brain interpreted the signals and defined obstacles that might be confused, distinguishing between a mountain, for example, and a thunderhead.

An amber scope glowed in the darkness above the main instrument panel. A pencil-thin beam of light swept around the scope leaving, here and there, blobs that trailed tails of luminescence like small comets. The two pilots, navigator, and engineer were trained to decipher the meaning of these blobs at a glance, "seeing" the terrain below and the path ahead.

High above the troop transports flew the shepherds: IAF Phantoms, keeping well away, their radar operators following the flock on compact screens. In each Phantom were devices to jam hostile radar and misdirect radar-directed missiles should an enemy attempt to intercept Thunderbolt.

By dusk the odd little airfleet was turning over Nairobi. For the troop transports there could be no question of landing on the way into Uganda. At the extreme of their flying range, they were entering the dangerous approach to Entebbe. No longer protected by commercial flight paths, they descended in the dark toward a sheet of water 3000 feet above sea level, the vast unseen source of the White Nile, mighty Lake Victoria.

Uri Dan describes the scene:

A LEGEND IS BORN

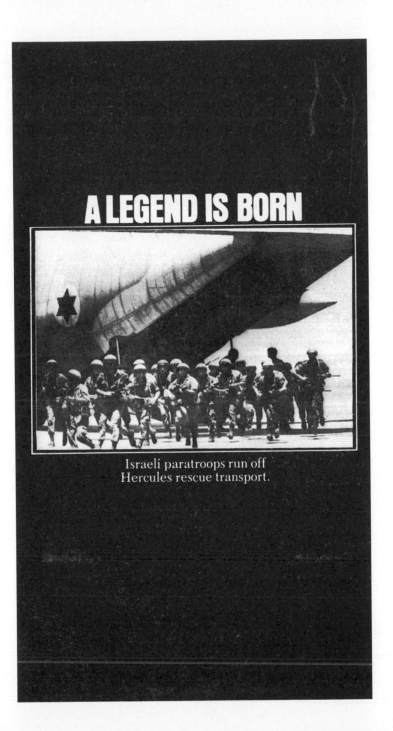

Israeli paratroops run off
Hercules rescue transport.

Left: Ugandan President Idi Amin with
Yasir Arafat, head of Al Fatah and PLO.

Left and middle: Fayez Abdul-Rahim Jaber and
Jayel Naji al-Arjam, hijackers killed at Entebbe. Right: claimed
to be Dr. Wadi Hadad, Chief of Palestinian terrorists.

Hijacked Air France airbus.

Idi Amin, in hat, talks with hostages released
by the hijackers at Entebbe Airport on July 1, 1976.
WIDE WORLD

Israeli commandos rehearse running from a Hercules transport that has swung around to provide covering dust storm.
BAMAHANE

Hercules, with long-range
fuel tanks, loading
equipment.
BAMAHANE

Seated left to right: Anonymous, Chief of Staff Mordechai
Gur, Brig. Gen. Dan Shomron, and Anonymous.
BAMAHANE

Israeli commandos study diagrams in rehearsal for Entebbe.
Faces marked out for security reasons.
BAMAHANE

Hercules C-130 transport takes off.
BAMAHANE

Prime Minister Rabin among rejoicing crowd at airport to
welcome Israeli commandos and freed hostages on July 4, 1976.

MICHA BAR-AM/MAGNUM

Rescued hostages emerge
from Hercules in
Israel. At left is Air France
pilot, Captain Michel Bacos.

Welcome home to Israel!

SHMUEL RAHAMANI

MICHA BAR-AM MAGNUM

ilCHA BAR-AM MAGNUM

WIDE WORLD

MICHA BAR-AM/MAGNUM MICHA BAR-AM/MAGNUM

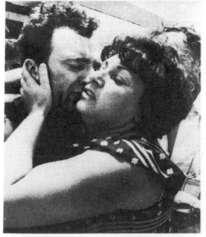 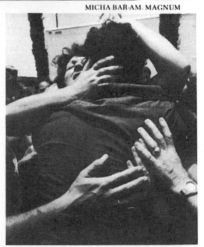

WIDE WORLD WIDE WORLD

Maj. Gen. Benny Peled,
Chief of Air Force.
ISAAC ISMACH

Brig. Gen. Dan Shomron,
paratroop leader.
WIDE WORLD

Chief of Staff, Lt. Gen. Gur gives press briefing
in Tel Aviv a few days after rescue.
Beside him is map of Entebbe Airport.
WIDE WORLD

Left: Lt. Col. Yonni Netanyahu,
field commander of the rescue force,
who was killed at Entebbe.
BAMAHANE
Right: mourners at
his funeral at home in Israel.
ISRAEL SUN

United Nations Security Council debate on
July 9 about Israeli rescue in Uganda.
Left: Israeli Ambassador Chaim Herzog;
right: Ugandan Foreign Minister Juma Oris.
WIDE WORLD

Mrs. Dora Bloch, 75-year-
old Israeli left
behind at Entebbe and
believed to have
been killed by Ugandans.
WIDE WORLD

As the Hercules flew toward Entebbe, flashes of lightning illuminated them as if to reveal their nakedness. Inside the planes, soldiers huddled in the darkness.

"David," commander of the force, was leading. He was overjoyed. Benny Peled, the IAF chief, chose him to bring the first plane into Entebbe. Some of the IAF's most senior pilots competed for the privilege, but the air force commander made no concessions to seniority. David was selected in accordance with the IAF routine work roster. He was considered a good pilot but his experience was not particularly rich. On the other hand, he had always fulfilled his duties well. The IAF commander saw no reason to deprive him of his due when his turn came. And so, quite fortuitously, David led the IAF's longest combat mission.

David listened to the muffled roar of the four turbojet engines, cruising at 350 miles an hour. His crew concentrated on a navigation plan worked out to permit the heavily laden planes to reach Entebbe, land, endure the confusion of a possible battlefield, take off again, and escape.

On the last leg to Entebbe, atmospheric disturbances were severe, requiring alterations in flight plans. Each Hercules was flying independently through the night, maintaining radio silence, descending into the Rift Valley, and relying on electronic aids to feel its way over Lake Victoria. The Hippos tossed violently and David pondered the justice of arguments he used when persuading young pilots to sign on for service with the IAF's transport unit. "When you fly a Hercules," he would tell them, "you'll see it has all the characteristics of a small plane. It's very maneuverable, and it can do almost everything except dogfight. It's well ahead of any other plane of its size."

A South African-born doctor complained of feeling unwell as the plane pitched and tossed in the stormy weather. Everyone understood—without saying it—that he was simply very agitated. "We were told there may be many casualties among the hostages," he said. "I have never worked under combat conditions." The soldiers tried to relieve his anxieties with jokes: "Look, doctor—you've got the chance to return home to South Africa from here." The doctor gave a sickly smile. But at Entebbe, under fire, he proved cool, swift, and devoted.

Another doctor on the medical team was Dr. Maurice Ankeleviecz, who had long experience in administering medical aid on the battlefield. When he was summoned to take part in the raid, he left his post at Shiba Hospital, Tel Hashomer, and reported for duty. The French-born Ankeleviecz, who had served for years as the doctor of the paratroopers, was far more tranquil than his South African colleague.

The operational plan, cleared with the army's chief medical officer, divided the doctors into two teams: ten were to attach themselves to the hostages; the rest would remain with the flying operation theater. Medical supplies included diluted milk—for hostages known to be suffering from intestinal ailments.

Dan Shomron and Yonni Netanyahu went over details of the operational plan with their subordinates again. Every now and then they clambered into the cockpit to ask "How's it going?" Yonni was even more content than Dan, now that zero hour was approaching. Before the operation was finally approved, Yonni said that he would not blame anyone if it was decided not to carry it through—even though he believed the raid was feasible. Now he was tense as a bowstring. In his view, the Arab states' hatred for Israel, and the actions of the terrorists, were a revival of Nazism.

Yonni was a man of contrasts. Born in the United States, he led an elite unit. The Six-Day War found him fighting in the Golan Heights, where he was wounded. He was discharged from the army as 30 percent disabled, and returned to the United States and his parents.

Defense Minister Peres had a personal interest in Yonni and stood as his guarantor when he returned to Harvard and sought further surgery on his arm. Doctors at Walter Reed Hospital worked to relieve the near constant pain caused by nerve damage that kept him from opening and closing his left hand. Surgery on the arm stopped the pain, but he was never able to regain full use of the hand. Technically he was still 30 percent disabled when he returned to Israel and talked his way back into the commandos.

"What can you offer?" demanded Major General Ariel Sharon, glancing at the crippled hand.

"I can recite by heart all the poems of Nathan Alterman," Yonni replied, referring to one of Israel's leading poets.

"Pass, friend," joked Sharon.

Two months before Thunderbolt, Yonni was promoted to command an antiterrorist unit.

17

INTO AFRICA

The 50-year-old chief of the Israeli air force circled Lake Victoria in the refueled 707 command aircraft. Benny Peled could both watch the raiders on radar and follow the operation on open radio mikes transmitting on a secret channel for relay to Tel Aviv. The silence below told him that Thunderbolt was going well, the Hercules flying at half-mile intervals. Thick mist covered the lake but Entebbe was clear.

In Defense Minister Peres's office in Tel Aviv, ministers gathered as zero hour approached.

"I walked over at about 10:30 p.m.," recalled Minister of Transport Gad Yaakobi, whose civil aviation responsibilities made him most conscious of the organization required to maneuver Thunderbolt along commercial routes and refuel camouflaged military aircraft at international airports. "After about fifteen minutes the prime minister joined us, and then other members of the task force. We sat quietly listening for the first sounds of action from receivers tuned to the raiders.

"At 11:03 there was the noise of gunfire."

In the old terminal building at Entebbe, the hostages had endured their sixth day in Uganda. Their captors lounged in chairs on the brightly lit tarmac outside. The prisoners were being guarded, during this shift, by the German man and woman. An Egyptian doctor, called to attend to the passengers, chatted casually with Jaber, the terrorist operations chief.

Many hostages were suffering severe attacks of diarrhea. Water in the toilets had run out. The toilet bowls filled up. Ugandan soldiers brought water in cans and filled up the roof tanks, but the pipes were clogged.

Moshe Peretz had kept the entries on this day very short.

Shabbat, July 3. 0530—Everybody gets up vomiting and suffering from diarrhea. Seems to come from contaminated meat, because the Orthodox people, who did not eat the meat, have not caught the ailment. Sanitary conditions are atrocious. The toilets are full of filth. There is no water in the taps.

0730—People are lying in their beds and vomiting. Some are taken for treatment at a nearby dispensary, and others lie down to sleep. Many people do not eat lunch.

1430—The Air France plane has been moved up close to the passenger building, with its nose pointed toward us.

1645—Amin arrives in air force uniform, wearing a blue beret and sporting his Israeli parachuter's wings. He announces that he has just returned from Mauritius, and everything is being done to try and save our lives. It is the Israeli government which is to blame, by not fulfilling the terrorists' demands.

This was the last time the hostages saw Big Daddy. "Your government is gambling with your fate," he warned them. According to Peretz, one of the Israelis respectfully asked to reply. "Field Marshal President Idi Amin," she began. Amin interruped, shouting: "Don't address me like that! My full title is 'Field Marshal Doctor President Idi Amin Dada!'"

Amin had bestowed the title of doctor upon himself. After all, his friends Wadi Hadad and George Habash were doctors as well as terrorist chiefs.

The group of terrorists dispersed. One, tall and wearing a white suit, picked up a short-barreled submachine gun and went off for his night's rest.

Those left to guard the hostages were some of the best of Wadi Hadad's professionals. Besides the Germans at the entrance, two Palestinians patrolled the hall. One was Fayez Abdul-Rahim Jaber, a PFLP special operations officer, with a cocked Kalachnikov rifle in his hand.

His thin, nervous companion, Abed el Latif, guarded another corner of the old terminal building. He too was one of Wadi Hadad's close advisers.

Jayel Naji al-Arjam, age 38, a short, sturdy Palestinian wearing a Carlos-style beret, was on guard in another part of the terminal. His function in the PFLP was to supervise terrorism in South America. There he helped recruit for the Terrorist International, whose leaders include Carlos, The Jackal. He assisted The Jackal in the attempt to assassinate the Jewish president of Marks and Spencer in London, Edward Sief.

Navigating with the aid of the Entebbe Airport radio beacon, the Hippos approached their objective. Just one more correction, shortly before arrival, because of weather difficulties—and, down below, the pilots saw the Uganda shoreline, illuminated by a crescent moon low on the horizon.

Inside the leading Hercules, Yonni and nine commandos were crammed into the repainted Mercedes, first in line before the rear ramp. Their faces were black. Their hands and Uganda-type pistols fitted with silencers were also coated in black. The Mercedes was black. They had not brought with them the dummy president. That particular deception was dangerous in the light of last-minute intelligence that Uganda's president had returned to Entebbe earlier in the day. It could be embarrassing if two Big Daddies confronted one another.

The transport planes split into two pairs. Entebbe Airport was approached by one pair aiming to land on the new main runway. The second pair were to land on the old runway, which is separated from the airport's modern extension by a slight rise in the ground.

The fleet covered the last ten-minute leg of the seven-hour flight at a sharply reduced speed of 180 miles an hour. They were within reach of the target at the Estimated Time of Arrival (ETA) calculated in Tel Aviv. Operational planners were delighted—and slightly astonished. The four Hercules had followed a difficult route comparable to a nonstop journey from New York to Moscow, without visual bearings or radio contacts, maintaining radio silence, and holding positions relative to the leader where in-flight decisions were made by the pathfinder.

The pathfinder said later: "We hit Entebbe on the nose, at the hour when it was felt the Ugandans would be sleepy, but the hostages not yet dangerously drugged with sleep. We hoped to catch some of the terrorists relaxed after drinking in Kampala twenty-one miles away.

"The soldiers knew the hazards of the flight. They saw the lightning and I felt sorry for them because nothing's worse than sitting idle in bad storms, hour after hour. Whenever I climbed down into the cargo hold, half the men were sprawled on the metal floor and the other half were rechecking notes or systematically disposing of documents. For them it should have been an agonizing seven hours—that's a hell of a long time groping through a void."

The pathfinder crept over the unseen waters of Lake Victoria, hanging the great bird on the four props, trusting the lives of his crew and 50 commandos to the accuracy of the radarscopes glowing in the dark. Shreds of mist condensed against the huge flight-deck windows and teardrops of moisture were flung back along the quivering perspex. The big wipers rocked rhythmically.

Suddenly runway lights appeared ahead. David blinked back fatigue and checked his instruments. Flying blind, a pilot is quickly disoriented. Airliners have tried to land upside down on the Milky Way when pilots transferred their eyes from instruments to visual contact with the world outside and mistook stars for ground beacons. David concentrated on the dimly lit panels that told him that he was flying straight and level.

Entebbe for some incredible reason was fully lit.

This was the moment over which so much argument had taken place in Tel Aviv. If the first Hercules got down and taxied with muted motors to the old passenger lounge without arousing suspicion, the safety of the hostages might be fairly well assured. If the airport was lit up because the terrorists already knew what was coming, the raiders were flying into a trap and the hostages were in grave trouble.

The first Hercules floated over the edge of the lake. Crew and soldiers had tightened straps for the tremendous jolt that comes with an assault landing. David watched the speed bleed away swiftly from 100 to 75 miles an hour. Inside the hull the plane seemed to fall out of the air with a shriek of twisted metal and protesting turbines. Outside, an observer would have seen the craft slide almost soundlessly onto the runway, the underinflated tires uttering a soft squeal.

The IAF Hippo had crawled over the muddy shore with the soft-footed grace of those nocturnal hippos that rise out of Lake Victoria to crop the grass at night.

David and his copilot kept the machine moving swiftly down the runway. No loud reversal of engines for braking, no standing on brakes, just the harmonious movements of two pairs of hands and feet juggling the controls and adapting swiftly to the new set of conditions. After a long and arduous flight the pilots had to maneuver with a different set of reflexes, eyes and ears alert for gunfire or the challenging glare of a searchlight.

Behind and below, the men took their positions in the cavernous hold, belly muscles tight, bodies swaying with the new and slightly sickening sway of the aircraft groping toward the enemy at 20 miles an hour. Behind the first Hercules, number two was coming down the alley, trusting the pathfinder had encountered no problem, flying hard on his tail and ready to pull up if for some reason the runway was blocked or the pathfinder stalled.

David kept moving at the same allotted speed, calculated in rehearsal to bring him within yards of the old terminal building without unnecessary noise. The turboprops scarcely disturbed the sluggish African night. The buildings came into view, dimly lit. David had an unreal sense of having seen all this before. In a way he had, during briefings and the previous night's dry run. He brought the Hippo to a gentle stop within sight of the long French windows of the lounge, so close that he felt he could reach out and touch them. The 70-ton Hippo, standing nearly ten stories high, wings spread more than 120 feet from tip to tip, growled softly at the guarded gates of what Yonni had called "the concentration camp."

The waiting commandos winced as the big ramp creaked open, letting in damp air and the faint unexpected light. The ramp struck the tarmac with a thud that seemed unbelievably loud.

"I know now what is meant by a deathly silence," David said later. "It didn't seem possible. No shooting. No movement. The stillness was more frightening than a burst of gunfire. It was a real silence of death and I sat there, feeling horribly exposed, one hand on the throttles, waiting and wondering when the trap would be sprung."

But there was no trap. Simultaneously, on the parallel runway and out of David's line of sight, the leader of the second pair of Hercules had dropped light as a feather in the same state of bewilderment.

18
"YONNI'S BEEN HIT!"

Brigadier General Dan Shomron hurled himself down the pathfinder ramp with such speed that the IAF liaison officer with him said afterward: "He moved so fast, I lost him. I couldn't believe this was the same man who'd been sitting at a desk all week."

Shomron's men scattered to take care of the terrorists. The Mercedes rolled down the ramp and swung off in the direction of the airport security guard, posted near the control tower. The car doors flew open as the Ugandans saluted. The black pistols fitted with silencers spat briefly and the guards collapsed. The ruse had worked. Yonni and his group wiped faces and hands with the grease provided by the makeup girl and removed black Uganda-style blouses so that their comrades would not make the same fatal mistake in identification committed by the Ugandan guards. Yonni had gone over each minute and movement of the ground operation, but he feared the hair-trigger reaction of other Israelis if they collided in the dark.

The Hercules behind the pathfinder bumped down and was almost abreast of the new terminal building when someone in the control tower must have taken fright. Suddenly the whole airport was plunged in darkness.

"It happened to suit us very well," reported the captain of the last Hercules. "I flew into a crossfire of tracers that opened unexpectedly from different points on the field. It was safer to land in complete darkness. This was what we were trained to do. Frankly, I'd been worried to see what looked like the lights of an amusement park on the approach. I was glad they went out. My job was to sit on the ground until everyone else was off, and then recover the last detachments assigned to destroy the Russian-built Mig fighters. I was a sitting duck for 90 minutes—the longest minutes of my life, because as my Hercules rolled to a stop, all hell broke loose."

This was the gunfire heard by the task force in Tel Aviv, some 2500 miles away, transmitted over hand-held radiophones and relayed from the IAF command plane circling overhead.

Benny Peled, the IAF commander over the scene of battle, required no reports from the Hercules pilots. It had been agreed that unless a major crisis arose, the air tacticians would draw their own conclusions from the sounds heard over the commandos' radiophones. The technique had been perfected during years of raids into hostile territory beyond Israel's borders. Twenty years before, Benny Peled himself had bailed out of his damaged fighter (the first IAF pilot to use an ejector). He had parachuted behind Egyptian lines, fractured an ankle, and hobbled into hiding. For several hours he dodged Egyptian search parties until a light IAF scouting aircraft found him and directed piston-engined Mustangs to fly a protective patrol until another Piper Cub retrieved him. Benny Peled learned then a lesson in the artful use of radio communications.

"There was no miracle," said another IAF chief,

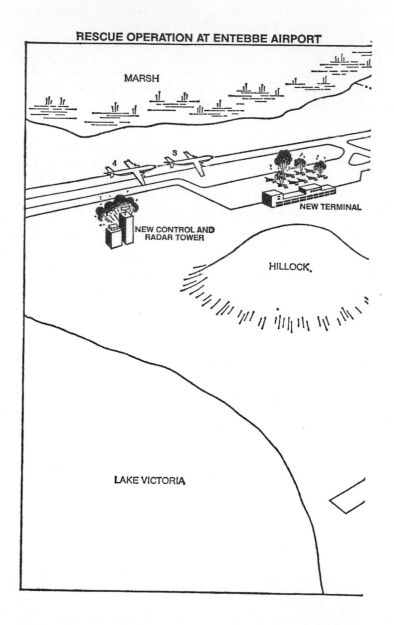

RESCUE OPERATION AT ENTEBBE AIRPORT

MARSH

NEW TERMINAL

NEW CONTROL AND
RADAR TOWER

HILLOCK.

LAKE VICTORIA

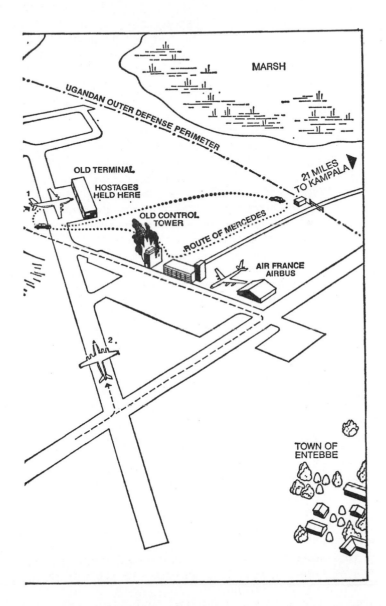

MARSH

UGANDAN OUTER DEFENSE PERIMETER

21 MILES TO KAMPALA

OLD TERMINAL

HOSTAGES HELD HERE

1

OLD CONTROL TOWER

ROUTE OF MERCEDES

AIR FRANCE AIRBUS

2.

TOWN OF ENTEBBE

Ezer Weizman. "This was a straightforward operation based on accumulated experience." Weizman, who planned the preemptive air strike of the Six Day War, was stressing what Israel's fighting men take for granted —that years of antiguerrilla warfare have developed discipline and a system that only looks fantastic to those unfamiliar with this daily grind.

Brigadier General Shomron took his command position close to the passenger building. The direction of the Entebbe operation was now in his hands. His skinny air-communications officer had found him again.

"Ilan," one of Yonni's men, ran toward the target assigned him—the German girl thought to be Gabriele Kroche-Tiedemann, the terrorist he called "that Nazi bitch." Her male compatriot, Wilfried Böse, stood outside a window with his back to the giant shadow of the Hippo literally breathing down his neck, unaware of the men sprinting toward him on rubber-soled boots.

Inside the dimly lit terminal, Baruch Gross, 41, and his wife Ruth holding their 6-year-old son Shai, were standing among the litter of bodies and mattresses. Gross himself had not slept since Idi Amin had announced that he was awaiting the final answer from Israel—before midnight. Watching the German through the window, Gross fancied the terrorist was about to squeeze the trigger of the Kalachnikov, its barrel pointing at the hostages.

Suddenly, with an expression of slow bewilderment, the German swung away and lifted his gun. A long burst of fire broke the silence. The German twisted and fell with the same look of astonishment on his face, the Kalachnikov still silent. Yonni's second-in-command jumped over the body toward his next target, and the youngster following stopped to roll the limp body face upward.

Gross hugged little Shai and told his wife to run for cover in the empty office of the East African Airways manager.

Ilan stopped breathing. Pacing him, near the entrance, with a gun in one hand and a grenade in the other, was the German woman. For a fraction of a second she seemed astounded and at a loss. Ilan pointed his submachine gun at her from a few yards' range and pressed the trigger, emptying the entire clip into her body. He had never fired at a woman before. With a feeling of shock he stepped over her body lying in the entrance and burst into the passenger lounge.

The raiders from the third Hercules reached the building just as Yonni's men broke into the lounge. Commands were shouted in Hebrew: "Lie down! On the floor! Down!" Whatever the warnings failed to do was made up by shock. The hostages froze in their places, stretched out motionless. Two Palestinian terrorists—Fayez Abdul-Rahim Jaber and Abed el Latif—were in the lounge. Both had time to open fire, one with an automatic rifle, the other with a revolver. Yonni's men pinpointed the source of the firing and poured a storm of bullets in their direction.

During those moments, the young hostage Moshe Peretz, completed his journal: "Several fellows jumped up suddenly and said they heard firing outside. I heard the sound of guns being cocked. Everybody got down on the floor. Some people fled to the toilets. People piled up, one on top of the other. Mothers covered their children with their bodies. The sound of shooting. I am in the toilet. I thought they were going to execute us one by one. Screams of alarm . . ."

One of the hostages, 56-year-old Ida Borochovitch, was bleeding profusely from a stray bullet. She was one of the pioneers of the Russian Jews' struggle for the right to emigrate to Israel. Her son, Boris Shlein, saw one of the terrorists—apparently Jaber—shoot her, only a few seconds before he himself was killed. .

Lizette Hadad, another hostage, said later: "Suddenly pieces of mortar began to fall from the ceiling. They struck me. A moment later Ida Borochovitch fell on me—and that was how I was saved."

Yosef Hadad, her husband, added: "We were lying down as usual, on mattresses laid out on the floor, trying to sleep. When the soldiers burst in I took a chair and held it over my head. I fancied that the German woman was beginning to shoot in my direction, and I began to say *"Sh'ma Yisrael."* I thought my life was finished. Suddenly we saw the Germans lying bleeding —and suddenly, we were outside . . ."

Young Benny Davidson related: "I did not know

they were Israeli soldiers. Suddenly we heard shooting. We ran toward the toilets. Everybody was running in that direction. We buried our heads on the floor. My father lay on top of my brother to protect him, and my mother was protecting me.

"I prayed. I don't remember precisely what it was that I prayed. It must have been a kind of private prayer. "God, protect us," I said. And then I added: *"Sh'ma Yisrael."*

The crowded lounge filled with smoke. Some hostages crawled under mattresses as more commandos burst through the windows shouting "Israel! Israel!" and then the Hebrew instruction to lie down—*"Tiskavu!"* Despite this carefully planned attempt to clarify a terrifying situation, some of the children milled about in bewilderment, and parents like Claude Rosenkowitz and his wife Emma threw themselves upon the children. One or two blankets appeared to have caught fire, frightening the two young daughters of Arye Brolsky, who pinned them to the floor and then tried in vain to make another girl keep her head down. She pulled free, rose to her knees, and was wounded.

The shooting inside the lounge lasted a total of 1 minute and 45 seconds. One victim was 19-year-old Jean-Jacques Maimoni, who had emigrated to Israel from North Africa only five years earlier. The other 103 hostages had nicknamed him The Barman. When others were sick or disheartened, Jean-Jacques raised spirits by brewing coffee or concocting drinks from fruit and coconut milk. He and Pasko Cohen, the 52-year-old manager of an Israeli medical insurance fund, had been the source of inspiration as more and more hostages became ill with colic or mild food poisoning. Cohen bore the tattoo marks of a concentration camp on his arm. Jean-Jacques, The Barman, worked beside him "as if we were father and son," said Cohen later. In the first seconds of gunfire, when most hostages fell flat to the floor or remained where they were on their mattresses, Jean-Jacques instinctively rose and caught the full blast from an Uzi that killed him instantly. His "father" Cohen, who had survived the death camps, tried to reach him and was in turn fatally injured.

Yonni and his men hunted for the remaining terrorists, combing the upper floor. In one of the toilets they discovered two terrorists with guns, hiding under a bed. The two were reported killed later. Another commando squad, operating in the northern wing of the passenger building, claimed a seventh terrorist—Jayel Naji al-Arjam, close personal friend of Wadi Hadad.

Doctors and medical orderlies, trained as combat troops,* moved swiftly to bring out the wounded—five civilians and four soldiers—and brought them to operating tables in the second Hercules. The battle on the airfield entered its second phase. The Israelis were fired upon from the nearby control tower, and Yonni's force advanced to take care of them. Bazooka shells and machine-gun fire were directed at the tower.

Someone shouted: "Yonni's been hit! Yonni's wounded! Orderly!" The call jolted the men. Yonni had been hit in the back and fell face down in the open space near the building's main entrance, bleeding heavily.

Yonni tried to stand up. He fell back again and lost consciousness. His second-in-command took over, reported to Dan Shomron, and continued with the movements planned by the men to whom the hostages owed their lives.

There were several small operations taking place. Each Hercules was under the guard of a dozen commandos, and the first plane had swung around to receive the hostages, who were directed toward its gaping hold by soldiers using bullhorns. From the other side of a 200-foot rise a glow of red fire illuminated the sky as the first of the Russian-built Mig jet fighters went up in flame.

Israeli half-tracks and jeeps armed with recoilless weapons raced for the outer defense perimeter, expecting to meet a column of armor coming down the Kampala road. President Amin's quarters, less than a mile from Entebbe Airport, were known to be heavily guarded by crack Ugandan troops. Instead of Russian-built tanks and infantry carriers, the Israelis encountered a squadron of Ugandan troops riding in light

---

*"Israel has the world's first army to produce medical teams capable of assuming all combat duties," the chief of staff claimed later.

trucks. By a margin of seconds, the Israelis reached the main airport gate in time to ambush the relieving forces, which were wiped out and on inspection seemed to have been rushing to the scene without much idea of what was happening.

The raid had begun one minute after midnight, Uganda time (which was one hour ahead of Israeli time), shortly after a pale moon had disappeared below the horizon. A thin rain had started to fall. The scene was wrapped in much the same fog that shrouded President Amin asleep close by. He was still unaware of the raid hours later.

19

DORA BLOCH VANISHES

James Horrocks, a British diplomat in Uganda, heard explosions and saw the black pall of jet-fuel smoke spreading over Entebbe. As chargé-d'affaires at the High Commission in Kampala, he had watched the progress of the drama since Flight 139's capture. One of his concerns was Dora Bloch, age 75, whose possession of a British passport entitled her to British protection. Dora Bloch was a hostage, as was her son Ilan Hartuv, an economist who had been interpreting for President Amin during the past week. Big Daddy had dubbed Dora Bloch's son "my translator."

On Friday Mrs. Bloch had been rushed to hospital after choking on some food. Ilan expected her return after receiving a message that she was now well again. Mother and son were on their way to the New York wedding of another son, Daniel, chairman of the Israeli Journalists' Union.

At midnight on Saturday, James Horrocks observed the raid with misgivings. In the previous four years Big Daddy had driven out 45,000 Asians holding British citizenship and whittled down the white European community from 3500 to some 500 Britons who were now hostages to fortune. The High Commission took a humanitarian interest in some 130,000 African refugees from neighboring states suffering from civil strife, and in several hundred Kenyans still employed in Uganda.

From many such witnesses, it was possible to piece together details of Thunderbolt kept secret by Israel's harsh system of security.

The destruction of the Russian Migs was undertaken by a team of experts. Another team rushed the main radar center and removed certain items of Russian equipment before blowing up the station to hide the evidence that devices had been stolen. Out of ten terrorists, seven were killed and their fingerprints and photographs recorded. Three other terrorists, it would seem, despite Israeli denials, were taken alive for interrogation.

A $1 million Israeli mobile fuel pump, adapted to serve the four Hercules from Entebbe's tanks, was left behind to make room for Soviet-built equipment and machinery taken from the quarters of Palestinian pilots learning to fly the Russian-built Migs.

The plan to refuel from Big Daddy's own tanks was abandoned. Thunderbolt proceeded faster than the planners expected. The first Hercules with hostages was lumbering out of Entebbe 53 minutes after the initial landing, 2 minutes sooner than predicted. Heavy gunfire, numerous small fires, the danger from exploding Migs, and the gauntlet that the Hippos must run to reach the fuel dumps caused Brigadier General Shomron to choose from several alternative plans. The Hercules, one with no more than 90 minutes of fuel left, should fly straight to Nairobi, 50 minutes flying time away.

All Israeli equipment, all trace of the raiders (except spent cartridges, the big fuel pump, and the general destruction) were cleaned up by the last group to leave. The senior pilot of their aircraft had sat for 90 minutes in the middle of continuous crossfire, knowing a stray shell could destroy the Hercules and remove the last chance for escape of the specialized intelligence and sabotage teams.

"I felt lonely and exposed, and each minute seemed like a lifetime," he reported. "It seemed a miracle that the preceding transports had escaped without incident. We planned for a meticulous schedule. My head told me that everything was going according to plan, ticking like a well-oiled clock. But my belly told me: Everything can't be that perfect—and you're the last one left."

Days later, home on a kibbutz where life is rural and the fields drowsy with summer heat, he found himself startled from bed by the rumble of thunder, convinced that he was back at Entebbe sitting on a planeload of explosives hit by shellfire.

In fact, none of the Hercules suffered damage. But the owner of the Mercedes complained, when it came back to him from its 16-hour escapade in the sky and at Entebbe, "I liked it white, the way it was. Look at it, covered in black paint. How—?"

Rather than answer his question, the IAF paid to have it resprayed.

The listeners in Defense Minister Peres's Tel Aviv office waited past midnight and then drifted next door into the chief of staff's quarters. From the IAF command 707 there was nothing to report after the brief news that the planeload of released hostages was en route to Nairobi.

From their flying command post above Entebbe, "Kutti" Adam, the chief of general operations, and IAF commander Benny Peled made no attempt to bother Dan Shomron. Thunderbolt's ground commander would keep informative transmissions to a minimum. The muffled sounds of firing, from 11:03 until nearly 12:30 a.m. on the morning of Sunday, July 4, Israeli time, were disturbing but not important so long as the ground teams remained silent.

"It's America's 200th birthday," said Adam as the 707 turned toward Nairobi. "And Israel is still in her twenties . . ."

At 1:20 a.m., Transport Minister Yaakobi telephoned the chairman of the semiofficial Committee for the Families of Hostages, Professor Gross.

"He couldn't believe it when I told him his brother and his sister-in-law were probably free, the hostages liberated," Yaakobi recalled. "Only a few hours before he had asked for another meeting with me this Sunday morning to discuss the deteriorating situation. He feared the start of executions. Ten minutes later, he recovered enough to begin phoning all the relatives of hostages. We knew perhaps two were killed, two or three injured. But we had no names. All families were invited to collect at the baseball stadium where we'd tell them where to meet the rescue planes. That was the worst part. There would be two families who rejoiced with the rest, and who would then go through the agony and the greater grief when they saw freed hostages stream into the sunlight—their own relatives not among them."

In the hospital where Dora Bloch had been taken, another British diplomat, Peter Chandley, checked to make sure she was safe. The elderly woman was sleeping quietly. The nurses said she was well and could rejoin her fellow Flight 139 passengers later. Chandley said nothing to the staff about the raid, and they seemed to know nothing about it. He tiptoed from the ward. No non-Ugandan would see her again alive.

20
"REFUEL AT NAIROBI!"

Golda Meir was awakened from a sound sleep, the phone beside her bed purring insistently.

"Ken—"

"Mrs. Meir, I thought you would like to know the hostages are on their way home," said Prime Minister Rabin. "Please excuse me for interrupting your sleep but—"

"You wanted me to know. Thank you. And congratulations."

Golda Meir put down the phone and looked at the time: 2:30 a.m. Outside her home in Ramat-Aviv, a gentle breeze stirred the heavy red flowers of a blossoming flame tree. The flame trees of Africa.

Later she wrote a dignified but indignant letter to the *Jerusalem Post* denying publicly an allegation "under the title ISRAEL SUPERSPY MADE ENTEBBE RAID POSSIBLE. It mentioned that I had urged the prime minister to go ahead with the mission and not surrender to the terrorists' demand and that I said that if he does not do it, he is not a man any more.

"I am dismayed by your quoting such a distasteful story.

"Of course Mr. Rabin did not 'consult' me nor did he have to. Mr. Rabin was gracious enough to phone me in the middle of the night, as soon as our people were on the way back, to inform me about the successful rescue operation—a call for which I am deeply grateful. For the action itself I am full of admiration, for him, for his cabinet, and of course for Zahal" (the Israel Defence Force).

There had been no superspy. There had been the swift drawing together of threads. How this was done in the last hours could be judged from computer-coordinated tapes of the laconic and brief messages acquired by IAF commander Benny Peled and General Adam in the flying command post. The messages between airmen, commandos, and special task teams during the 90 minutes at Entebbe were models of brevity. Yet they conveyed drama and the fast collection of field intelligence.

They went something like this:

"Twenty aboard," referring to hostages. "Twenty-one . . . Now another group of ten . . ."

"Do we go for Jumbo?" referring to Nairobi and the difficulty of refueling at Entebbe.

From each pilot in turn: "Yes." "Yes." "Yes. "Yes."

"Don't harm the gogglies in Apple," referring to Ugandan troops in the old terminal where hostages had warned the commandos not to shoot the African soldiers. "They were only helping us."

But one group of gogglies—another mobile force of Ugandan troops—did not come with helpful intent. Two commando units caught them near the main control tower and estimated they killed 20. Later counts indicated that at least 45 Ugandans died in actions that the commandos sought to avoid. No sure figures were possible because of the later wave of vengeance murders by Uganda's secret police.

Yonni's body was carried to the Hercules slated to leave with the hostages. His men, sweeping beyond him in the skirmish, thought he was only injured. They caught a brief glimpse of hostages streaming into Yonni's machine, some pushing past stretchers, a few clearly frightened and desperate to reach the safety of the big Hercules.

A young woman stripped to her bra and panties was wrapped in a blanket as she fell breathless inside the ramp. A young boy kept shouting, it seemed, for his mother. A Hercules guard reprimanded him: "You're a grown man—stop calling for mama!" In the confusion none of the rescuers understood the distress of Dora Bloch's son. Near the lounge a young Israeli found himself with two Ugandan prisoners and a couple of minutes to spare. He tied their wrists and ankles and then gave them a quick lesson in Hebrew: "Tell President Amin that Danny from Kibbutz———was here. That's all. I have come to Africa and I want to leave a souvenir for your chief. Understand?" He spoke in English and then repeated the treasured Hebrew phrase: "Danny from Kubbutz———was here."

The first Hercules down was to be the last out. The chief pilot turned down the cockpit lights after stopping engines, and reviewed the situation. The two runways were not within sight of each other and the old runway was used for the two known squadrons of Russian-built Migs and other military aircraft. Explosions and fires were visible, but not their cause. Airmen detailed to make a swift survey immediately on landing were reporting that fuel tankers had been moved to the far side of the field.

Fifteen minutes into the ground-attack phase of Thunderbolt, terse consultations were held between the pilots. Was it worth taxiing through areas of fire and possible ammunition explosions? Since airworthiness was paramount, a decision was made to refuel in less hazardous conditions. An IAF commander said: "We knew that if one or more Hippos could not get out, some men would have to be left behind. The soldiers knew this. We knew it. If you consider the normal delays when airliners cover lengthy routes, and how a small malfunction grounds a plane, you have an inkling of how we felt. A stray bullet, some moment's neglect, and there would be no forgiveness. Even a slight delay in leaving at the end of the operation would be fatal. We were all acutely aware of this and it tightened my guts."

One of the Hercules, loaded to full capacity and ready for takeoff, struggled with one set of wheels inexplicably pushing against mud. The light drizzle had made the tarmac slick and slippery, the soil marshy. The pilot felt the hesitation and peered ahead at the white line by which he was steering. "Stick your head out," he ordered his copilot. "That line—"

"It marks the edge of the runway, not the middle!" yelled the copilot. "Turn starboard—"

The pilot pushed the throttles wide and wrenched the Hercules away from the mud, having lost precious yards in the hazardous last stage of takeoff. Lake Victoria was coming up fast. The pilot switched automatically to the emergency procedure for maximum effort takeoff. Stand on the brakes, pour on power . . . down went the nose. He selected full flap and released the brakes. Up came the nose and the machine lumbered forward. At about 60 miles an hour the plane came unstuck, behaving partly like a conventional aircraft and partly like a helicopter with the props as rotor blades. The big Allison turbos were hauling the load skyward. The total run was later estimated at 600 feet and the Hercules' angle of attack an incredible 45 degrees.

Close shaves like this were not heard at defense headquarters in Tel Aviv. What was retrieved in code words and hasty exchanges built up a powerful sense of tension. A task force minister said later: "The clipped transmissions created a mosaic of action. Any hostile eavesdropper would have been baffled. Doubtless the Russians, who snatch every broadcast down to the lowest frequencies, were now conscious of the operation. The Arabs? They'd guess. But an informed listener could only conclude that a fantastically efficient long-range raid was ending. The voices were very calm, almost matter-of-fact."

The air talk in Hebrew sounded totally mystifying, a shorthand of acronyms and numerals between sender and receiver. To the chief of staff, General Mordechai

Gur, it meant more now than the previous night when he sweated through landings and takeoffs by pilots determined to convince him that such operations were feasible and safe. Gur, listening to the jargon, was glad to have been convinced by sharing the flight deck of a Hercules performing circuits and bumps in the darkness of an Israeli desert. "It was enough to shatter any man's nerves who isn't a flier," acknowledged a pilot. "It can blow the mind of a man who *is* a flier—unless he knows the procedures."

Brigadier General Dan Shomron, first on the ground at Entebbe, was also (like his Hercules) last off. His IAF aide became a walking flight controller. The last groups ran back from the shattered Entebbe control tower and the sabotaged radar station. Field security made a rapid check of the scene for lost documents or dropped Israeli equipment. The dead terrorists had been photographed and fingerprinted.

Shomron walked backward onto the Hercules ramp. Fires were spreading beyond the hillock where the Migs burned in their revetments. Shots continued from the direction of the burning tower. Slowly the ramp creaked up, hydraulic pistons hissed, and the Hippo began to shudder as the turboprops picked up speed with the final clunk of closing ramp doors.

Somewhere The Jackal and Dr. Hadad would lick their wounds. Flight 139, the Air France airbus, stood unharmed, a symbol of the compromises and weak policies that in Shomron's opinion forced Israel to risk lives and limited resources in what should have been an international police action.

"If we can do this in Africa, we can do it anywhere," he reported later. He had argued that hostile bases should be dealt with in this summary fashion. "Surgical operations," he called them. When a nation covered the tracks of assassins, it should know that Israel would strike. Airports and oil wells could be tidily knocked out in reprisal raids. A score of targets were filed at headquarters, indicating the method of attack—paratroops, helicopter-borne commandos . . . But none of this would be needed if an international antiterrorist agency emerged from Thunderbolt.

Brigadier General Shomron watched the men strip to the waist again and stretch out under the battle-scarred half-tracks, sinking back into sleep as if nothing had happened.

21
IDI GETS THE NEWS
FROM TEL AVIV

In Cairo the first stir of common sense was felt by Arabs with more to lose than gain from continued terrorism. President Anwar Sadat was called from bed to hear a preliminary report. Egyptian leaders had followed the changing fortunes of terrorism, noted the development of guerrilla bases in other more radical Arab territories and in Somalia, and some felt they had more in common with Israel than with the forces that armed these artists in modern revolution.

"It is no secret that the archterrorist Carlos, The Jackal, is back in Libya," Sadat dictated later to the editor of *Akhbar el-Yom*. "I want al-Qaddafi [the Libyan leader] to hear this. The Jackal moves now to South Yemen, now to the Sudan, in support of a superpower, seeking to make the naive leaders of inexperienced nations mere tools in the game of this superpower." Sadat stopped short of identifying the Soviet Union, but referred later to Russian support for Libya.

President Amin was aroused at 2:20 a.m. on Sunday, Uganda time, by a phone call from the Tel Aviv store where "Borka" Bar-Lev sat by the radio.

"Tell your government it must accept the demands of the hijackers," said Big Daddy.

"I see," Bar-Lev replied solemnly.

"It is not a matter for more negotiation," said the president of Uganda.

"Well, thank you for what you have done," said Bar-Lev.

"Thanks? What for?" said Big Daddy.

Bar-Lev put down the phone. A radio report from Paris had already broken the news of the raid on

Entebbe. Evidently Amin still knew nothing about it. The hostages were out of his reach. The terrorists who brought him fresh fame were dead.

A few hours later, at about 5:00 a.m., the situation was reversed. This time it was Amin who phoned his Israeli friend.

In a choked voice he asked Bar-Lev: "What have you done to me? Why did you shoot my soldiers? After all, I looked after the Israelis, I treated them well, I gave them services, blankets, mattresses, I hoped that we would soon make the exchange—and look—you killed my soldiers."

Bar-Lev said that Amin's voice indicated confusion and shock. Amin still did not understand what had happened at Entebbe.

Amin: "They shot my men . . ."

Bar-Lev: "Who shot? Did the hostages have guns?"

Amin: "The hostages didn't shoot. Planes came and shot."

Bar-Lev: "Planes? I didn't hear that there were planes. You woke me from my sleep. I'm at home, and I don't know a thing."

In the course of the conversation Amin pulled himself together. Bar-Lev asked him if he wanted to talk to his wife Nehama, whom Amin knew well. The president declined, but sent his regards to her and to the children.

Before he hung up, Amin recovered his flamboyance. "Not as a politician, but as a professional soldier, I must tell you that the action was very good indeed and your commandos were excellent."

Daylight brought second thoughts. Big Daddy called again with a request that Israel provide his armies with "a few spare parts." Some of his guns and armor were not in good order and it sounded as if the Russians were not pleased by the loss of their Mig-17s and Mig-21s. Replacements from the Soviet Union were likely to come with strict orders for their protection. As an Israeli military spokesman commented: "The Russians have invested $20 billion in that area these past few years, and they have to choose between unstable leaders like Amin or terrorist groups to guarantee the investment.

"The raid on Entebbe hurt the credibility of the PFLP and the PLO groups. God knows what it did to Amin."

Perhaps Big Daddy had an inkling. Thunderbolt's aircraft were delivering the hostages to Israel when the Ugandan president spoke to Uri Dan in Tel Aviv: "I am carrying in my arms the corpses of my soldiers who were killed by the bullets of your men; I think you have repaid me with evil for good," President Idi Amin told the author. News agencies had already sent out fragmentary reports about three mysterious planes landing at Entebbe and producing a tremendous upheaval in which they had spread death and destruction before leaving again. An Israeli military spokesman had issued a dry, one-line statement: "The hostages have been liberated from Entebbe by an Israeli army force."

The first frantic international phone calls multiplied into a veritable deluge of questions for Israel from all over the world. Everyone wanted details of an operation which shocked and astonished friend and foe.

"Yet Idi Amin himself knew very little about what happened under his very nose," reported Uri Dan. "It was with great difficulty that I persuaded a frightened assistant to call his president to the phone. When I heard his shattered voice, I grasped that he had taken the beating of his life. He was like a man who had had the carpet pulled from under his feet."

Amin said: "I am speaking to you from the airfield. I am counting the bodies of the soldiers who were killed during the night."

His tone at first was cringing. He presented himself as the protector of hostages, the innocent victim of Israeli deceit. He denied collaborating with the Palestinian terrorists.

"Today I had intended to work for the release of the Israelis. For this purpose, I advanced my return from the OAU conference in Mauritius. All that's left for me now is to count the victims."

Amin refused to say how many of his soldiers had been killed at the airfield. Uri Dan had the impression that Amin did not really know what had happened.

"Your Hercules planes came, and my soldiers did not want to fire at them, for otherwise we would have shot them down."

The conversation lasted 30 minutes.

Question: "Why were your soldiers there? Were the hostages the captives of your soldiers, and not just of the Palestinians?"

Amin: "The hostages were not in the hands of the Ugandan army. They were in the hands of the Palestinians. If my soldiers had wanted to fight, they would have fought. But they were killed. My soldiers were 200 yards from the building, and the Palestinians were inside. Ask your people when they return to Israel."

Question: "Is it your intention to come to Israel to clarify the issue, the situation which has been created?"

Amin: "Why should I? I have no reason to come. It's all quite clear . . . I was very good to the Israeli hostages. I will help anyone in the world to bring about peace. I'm sorry you killed innocent people."

Question: "Why did you permit piratical deeds on your territory for a whole week?"

Amin: "Only yesterday, I spoke to the UN secretary-general and told him that I received a message from the [Air Force] plane that it only had enough fuel for another 15 minutes. Then I said I had to give it permission to land at Entebbe. Since then I have been engaged in negotiating to save them."

Amin's voice broke, and he went on, almost crying: "We looked after them very well. We did everything for them. We gave them food, we gave them toilet requisites, and we guarded them so as to be able to exchange them. And now, what am I left with now? Instead of thanking me, you kill my people."

He added: "God will help everyone to bring peace. God wanted my people to die today. It's very bad . . . very bad. I am collecting the bodies of the dead. I know it comes from God, and I will help him, and everyone, to bring peace. I don't want there to be war,

for we are all children of God. In the Middle East too.
I want to make peace between you and the Palestinians."

Uri Dan asked him: "Why do you collaborate with
the Palestinians—even letting Palestinian fliers learn
to pilot your Migs?"

Amin: "I don't collaborate with the Palestinians.
Those who hijacked the plane were not just Palestinians. There were also Germans and French and others.
It's not true that the Palestinians fly my planes. My
pilots fly them."

Uri Dan asked how it was his soldiers who were
killed, if there was no cooperation between them and
the Palestinians.

Amin: "The soldiers were there to protect the lives of
the Israelis. I saved their lives, and tell them, when
they come to Israel, that I wish them a happy life. I
even said that to Colonel Bar-Lev, who I just talked to
on the phone. If my soldiers had fired at the airplanes,
they would have killed your soldiers. But we didn't
want to fight. We can fight—when we want to. All we
wanted was to solve your problem. I'm sorry, very sorry,
about what happened. What you did was a bad thing."

Question: "Mr. President, nevertheless, was it essential that you give a safe haven to pirates for a week?
Instead of throwing them out, why did you allow the
Palestinians to intervene in your country's internal
affairs?"

Amin: "They did not interfere in Uganda's affairs. I
wanted to protect your people. But the Palestinians—
and not just the Palestinians, the Europeans, the French
and the Germans—they laid explosives in the building,
and threatened to blow it up. I put them into the
building, because I wanted to give the people good
conditions. But it's not true that I collaborated with
them. I tried to save the lives of the passengers."

Question: "Do you intend to proclaim a state of
emergency? Aren't you afraid that, after an operation
like this, and after such a blow, you are likely to lose
the presidency of Uganda?"

Amin (hesitating, sounding worried): "No, no!
Definitely not! My soldiers are with me, and they are
helping me, and there are no difficulties at all."

Question: "Will you proclaim a state of emergency?"
Amin: "Yes."

A moment later he changed his mind, and in response to a further question concerning a possible state of emergency, replied: "Why?"

Uri Dan said: "So that your regime can survive . . ."

Amin: "No. My country is well protected. What happened is a small thing, and we'll see to it."

"A last question, Mr. President: Will you approach the United Nations on this matter, or the Organization of African Unity?"

Amin: "I can't talk about that over the phone. Thank you."

Uri Dan wrote later: "From the moment I heard of the plane being hijacked to Uganda, I could not stop thinking of the scene in a documentary film about Idi Amin Dada, where he rows in a boat on Lake Victoria and talks to the crocodiles. While I followed the exhausting negotiations, through the so-called mediation of Amin, I fancied a crocodilelike conversation, though I could not make up my mind. When I completed my conversation with Amin, it was clear to me that the crocodile was on the other end of the line."

22
"I AM DISTRESSED FOR THEE, MY BROTHER JONATHAN"

The *Sunday Nation* in Kenya published a front-page account of the raid that morning. It may have been incautious on the part of editor Goerge Githii, who had left Israel only hours earlier. Still, it was a scoop. Only those who knew the technicalities of newspaper production, and the sleepy routine of putting the Sunday edition to bed on Saturday afternoon, may have wondered.

President Jomo Kenyatta had put his fellow Kikuyu into *The Nation* for political reasons and he kept a discreet distance. Nobody else in the one-party state would disturb the discipline imposed by Jomo, the old Mau Mau chief who knew a few things about terrorism himself. So when the *Sunday Nation* published its scoop, editor Githii was unlikely to have acted without his president's approval. Kenya is too small. And Amin in Uganda had been getting too big. It would have been easy to keep secret the scene at Embakasi Airport, several miles from Nairobi with a game park between, although the airport had been busy all through the night.

The unusual activity began when an unscheduled Boeing 707, El Al charter flight LY 167, landed at 11:26 p.m. local time and taxied to Bay 4, reserved for aircraft requiring security precautions. The 707 was quarantined at once by Kenyan GSU men and El Al staffers. The civil registration number on the tail was 4XBY8, which conflicted with the air control log that recorded this as Flight 169. Almost two hours later another 707 contacted Nairobi control and announced itself as Flight 167 from Tel Aviv.

Slightly bewildered, the Nairobi air controllers accepted the captain's report that he was delayed by engine trouble. Then they called El Al's station manager to ask for clarification. This was enough to tell the El Al manager that the rescue planes were on their way to Nairobi from Entebbe. At 2:06 a.m. Nairobi time, both the second 707 and the first of the Thunderbolt Hercules landed together. Within the next 30 minutes, three more Hercules landed and joined the rest of the fleet in Bay 4. A fully equipped hospital inside the first Boeing 707 received the casualties brought by the Hercules. Ambulances sped ten of the more seriously wounded to the Kenyatta State Hospital where a Canadian nurse on night duty heard the call for blood. She was "astonished to see burly Israeli soldiers arrive to give transfusions. They already knew the type of blood required." In the case of Pasko Cohen, the survivor from the Nazi death-camps, they were too late. He died shortly before dawn.

The big transports gulped fuel for the long flight back and some of the released hostages left the security area for coffee and sandwiches. It was obvious that regular services were being extended beyond the normal daytime period. They were asked not to "make any fuss" about this hospitality, by officials of the East African Directorate of Civil Aviation who feared retaliation against their colleagues at Entebbe. In the event, four were reported by the directorate to have been murdered by Ugandan soldiers, apparently in revenge for failure to challenge the incoming Israeli planes.

The last Hercules left Nairobi less than two hours before dawn. The Boeing 707 hospital followed, leaving two seriously wounded Israeli soldiers and an injured hostage in Kenyatta State Hospital. By daylight, the sole evidence of the night's activities, reported *The Nation*, was bloodstains where the rescue planes had parked. Elsewhere on Embakasi Airport, however, squatted a P3 Orion long-range reconnaissance aircraft, the first U.S. Air Force plane to be based—however temporarily—in Kenya.

About midnight, in Tel Aviv, the general staff, the task force ministers, and senior officers moved to the prime minister's office—the red-tiled former barracks in Tel Aviv's muddle of military and ministerial compounds. There they were met by Menachem Begin, the opposition leader, who, punctilious as always, arrived in suit, shirt, and tie despite the heat. He came at Rabin's request.

"*Kol hakavod*—well done!" Begin hugged the prime minister.

"A drink?" Gur waved a whiskey bottle in Begin's direction.

"Tea." Begin loosened his tie. It was the first sign of concession. He had maintained his old-world courtesy, his abstemious habits, his careful sense of dress almost as if to live down his reputation as the terrorist that the British once sought to "string up," as he put it. He continued to relive the period of his Irgun resistance movement over and over, hour by hour. He was still Commander of the IZL—Irgun Zvai Leumi—though it was 30 years since Black Sunday when British and Jewish moderates moved against him.

"Tea it is then," said Gur, producing a glass of tea-colored liquid.

Begin sipped it, made a face, then grinned. "To health
—*Lechaim.*" He swallowed the raw whiskey. "Today I
make an exception."

The eyes of Herzl and Weizmann seemed to twinkle
from the portraits on the wall.

"You know how many fighters we lost during the Irgun campaigns?" asked Begin.

"Several hundred," guessed a young aide.

"Thirty-five!" The opposition leader had taken off
jacket and tie now. "The lives were always our priority.
When operational planners came up with schemes, my
first question was always: Is there a safe way back?"

The question had been asked and answered on this
anniversary of Black Sunday, just as it was at the birth
of Israel. Many more had come back from Thunderbolt than the pessimists expected, because of the same
obsessive concern for life, "an obsession," Begin had
once said, "that only comes from seeing one's people
nearly exterminated."

And so he broke his own rules and toasted the rescuers—nearly five hundred men and women in front-
line roles, from agents to commandos. They had suffered the loss of Yonni, but nobody else.

The sense of relief washed over Begin a few hours
later when crowds mobbed him at Ben-Gurion Airport
where he arrived with the task force to greet the
released hostages. For eight hours, since 3:00 a.m. when
the army radio first broadcast the news, families had
received word through friends or from their committee.
They gathered first at Yad Eliyahu baseball stadium at
dawn. By then, the four Hercules had split and were
moving toward secret bases to disgorge military equipment and the commando teams. Each of the big transports buzzed Elath Airport at the head of the Gulf of
Aqaba and made low passes over other communities
where civilians could be seen out in the streets, waving.
The planes unloaded the human cargoes and equipment
that still required top security protection, refueled, and
reassembled at Ben-Gurion. It was 11:00 a.m. and the
families of the hostages had moved to the airport from
the stadium. When the crowds saw Begin, they seized
him and began pushing him over their heads, passing

him along in a spontaneous recognition that he represented tradition.

A cable was sent to the parents in Boston, Massachusetts, reporting the death in action of Colonel Yehonatan Netanyahu, Yonni, son of Ben-Zion. Those who knew his father were sure that when he heard how Yonni died there would be no tears. And this was so. The parents flew back to receive Yonni's body in Jerusalem. The father, steeped in Jewish history, a teacher of Jewish history at Cornell University, understood what prompts every Israeli soldier to take risks to recover the corpse of a fallen comrade and knew that grave risks had been taken to bring back this boy.

"Yonni took me from the streets, literally," said one of the commandos who visited the parents during the seven days of mourning. "I would be a criminal today, or going from job to job. I was lucky to get into his unit. He did more than teach night marches through the desert, jumping from planes, moving fast from a helicopter in battle. He knew all the weapons but he made me see them as the means of preserving the nation. He taught me history and opened my eyes. Because of him, I went to college."

Ben-Zion the father listened to these comrades of a fallen son and nodded and said little. He had completed his massive study of religious persecutions and his work in the United States had removed him only physically from his home in Jerusalem. He received Defense Minister Shimon Peres, who would deliver the eulogy at Yonni's funeral. Peres reminded him of Ben-Gurion's fine dedication of the first *Scrolls of Fire* to Reuben Avinoam: "To Reuben who lost his son and discovered his generation." The defense minister added: "Ben-Gurion learned anew the astonishing human riches of our people, and the abysmal tragedy of the premature death of the best of our sons."

Later, Peres stood over Yonni's body and intoned: "I am distressed for thee, my brother Jonathan: very pleasant has thou been unto me," quoting from 2 Samuel 1:26. Then he added, "It is a short path from Jonathan, son of Saul, to Jonathan the son of Ben-Zion."

A PERSONAL NOTE

You have to share Israel's communal life to recognize the integrity of the sentiments expressed by Defense Minister Shimon Peres, whose love for his people was expressed in his words over the body of Yonni. The name in English, of course, is Jonathan and in the aftermath of the raid on Entebbe, in a gesture that reflected a national sentiment, Peres and the rest of the cabinet agreed that the mission should be remembered under the title Operation Jonathan.

A young nation needs its heroes. Israelis are not a notably melodramatic people. Their romanticism is expressed in less obvious ways. The last few years had been hard and sometimes discouraging, and outsiders are apt to forget the strain.

When I returned to Israel after the War of Attrition in the 1970s, the mood had changed on the surface. The people were adapting to new threats. There had been the struggle to build a nation; the struggle to resist attacks upon settlements; and then the wars, frontal and clandestine, growing more and more technical until it seemed the burden must pass beyond endurance.

Then Israel took on the Russians—the smallest of modern states pitted against the largest totalitarian regime in history, with unlimited resources in weaponry.

I remember fearing that Israel had gone too far— stealing modern Soviet missile systems, lifting out of Russian's client Arab states the most secret weapons, recovering Russian warplanes that were still unknown to the West—in general, making the Soviet Union— which has become arrogant and imperialist—look silly.

I remember Motti Hod, the Israeli-born chief of perhaps the best tactical air force in history, warning Washington: "The Russians are flexible and fast. Don't make the mistake of supposing they are weighed down by the bureaucratic delays of dictatorship. In matters of war, they respond within minutes to situations that you mull over for months."

Russia's response to Israel, since she exposed weaknesses in Russian weaponry, has shifted. Part of the shift is terrorism, the supply of arms, the training of fanatics, the provision of experts, done through clients who have no visible link with Moscow.

Israel would become a nation of hostages. Her close enemies pursued the logic of earlier attacks, to isolate the state of Israel.

Terrorism was a refined weapon in the hands of these traditional enemies. Groups of fanatical malcontents could be recruited in any country. The Palestinian cause was only one, created from the deliberate isolation and the world's neglect of refugees on the borders of Israel in the 1950s.

Terrorism graduated from bazooka attacks against a kibbutz to the hijacking of aircraft for political ends. All forms of guerrilla warfare sap the victim's energies.

If terrorism succeeds against Israel, it is only a matter of time before every democracy confronts the same threat on the same scale. For as Daniel Moynihan said at Hebrew University, at the time of Thunderbolt, "Israel has become the metaphor for democracy as much as the utterly unprincipled attacks by terrorists on Israeli civilians has become a metaphor for the general assault on democracy and decency which is the sustaining ethos of totalitarianism in our time."

After Thunderbolt I talked with the task force ministers and generals, the soldiers and airmen, and remembered again how this democracy works and why it is both an offense to the Russians and an invitation to further attack.

The soldiers and the politicians were exhausted. Thunderbolt was, as one said, "just a routine commando raid that happened to be a bit further in distance." But it had taxed the conscience of those who made the decision. Then, while it took place, everyone came together in a formidable and talented team.

When it ended, old arguments revived—arguments that invite Israel's enemies to underestimate her in a crisis. Certainly, the habit of democratic argument is precisely why the best possible solution to the case of

Flight 139 was discovered. Nevertheless, the habit of argument encourages her enemies to think that next time the community will collapse.

These enemies fail to understand the role that deeply felt emotions play. The romanticism of Israel is its final and decisive weapon. This sabra mentality, prickly outside and soft within, came out best in the story of an entire Israeli family that was captured on Flight 139 and taken backward in time to the days of the pogroms and the concentration camps: the Davidsons, Uzi the father, Sara the mother, Roni (17) and Benny (13) their sons.

Sara, the mother, is a handsome and unafraid young woman—unafraid of physical danger or intellectual challenge, as she demonstrated in conversations with the Germans who held guns to her head. Here are excerpts from her diary, and that of her husband, delivered with the first Hercules to return.

Uzi looks at me, and I look at Uzi. As though we had reached an agreement, we tell the boys: "We won't die. We'll get home, to Israel. We'll be together, all the time."

I said "together" and a great fear arose in my heart . . . You know, you say something and suddenly you understand how important that "together" is, and what danger awaits us if we are separated and that togetherness is destroyed.

The whole family understood. Without a word, we snuggled up together, within ourselves, hugging one another. Uzi was like the commander of a little unit. He whispered: "If they take the men and separate them from the women, you boys, stick close to mother, all the time with mother. You, Ron, you're the older, you understand . . ."

My little men. Ron and Benny. Only yesterday they were my little children.

Not everyone can keep calm. Our children are quiet and sad. From various directions, I have heard hysterical voices—"They'll kill us, they'll massacre us. They're waiting to slaughter us."

I had a long talk with the German hijacker. I asked him: "When we were flying from Athens how did you know that the pilot was really heading toward Benghazi? He could have pretended to obey your instructions, but fly to Lod or some other place." He looked at me, smiled, and said: "I learned the subject thoroughly in several Arab countries. I spent several months learning to read maps and instruments. I knew where the plane was flying."

He was silent and then said: "You have a beautiful country, really beautiful." I asked, "Have you visited my country?" He did not reply. In place of an answer, he smiled again. I said, "Maybe I shouldn't have asked you that," and he smiled again.

The German "captain" reads a statement: "The French are the enemies of the Arabs. They gave Israel a nuclear reactor. The Americans are the enemies of the Arab people: they give the Israelis murderous weapons. But the principal enemy is Israel, and the Israelis."

A nice feeling! We are being prepared for our fate, different from the others. The "captain" reassures us. "No harm will come to you. The whole history of hijackings proves that we did not kill the passengers. We shall negotiate. We have demands. If they are met, we shall release you and you'll return home."

The handclapping kills me. It makes my blood boil. Every time the "captain" makes a speech: handclapping. Every time Idi Amin appears: a storm of applause. I'm no heroine; there's nothing I wouldn't do to save Uzi and the boys. I can't do what I would really like to do—to straighten up and tell Idi Amin, or the terrorists: "I don't give a damn about you! I'm a Jew! I'm an Israeli!" But as long as we can preserve a little human and national dignity—what's the point of humiliating ourselves, welcoming them with handclaps? We have to show respect toward Amin, because we're in his hands and he can determine our fate. Respect—all right! But not fawning, not this self-abasement! It seems that under these circumstances it's hard to keep one's human and Jewish stature erect.

Rumormongers. The Ugandans are laying strings outside. What's this? One rumor says it's a way of eavesdropping on everything we say. The area is being prepared for booby-trapping with explosives, says another "report." A Ugandan soldier comes in: "We've put up strings for you to hang up your washing. Every woman can do her laundry in the toilet and hang the clothes outside."

What a relief! Not mines, not eavesdropping, just washlines. There's a human touch about it.

The "captain" smiled at me. I plucked up the courage to go up to him. He was not nervous. I asked about the fate of our luggage.

He explained they were prepared to let us have it, but the suitcases were inside the plane, in special containers, and Entebbe did not have the equipment to unload them. He spoke freely. I thought: Should I stop? Go away? Something about him encouraged me to go on talking. I said, "How can you keep us in such conditions, without mattresses or blankets, so crowded?" He brought out a piece of paper and a pen, and wrote down my requests: mattresses, blankets, soap and washing power, thorough cleaning of the toilets. He promised to take care of it. But here he was no longer in command—he was the leader only on the plane. Here it was the Arabs who were the bosses, and he was a soldier who obeyed orders.

The man aroused my interest. He was a cipher to me. I could understand the Palestinians, from their point of view. But he, a German, made the impression of being a well-educated and intelligent young man. I asked, "Why are you here?" He hesitated for a moment, and then replied at length. He believes in the rights of the Palestinian people. They're an unfortunate people, without a homeland. He can't live his life indifferent to their fate. He had to help them. Therefore he was here, and he was prepared to do everything for this unfortunate people.

I said: "Let's suppose that you and the 'Front' and all the other enemies of Israel in the Arab countries and elsewhere succed in destroying Israel, heaven forbid, and the surviving Jews will be dispersed all over the world again—what will you do? Hijack planes to help the Jewish people return to their homeland, or do you only do that for the Palestinians?"

He said: "I agree that you should have a state of your own."

I said "Are you in favor of the existence of Israel?"
He said "Yes, certainly. But, either a Palestinian state
should be established alongside your state, or you
should live together with the Palestinians in a single
state."

I said: "That goes contrary to the concepts of the
people in whose service you are operating, and risking
your life. They aren't prepared to recognize Israel's
right to exist."

He replied "I'm not the spokesman for the front. I
have views of my own. Have you ever seen a Palestinian refugee camp? Have you ever seen how those
people live? Have you seen their children?"

"In the end," I told him, "the Middle East problem
will find its solution. The war can't go on forever.
What will you do then? Where do you belong?"

He was almost offended. "I'm a German. I love my
country. Not as it is now. I want another Germany. I
live in hiding. In constant flight. The German police
are looking for me all the time. I know that I'll end
my life either with a bullet in the head, or sitting in prison for a long time. I have a feeling that my time is
drawing near . . . it will soon happen."

I said: "You are wasted, young man. You have high
intelligence. If you studied something useful, you could
serve humanity and its values far better than in hijacking planes. You are living within a framework where
you are wasting your strength in vain."

He said apologetically, "I've studied a lot, though I'm
young."

"Maybe," I said. "But you are wasting yourself, and
you are not made proper use of."

He was silent.

I said: "Tell me the truth: How do you feel, standing
before women and these children at play, with your
machine gun cocked, as it is now? If you have to fight
us, we have soldiers. Why don't you fight against our
soldiers?"

He lowered his eyes. "Believe me, I feel bad, standing like this, facing the children and you . . ."

All these years, I could not comprehend the Holocaust. Year in, year out, I read what is written on the

subject, and I see the films and hear the horrifying
testimonies—and I don't understand. But why did the
Jews enter the gas chambers so quietly? Why did they
go like sheep to the slaughter, when they had nothing
to lose? I needed that nightmare at Entebbe to comprehend, and now, but only now, I do comprehend. It's
easy to trick people when they so want to live. The
Jews in the Holocaust did not know what was in store
for them, and believed the lies about the work camps
and the showers. We were also easy to deceive. The
German woman was like a wild animal. Frustrated as
a person and as a woman. But she was less dangerous.
Because she was frank about what she was, and wore
no mask. It would never have occurred to me to talk to
her. She was an open enemy.

The German man adopted a pleasant manner. He
was a concealed enemy, pretending, tempting his victims to believe in his good intentions. He was so quiet,
so pleasant, so affable—that, after my conversations
with him, I found myself accusing myself: You believed him! He succeeded in deceiving you!

If he had said to march in a certain direction,
where his colleagues were awaiting us with machine
guns, ready to mow us down—we would have gone. Because he knew how to smile and pretend. He didn't
miss any opportunity to tell us: "You are not to blame.
You are all right. Nothing will happen to you. Don't
worry. Your government will agree to an exchange,
and you'll go home."

And because we so wanted to believe that he was
different from the others, better and more easy-go-
ing than the others—we believed him. It's easy to
believe. If the matter hadn't ended as it did, no one
would have had to urge this "good German" to fire off
his cartridge clips at our children and us, or to blow us
up with the grenades and explosives.

It's the first time I've comprehended the Holocaust.

Uzi Davidson kept notes too:

On the last night of our captivity, I was reading
about Winston Churchill—and from outside, I heard
two or three bursts of fire. Then another single bullet.

I raised my head, and saw the hijackers jump from their places. We were at the edge of the hall. I had no idea what was happening. I thought one of the Ugandan soldiers had accidentally fired his gun. I feared there was going to be trouble.

I lost any sense of time, but I think that within two seconds I had the family crawling toward the toilet. There was a wall there where we could take cover. I thought it better to get there. I don't know how long we lay there. It must have been minutes. It seemed like five years, going on and on.

Outside, there was a serious clash in progress, with shooting and explosions. We did not exchange a word. I did not see the terrorists.

Somebody in the hall straightened up and called: "Yes, yes, Israeli soldiers, Israeli soldiers," and while I was still wondering why the man was shouting such nonsense, I saw one of the most wonderful sight I have ever seen: Next to us there stood an Israeli soldier, of Yemenite extraction—short, thin, carrying a Kalachnikov rifle two sizes too large for him. He was as cool as though he had dropped by to invite us for a drink, just by chance. He said *"Shalom,* fellows. Everything is all right. Get up calmly, and come with me. We're taking you home."

It seemed unreal and impossible. I didn't know for sure whether I was dreaming or not, daydreaming, or taking part in some abnormal drama—but that quiet voice was so convincing, so simple, so undramatic, that we stood up and followed him to the plane and we boarded it quietly ... as he requested.

Sara's last entry was this:

There is a verse: "The Lord's redemption cometh like the twinkling of an eye." When we heard the sudden shooting I repeated the *"Sh'ma Yisrael!"* that a Jew says when the hour has come.

And a soldier leaped toward me with Hebrew on his tongue. I felt goosepimples. I would not die, but live to tell the deeds of the Lord.

Ninety minutes at Entebbe arose because Israel refused to barter innocent lives for terrorists. Three days later, the very woman whose freedom was demanded by Flight 139's hijackers was helped to escape from a maximum-security jail.

Terror International had again exposed Israel's isolation in the struggle against a worldwide conspiracy to destroy civilized society.

The terrorist whose freedom had been demanded against the lives of innocent civilians, women, and children was Inge Viett.

When the Entebbe attempt at blackmail failed, Inge Viett's freedom was secured by another branch of Terror International. With guns smuggled into their cells, Inge and three other German women terrorists overpowered the guards in their West German prison and vanished into the night.

"Words fail me," said Justice Minister Hermann Oxfort in West Berlin. And well they might.

Inge Viett was imprisoned as a terrorist who secured the release of five other jailed anarchists by helping to kidnap Peter Lorenz of the West Berlin assembly. Lorenz was threatened with execution until the anarchists had been delivered at West German expense in the luxury of their own airliner to freedom in South Yemen.

Any defeat inflicted by Thunderbolt on Terror International was diminished by Inge's escape. With her terrorist companions, she was out of Europe within 48 hours, in time to read the opening debate in the United Nations Security Council where Israel stood accused of "flagrant violation of Uganda's sovereignty."

The juxtaposition of his ironic debate and the terrorists' breakout may appear to future historians to have been inevitable. Inge Viett, The Jackal, Dr. Hadad, and the terrorist operational commander killed at Entebbe would be comforted by it.

The debate was greeted elsewhere as a vindication of Israel. This was surely a measure of how international morality has been corrupted. In the nine years since the Six Day War, virtually every United Nations resolution condemning the Jewish state has passed—except in the Security Council where the U.S. veto has saved us from total disgrace.

In the week after Entebbe, the UN's huge anti-Israeli bloc tried again. A motion to censure Israel by the Organization of African Unity failed from lack of support. The Security Council at long last was unable to turn a blind eye to political terrorism. But it was still sufficiently intimidated to say nothing *against* terrorism.

"Israel was not condemned and was therefore vindicated," ran the argument of those who greeted the outcome as a victory.

What a dismal comment upon international morality! *Israel was not condemned!* Values have been upended. Peace at any price is now the objective of a world forum born out of the Holocaust to preserve the humanities—not to sacrifice them for survival at any cost.

Israel's sense of isolation in the days before July 4 was deepened by that Security Council performance. I remembered the words of a deputy Israel Air Force commander in the rear cockpit of a jet while I maneuvered above the wasteland where Solomon once pulled down the Temple.

Yerucham Amitai said over the intercom: "You think we'd do it again?"

"I have that feeling," I replied. We were flying at a time when terrorism had found new ways of eating into the state of Israel. The War of Attrition. Something that nobody quite knew how to handle, because in fighting such terrorism there was a danger of losing your own sense of right and wrong.

"You're right," replied Amitai. "We'll never submit to liquidation again."

Amitai had survived the death camps to fly for Israel. He had told me about Warsaw, the underground, his escape from Nazi hands. He had worked as a bricklayer in Palestine to learn to fly. He became so good that he flew almost every plane in service. He trained the Uganda Air Force. He trained the airmen of Singapore and other small states. It became a mission—to teach the weak to protect themselves against the bullies. When he was killed in a pointless crash, I felt a sense of failure. His story haunted me and yet I had never known how to voice for him the underlying sense of unyielding resolve.

But there is a time for the dead to speak.

Amitai would have heard the Security Council speeches and he would have shrugged.

"We depend on nobody," he would have said, repeating his words to me. "If Israel should ever fail to protect her own, she would cease to have meaning. We have been forced into aggressive defense and the stakes keep getting higher.

"In the end, we may have to choose between action that might pull down the Temple of Humanity itself rather than surrender even a single member of the family to the executioners.

"Survival in other circumstances is not survival at all. And all of us, whatever our race, won't be worth a damn if we buy our lives at the cost of our conscience."

UNITED NATIONS SECURITY COUNCIL DEBATE

Excerpts from the Provisional Verbatim Record
July 9, 12, and 13, 1976   New York City

UGANDA. Lieutenant Colonel Juma Oris Abdullah, Minister for Foreign Affairs: The Ugandan delegation wishes to express its thanks to the members of the Organization of African Unity for requesting the convening of the Security Council to consider the aggression of Zionist Israel against the sovereignty and territorial integrity of Uganda. My delegation would like also to thank you, Mr. President, as well as all the other members of the Security Council, for agreeing to convene this meeting.

At about 4 o'clock East Africa Time, 0100 hours GMT, on 28 June 1976, His Excellency Al-Hajji Field-Marshal Dr. Idi Amin Dada, V.C., D.S.O., M.C., Life President of the Republic of Uganda, was informed by a telephone call from Entebbe Air Control that a hijacked French plane with 250 persons on board was circling over Entebbe, having only 15 minutes' fuel left, and was seeking permission to land.

President Amin was placed in a dilemma: whether to refuse permission for the aircraft to land, thereby risking every likelihood of crushing and killing all those aboard, or to allow it to land safely at Entebbe and face the consequences of a hijack situation.

Taking those facts into account, and motivated by humanitarian considerations, the President directed that the aircraft be allowed to land safely at Entebbe airport. A contingent of security forces was positioned to guard against any possible danger. To avoid interference with the normal air traffic and also to enable the Ugandan authorities to ascertain the character and nature of the hijackers, the plane was directed to taxi to the old airport, which is about one mile away.

It took several hours before the initial contact with those in charge of the aircraft was made. After the initial contact the Ugandan authorities learned that the hijackers of the aircraft were members of the Popular Front for the Liberation of Palestine (PFLP) and that they had with them over 250 hostages on board of different nationalities and different age groups. The hijackers stated that they did not want anybody to go near the aircraft and that, whatever security arrangements the Ugandan authorities intended to make, the security officers concerned should not go within a radius of 50 metres of the aircraft. After further communication with the hijackers, the President of Uganda was able to convince them to allow the hostages to be supplied with refreshments. At that point the hijackers informed the Ugandan authorities that they were waiting for further instructions from their leaders and to that end they wanted the fact of their being at Entebbe to be publicized. It was also at this point that they issued a long statement of general policy of the PFLP, demanding that it be given as wide publicity as possible. Being anxious to co-operate for the sake of the hostages, the Ugandan Government agreed that the statement would be repeatedly broadcast by the Uganda Broadcasting Corporation and publicized in the local press so as to keep the hijackers appeased.

Initially the Ugandan authorities' intention was to offer the hijackers fuel and food supplies and request them to proceed elsewhere. They were extremely reluctant, and refused to proceed anywhere until they had made contacts with their leaders and made their motives for the hijacking known. This situation continued for most of that day, during which very tricky and delicate negotiations were being conducted by President Amin personally, resulting in the hijackers agreeing that the hostages still under their guard would be allowed out of the aircraft and securely transferred to the old airport building. That process was a very delicate one, carried out at a time when the hijackers had become highly irritable and very suspicious of any possible disarming action by Ugandan authorities. It involved the aircraft being moved as near as possible to the old airport transit launch. For this process, the hijackers demanded that they first inspect the transit launch and the entire building to ensure their own security and that of their hostages. Some of them accordingly went ahead of the aircraft, placed explosives in strategic positions and demanded the withdrawal of the Ugandan security forces to a position 200 metres away from the aircraft terminal buildings.

At this point it is relevant to mention that, in addition to having high explosives which included hand grenades, the hijackers also had automatic weapons. As Uganda has clearly stated in various communiqués on the hijacking, the Ugandan armed forces were not allowed by the hijackers to go near the airport building. That was part of the bargain. However, once the hostages and hijackers were in the airport building, after further bargaining, many facilities were made available to the hostages, such as medical and food supplies and other welfare maintenance, which were administered by the few civilians while negotiations continued with the hijackers.

Most of 29 June 1976 was spend in finding out the modalities of concrete negotiations while waiting to learn the wishes of the hijackers. By the end of the day, the hijackers proposed that the Somali Ambassador to Uganda, in his capacity as the dean of the Arab League, should be their spokesman. Also during the course of the day, the hijackers circulated a questionnaire to the hostages seeking information about their nationalities, professions and ages. The demands of the hijackers had not yet been made known by the end of that day. Also during that day, the hijackers accepted the Ugandan authorities' request that, in addition to food supplies, a medical team consisting of one doctor and several nursing staff be made available to hostages in need of medical attention.

On 30 June, following the report by the medical team and President Amin's persistent appeals, the hijackers agreed to release 47 hostages including the old, the sick and some children. It was on the same day that for the first time the hijackers issued their demand. This was for the release of certain persons imprisoned in Israel, Germany, France, Switzerland and Kenya, totalling in all 53. The demand was given to the Somali Ambassador as well as to the Ugandan authorities. The Ugandan authorities in turn passed it on to the French Ambassador. On that occasion also, the hijackers set a new deadline of 2 p.m. East

African Time, 1100 hours GMT, 1 July, by which time all the persons whose release they had requested should be transported to Entebbe for an exchange of hostages.

On 1 July 1976, which was the first deadline the hijackers had set for the release of the 53 persons who were allegedly held by the five Governments referred to above, President Amin was not only able to persuade the hijackers to extend the deadline to 4 July 1976, but also continued to plead for the release of the remaining hostages.

The response received from the hijackers was the release of 100 hostages belonging to nations other than Israel or having dual nationalities, and the extension of the deadline to 1100 hours GMT on 4 July 1976 in order for the hijackers to secure their demands. Up to this point, as can be seen, President Amin had personally played a very vital part in talking the hijackers into agreeing to the release of their hostages. He had spent virtually the whole time without any sleep. In appreciation of his efforts, for example, he received a number of messages from world leaders, such as the President of France, who, in two messages within two days, expressed his deep appreciation for the strenuous efforts President Amin was exerting to have the hostages released, and urged him to continue so that all the hostages could be released.

On 2 July 1976, President Amin had to go to Mauritius, where he was to open the thirteenth session of the Organization of African Unity's Assembly of Heads of State and Government, and also to hand over the chairmanship of the Organization to the new chairman. While in Mauritius President Amin took the opportunity fully to brief his colleagues on his efforts to have the hostages released. In his statement to his colleagues, President Amin included an appeal to all Governments concerned to do everything possible to save the lives of the remaining hostages. He also took the occasion to brief the Secretary General of the United Nations, Dr. Kurt Waldheim, fully on the matter, urging him also to use his good offices to impress upon the Governments concerned the gravity and urgency of the matter.

Because of the delicate situation back home, President Amin had to cut short his stay in Mauritius to return home early on the evening of 3 July 1976. Immediately on his return, the President quickly re-established contact with all those concerned, including the hostages, whom he personally addressed in the presence of the Somali Ambassador, now for the third time, reassuring them of his untiring efforts to secure their release. Specifically, the President took the occasion to thank the hostages for the message of appreciation which they had issued earlier in the day for the efforts he was making on their behalf.

Hardly had President Amin settled down when Israel's invading force landed at Entebbe. As you were informed, Mr. President, in a message sent to you by my President on 4 July, at 2120 hours GMT, three Zionist Israeli transport planes landed by surprise and without any authority from the Ugandan Government at Entebbe International Airport. Soon after landing, they proceeded straight to the old airport building where the hostages and the crew of the French airbus, which was hijacked in flight between Tel Aviv and Paris, were being held by Palestinian commandos. Out of the aircraft, two military jeeps drove and the invaders, using hand grenades, machine-guns, bazookas and other explosives, indiscriminately attacked the airport building and the Ugandan soldiers who were guarding the building at a distance of 200 metres and who were armed only with light arms in accordance with the conditions laid down by the hijackers. As a result of this attack on the building, the invaders killed seven hijackers and some hostages and a number of Ugandan soldiers, injuring many others as well. The Israeli invaders also blasted the old airport terminal building, damaged the runway and destroyed a number of Ugandan aircraft and extensive installations.

I should like to draw the attention of this Council to some aspects of the Israeli invasion that clearly indicate that Israel did not mount the invasion without the knowledge, collaboration and assistance of a few other countries. Africa should not allow any part of its soil to be used by the Zionist Israelis and their imperialist masters or collaborators to attack another sister country. According to the information available to us, which information has been confirmed by the international press, Zionist Israel's plan to invade Entebbe was decided upon in Tel Aviv on the first of this month. That is the very day President Amin had convinced the hijackers to extend the deadline for their demands and had also succeeded in getting the hijackers to release more of the hostages.

The Ugandan delegation has further knowledge that the Israeli plan to invade Entebbe must have been conceived as far back as when the hijacked plane touched down in Uganda. It is of interest to note, for example, that on the very night of the invasion, exactly one hour and forty minutes after the Israeli force landed at Entebbe, the Voice of America was broadcasting the success of the mission. This was in its broadcast of 2 a.m., East African Standard Time, 2300 hours GMT. All the British Sunday papers that normally are published by midnight of Saturday had, in great detail, the story of the so-called successful operation at Entebbe.

The Sunday Express, for example, in its edition of 2:30 a.m. of that same morning, gleefully reported that

> "An Israeli commando force today resuced all hostages held by pro-Palestinian guerrillas at Entebbe Airport, Uganda, an Israeli spokesman said in Tel Aviv early today. The Air France crew was also freed, the spokesman said. Explosions rocked Entebbe Airport after three Israeli aircraft swooped down."

I should like to make it clear that Uganda has never and will never condone international piracy. It is not therefore true to say, as has been alleged by the ruling circles in Israel, that Uganda collaborated with the hijackers. The Ugandan Government got involved in this affair accidentally and purely on humanitarian considerations. Perhaps the crew of the French airbus will be in a better position to tell us how the hijacking ended in Uganda. According to what we know from press reports, the French airbus belonging to Air France, flight 139, started from Tel Aviv en route to Paris via Athens. It was after it took off from Athens that the hijackers took over and forced the aircraft to land in Benghazi, from where it took off after refuelling. Its request to land at Khartoum was refused and, possibly, that is why it ended up at Entebbe with only a fifteen minute supply of fuel. It can be deduced from this story that the hijackers wanted to go to Khartoum.

Uganda gave all the help and hospitality it was capable of giving to all the hostages. The response to this humanitarian gesture by Zionist Israel—the vehicle of imperialism —was to invade Uganda, once again living up to its record of barbarism and banditry. By this act of naked aggression against Uganda, the Zionists killed Ugandans who were trying to protect the hostages and inflicted great damage on Ugandan property.

Is this a worthy Member of this Organization? Uganda has made its view on Israel's membership in the United Nations repeatedly clear in many international forums, the last of which was the address to the thirtieth session of the General Assembly by President Amin.

We call upon this Council unreservedly to condemn in the strongest possible terms Israel's barbaric, unprovoked and unwarranted aggression against the sovereign Republic of Uganda. Uganda demands full compensation from Israel for the damage to life and property caused during its invasion. Our authorities are in the process of working out the particulars of the claim arising out of the damage.

I can only hope that no other African State can in any way be tainted with suspicion in this sordid affair, for this would mean that no one on the whole continent could trust or support the ideal of African unity. This unity has been forged through the sweat, brains and blood of all our African brothers. Let not today be, even in doubt, a day of suspicion.

I wish, on behalf of President Amin, the Government and all the people of Uganda, to end my delegation's submission by expressing our thanks to all those countries and organizations, especially the Organization of African Unity, that have since the unwarranted aggression against the innocent people of Uganda sent messages of sympathy, solidarity and support, which we very much appreciate.

ISRAEL. Chaim Herzog, Ambassador to the United Nations: From a purely formal point of view, this meeting arises from a complaint brought against the Government of Israel. However, let me make it quite clear that sitting here as the representative of the Government of Israel, as I have the honour to do, I am in no way sitting in the dock as the accused party. On the contrary, I stand here as an accuser on behalf of free and decent people in this world.

I stand here as an accuser against the forces of evil which have unleashed a wave of privacy and terrorism which threatens the very foundations of human society.

I stand here as an accuser of all those evil forces which in their inherent cowardice and abject craven attitude see blameless wayfarers and innocent women and children —yes, even babes in arms—a legitimate target for their evil intentions.

I stand here as an accuser of the countries that, because of evil design or lack of moral backbone, have collaborated with these bloodthirsty terrorists.

I stand here as an accuser of all those in authority throughout the world who for reasons of cynical expediency have collaborated with terrorism.

I stand here as an accuser of this world Organization, the United Nations, which has been unable, because of the machinations of the Arab representatives and their supporters, to co-ordinate effective measures in order to combat the evil of world terrorism.

I stand here as an accuser of those delegations to this Organization which for reasons of political expediency have remained silent on this issue—an issue which is bound to affect every country in this Organization. In so doing they have become themselves accomplices.

Seated in the dock today with the accusing finger of enlightened world opinion directed against them are the terrorist organizations which are plaguing this world, and whose representatives have in the past been seated here by the world body with rights equal to those of Member States. In the dock are all those countries which have collaborated with the terrorists and which have aided and abetted them. There stand here accused those countries which have blocked every international move to deal with this plague of terror which besets the world.

In the dock before us stand all those countries—they are all too numerous—that cry to the high heavens when they are affected by terrorists, that fulminate at this Security Council table when their citizens or diplomats are threatened, and that remain silent when the same happens to citizens of other countries. Some of them do not even have the doubtful grace to remain silent; they have the wicked effrontery to join in condemnation of a country which tries to prevent these acts.

In the dock before us stand the representatives of all those countries which stood and applauded the entry into the hall of the General Assembly of a gun-toting terrorist who, according to the President of Sudan, personally gave the order to execute the American and Belgian diplomats bound hand and foot in the basement of the Saudi Arabian Embassy in Khartoum on 1 March 1973.

Yes, before us stands accused this rotten, corrupt, brutal, cynical, bloodthirsty monster of international terrorism and all those who support it in one way or the other, whether by commission or omission. Facing them today are the ordinary decent human beings throughout the world who seek nothing more than to live a life free from terror and from intimidation, free from the threats of hijackers, the indiscriminate bombs of terrorists and the blackmail of criminals and murderers.

Israel's action at Entebbe in order to release its hostages has given rise to a worldwide wave of support and approval, such as has rarely been seen from every continent, including Africa; from every walk of life; from countries hostile, as well as friendly, to Israel. The ordinary man and woman in the street have risen behind us and proclaimed "enough" to this spectre of terror, have cried out "enough" to this world body of pontificating diplomats in which on so many occasions moral cowardice and cynical expediency have combined to drag it down to the depths to which it has plunged.

In more ways than one, this Organization is in the accused stand today. Mankind will judge it by its behaviour on this occasion, because never has the issue been clearer; never has the issue been so clear-cut. There will be no excuse in history for this body, or for the constituent Members of this body, if it fails to condemn terrorism. The issue before this body is not what Israel did at Entebbe Airport: the issue before this body is its own future in the eyes of history.

The representative of Uganda has very conveniently

avoided the main issue before us. Let me recount the events as they occurred.

On Sunday, 27 June 1976, an Air France airbus, flight 139, en route from Tel Aviv to Paris, was hijacked by a group of Palestine Liberation Organization (PLO) terrorists with 256 innocent passengers aboard in addition to a crew of 12.

The terrorists took advantage of the lax security measures obtaining at Athens airport and brought on board pistols and approximately 20 grenades.

Thus began a methodically planned and carefully executed act of air piracy by the Popular Front for the Liberation of Palestine, one of the several terrorist groups joined together to form the PLO. Thus began another in a long list of PLO crimes against innocent civilians.

Having commandeered the aircraft, the hijackers forced the French pilot to land in what is by now internationally accepted as the first haven for such criminals, namely, Libya.

This was, it will be recalled, the first stop in the flight of the ministers of the Organization of Petroleum Exporting Countries (OPEC) kidnapped in Austria last year. The Council will recall that the hijackers, holding at pistol point the ministers of the member countries of OPEC, of which Libya is a member, were greeted effusively by Prime Minister Jalloud of Libya, who embraced the criminals who at that time were holding his Arab ministerial colleagues as hostages and who had only the day before killed a member of the Libyan delegation in Vienna.

On this occasion which we are now discussing, last week the Prime Minister did not greet the terrorists. He was doubtless preoccupied with preparations for a Libyan sponsored coup d'état in Sudan, judging by the complaint submitted by my Sudanese colleague to this Council. All these in addition to his preoccupations with bringing in so-called Libyan peace-keeping forces to Beirut in order to fan the flames of hatred, to enlarge the scope of murder, and to increase the peril for the Christian population in Lebanon.

Having mentioned Libya, I think it is appropriate to draw attention to the central role which this country plays in the promotion and encouragement of international terror in the world today.

This is the country which has for years acted as paymaster of international terror movements, Arab and non-Arab, throughout the world.

This is the country which has been condemned by Sudan and Tunisia only recently for its acts of terror and for the sinister and dangerous part it has played in planning to assassinate the leaders of these States and to overthrow their Governments.

This is the country whose ambassador was expelled but a few days ago by the Government of Egypt for its subversive activities.

It is, I submit, a disgrace to this world Organization that the representative of this world sponsor of terrorism is seated as a member of the Security Council, the purpose of which is to encourage the maintenance of international peace and security.

To return to our story, the Air France plane was refueled in Benghazi. The destination of the hijackers was, in accordance with a previously prepared plan, Entebbe Airport, outside Kampala in Uganda.

The airbus landed at Entebbe Airport on Monday, 28 June, and the hijackers were met by a reinforcement of terrorists, who awaited them at the terminal armed to the teeth with sub machine guns and explosives.

President Idi Amin of Uganda arrived at the airport shortly before the hijacked plane landed and embraced the hijackers in a gesture of welcome and a promise of support and assistance. Ugandan soldiers were then positioned with their guns trained, not on the hijackers, but on the innocent civilians—men, women and children.

On Tuesday, 29 June 1976, the hijackers spelt out their demands. These included the release of 53 terrorists gaoled in Israel, West Germany, France, Switzerland and Kenya by a deadline of 3 p.m., local time, Thursday, 1 July. They threatened to put the innocent passengers to death if their terms were not met.

When the hijackers released 47 women and children and some passengers on Wednesday, 30 June, it gradually be-

came apparent that President Amin was in fact co-oper-
ating with the terrorists under a cloak of deception and
false pretence. This was the situation on the evening of 1
July, the first deadline set by the terrorists. It became
obvious that the Israeli passengers—men, women and
children—were in serious and grave danger of their lives.

When the hijackers released a further 100 hostages, there
story, when they arrived in Paris, revealed an ominous
development. They described to the waiting reporters how
Ugandan soldiers, under direct orders of President Amin,
supervised the separation of Jewish passengers from non-
Jewish passengers.

This was a development of a nature so sinister and so
pregnant with memories of the past that no member of the
Jewish people, whether in Israel or abroad, could fail to
recall its horrible significance.

There flashed immediately upon the inward eye of every
member of our people the memory of the terrifying selections carried out during the most horrifying holocaust that
mankind has ever seen and which beset our people. We
recalled the selections carried out by the Nazis in the
concentration camps as members of the Jewish people were
singled out for the gas chambers and extermination.

Following the never-to-be-forgotten experience of the
holocaust in Europe during the Second World War, an
oath was taken—whether consciously or unconsciously—
by every member of the Jewish people, wherever he or she
might have been, that never again would this happen; that
never again would circumstances be allowed to develop
in which such a catastrophe could happen; that Auschwitz,
Dachau and Buchenwald belonged to the past and would
never again return.

On this occasion, I solemnly reaffirm before this body
the oath which has been taken by our Jewish people,
wherever they may be. It will never happen again.

And so, when this ominous reminiscent selection began,
when the separation of the Jews was undertaken, it became apparent to the Government of Israel that there was
no alternative but to conduct a rescue operation to save
the lives of its citizens.

The Government of Israel's apprehension was heightened
by a knowledge of President Amin's attitude towards the

Jewish people. In September 1972, President Amin sent a cable, which was published on 13 September 1972, to the Secretary-General of the United Nations, Mr. Kurt Waldheim, with copies to the Prime Minister of Israel and to the leader of the PLO, Yassir Arafat. In this cable, President Amin applauded the murder of the Israeli sportsmen at the Olympic Games in Munich who, bound hand and foot, were gunned down by the PLO. Moreover, in the same message, he had the obscene ghoulishness to praise Hitler for his role in destroying over 6 million Jews.

The members of the Council will recall that but nine months ago, in the General Assembly of the United Nations, President Amin called for the extinction of Israel as a State. The combination of the move to separate Israeli and Jewish passengers from other passengers, the official endorsement of Hitler's policies by the President of Uganda, his call for the extinction of Israel and the horrible fate of hundreds of thousands of his own countrymen who did not find favour in his eyes—in this connexion I refer members to the terrifying recital of the brutalities of what it refers to as the "dictatorial fascist ruler of Uganda" published on 7 July by the Government of Kenya—all these taken together bring home to the Government of Israel the realization that, unless action were taken, the hostages, men, women and children, were doomed and could expect no mercy in Entebbe.

What more sinister indication of the wicked and maniacal intentions of the hijackers and murderers and of their Ugandan allies could there have been than that among the hostages held until the last moment before the deadline were 11 children and 34 women doomed to be shot in cold blood by those bloodthirsty murderers?

There, under the watchful guns of Terror International and President Amin, a kindergarten was organized by the hostages in the shadow of impending death. The tragic scene this evokes in one's mind is devastating. It is so much in character with the style of these bandits. They were there prepared to shoot down a kindergarten of innocent children, just as their colleagues in Somalia but a few months ago—as we were informed by the French Ambassador here—threatened to cut the throats of 30 French children aged six to twelve who were being held hostage.

At this point, let me quote from the statement of Prime
Minister Rabin to the Knesset on 4 July:

"The time of expiry of the ultimatum drew increasingly closer. The release of non-Israeli passengers more
and more exposed the evil conspiracy against Israeli
citizens. The political efforts bore no fruit. The sand
in the hourglass was about to run out, leaving no possibility for any independent rescue effort. Under these
conditions, the Government of Israel decided unanimously to take the only way left to rescue our people and declared its readiness to release terrorists
detained in Israeli prisons. Following the Cabinet's
decision we accordingly informed the French Government, through which the negotiations were being
conducted with the terrorists. We were prepared to
adopt even this alternative—in default of any other—
to rescue our people. This was not a tactic to gain
time, and had this choice alone been left, we would
have stood by our decision as a last resort."

The hijackers raised their demands. They announced that
Israel would be held responsible for all the terrorists whose
release they demanded, including those terrorists not held
in Israel, and they refused to allow the exchange to be
made in France or on neutral territory outside Uganda.
Their sinister tone and new demands boded evil for the
hostages. The Government of Israel was left with no alternative.

On the night of 3-4 July 1976, the Israel Defence Forces
mounted a most remarkable operation which will go down
in history, rescued the hostages and escorted them to
safety.

I wish to reiterate on this occasion that Israel accepted
full and sole responsibility for the action, that no other
Government was at any stage party to the planning or the
execution of the operation. The operation was planned and
executed by Israel. We are proud of it.

During that rescue operation, three of the hostages were
killed by the terrorists before the terrorists were gunned
down by Israeli troups. A senior Israeli officer was killed,
shot in the back, and several soldiers and hostages were
wounded.

The weight of evidence before us reveals prior knowledge and active connivance on the part of the Government of Uganda in this whole episode. Even if the evidence were not available—and I say it is available in abundance—it is sufficient to read the letter addressed by President Amin to you, Mr. President, on 4 July 1976 (S/12124, annex), in order to reveal that he implicated himself in his own statement. It is quite evident from his letter that the Ugandan troops mounted guard not over the terrorists and the hijackers but over the hostages. In the fourth paragraph of his letter he states, "I directed that the plane be guarded properly". He then goes on to make the most incredible statement: ". . . the Uganda Armed Forces were not allowed by the hijackers to go near the airport building". This is known to be false. The Ugandan troops were in and around the building.

He then reveals his complicity in relating the story of the release of the 147 hostages on 30 June and 1 July by openly admitting his part in separating the Israeli passengers from the other passengers. We learn also from his letter of the sinister part played by the Somali Ambassador to Uganda, the representative of a country which has become a prime troublemaker in the area and a threat to its neighbours in Kenya, Ethiopia and the area of Djibouti, and which only a few months ago was involved in holding hostage 30 French children, on which occasion the Government of France, motivated by the same sentiments which motivated the Government of Israel this time, took armed action in exercise of its rights under international law to save the children from Somalia.

It is no coincidence that one of the terrorists at Entebbe Airport was the head of the PLO office in Somalia.

The entire story is one of collusion from beginning to end on the part of the Ugandan Government. Let me spell out only a small proportion of the facts as recounted by members of the Air France crew and the hostages who were released.

On advance complicity,

(a) The captain of the Air France plane has stated that the German hijacker, Wilfred Böse, knew in advance that Entebbe was the plane's destination.

(b) When the plane landed at Entebbe, the German

woman hijacker declared, "Everything is OK; the army is at the airport."

(c) Böse announced to the passengers when they landed that they had arrived at a safe place.

(d) Immediately on arrival, Ugandan soldiers surrounded the plane. They were accompanied by five armed Arab terrorists who embraced and kissed the hijackers on the plane. After that, the terrorist reinforcements took part in the guard duties and in the negotiations.

(e) Before landing, while they were still in the air, the hijackers advised the passengers that buses would come to collect them.

(f) After the passengers had been concentrated in the terminal's large hall, President Amin was seen embracing and shaking hands with the hijackers.

(g) As the plane landed and was taxiing along the runway, a black Mercedes car drove up, two terrorists emerged and one of them took over control of the operation thereafter. He boarded the plane, embraced Bose, the German hijacker, and talked to him.

(h) Michel Cojot, a French company executive who acted as a go-between for the passengers and the hijackers, reported that when the airport director brought supplies for the hostages, he, the director, said he was prepared with supplies as he had been told to wait for approximately 260 passengers and crew.

Now, on the detention of the hijacked passengers,

(a) In the first 24 hours, guard duty was done by Ugandan soldiers, and the hijackers were not in sight. When the hijackers returned refreshed, the Ugandan soldiers supplied them with sub-machine-guns to guard the hijacked passengers. I ought to mention here that the Foreign Minister of Uganda had said that the hijackers were armed with sub-machine-guns. What he omitted to mention was that on the plane all they had were pistols and grenades. The sub-machine-guns were supplied to them when they landed at Entebbe.

(b) In the following days the Ugandans were on guard outside the building, while a large force of them was concentrated on the first floor of the building.

(c) Ugandan soldiers escorted the hostages to, and guarded them in, the toilets.

(d) The terrorists came and went as if they were at home with two cars driven by Ugandans, one of them in uniform, at their disposal.

(e) The hijackers received logistic aid and were supplied with arms—sub-machine guns, pistols and explosives—at the airport. They also received a mobile communications set.

(f) The terrorist who took control of the operation in Entebbe took hostages aside, under Ugandan guard, for interrogation.

(g) Every time President Amin appeared in the area of the terminal and before the passengers, he was closeted with the terrorists in a most friendly atmosphere.

(h) At the outset of the negotiations President Amin dismissed the French Ambassador and prevented him from establishing contact with the terrorists. This contact was conducted by him in person.

(i) President Amin warned the hijacked passengers not to dare to try to escape.

(j) Apparently for reasons of bravado and to frighten the hijacked passengers, two jet aircraft overflew from time to time the terminal in which they were being held. Near the building an armored vehicle armed with a heavy machine-gun was parked, and close to it stood two helicopters.

(k) A mixed guard of hijackers and Ugandan Army men guarded the hostages; contact between them was constant and free. The Ugandan soldiers were on guard both inside the hall, on the second floor of the terminal, and on the plane.

(l) The hijackers were unconcerned and very relaxed during the period on the ground. They left the airport building from time to time and acted with an obvious feeling of assurance that the Ugandan Army would not attempt to overpower them. Mr. Tony Russell, an official of the Greater London Council and one of the Britons freed from the hijacked Air France airbus, in an interview with the London Times on 5 July, said that President Amin had been in a position to release all hostages if he had wished. "Once we were moved from the aircraft", he said, "the terrorists were not in a commanding position. I have the feeling that if Amin wanted to free us after we were transferred to the airport building, it could have been done. The terrorists had had no sleep for 30 hours and had no powerful weapons at their disposal", said Mr. Russell.

(m) The commander of the hijackers in Entebbe spent all his time in the company of President Amin, who, incidentally, recounted this fact by telephone to a Colonel Bar Lev, who spoke to him from Israel.

(n) While the passengers were being held, Radio Uganda broadcast an announcement of the hijackers praising Amin for his stand against Zionism and imperialism.

(o) And finally, the hijackers were buried with full military honours together with soldiers of the Ugandan Army.

Uganda maintains close ties with the PLO, which has a large presence there. The PLO office, operating in Kampala under Khaled al-Shaykh, organizes propaganda activities throughout East Africa. The Popular Front, under George Habash, has an intelligence office in Kampala responsible for the activities of the Organization in the whole of Africa. This office is subordinate to Wadia Haddad, the head of the branch for overseas terror-strikes of the Popular Front. Hundreds of Palestinians are employed in administrative posts in the administration and public services in Uganda as substitutes for the Asians who were expelled from that State.

Uganda and the PLO maintain close co-operation also at the military level. In Uganda there is a centre for the military training of Palestinians. Palestinian pilots train in the Ugandan Air Force on MIG 21 planes. Members of the PLO are to be found among the bodyguards of President Amin.

The extent of Ugandan collaboration can be gauged from the news broadcasts in English on Kampala Radio after the aircraft landed at Entebbe. Records of these broadcasts are available from monitoring reports supplied by the British Broadcasting Corporation.

If the representatives will take the trouble to read the reports, they will reveal a complete identity of purpose with the hijackers and their demands on the part of the Ugandan authorities.

There is no attempt in the broadcasts to hide an atmosphere of euphoric ecstasy over the hijacking, and of identification with the hijackers on the part of the Government of Uganda.

Thus the enthusiastic broadcast on 29 June opens with:

"We now bring you the special announcement you have been waiting for. The following are the demands of the Popular Front for the Liberation of Palestine". The announcer then read out the six-point statement issued by the PFLP.

One does not really require all this evidence in order to prove that Israel was entirely justified by every norm of natural and international law in taking the action which it took. In viewing the facts of the case, one must reach one of two conclusions: either the Government of Uganda was directly implicated in holding as hostages innocent passengers, men, women and children, or the Government of Uganda does not exercise sovereignty over its territory and was incapable of dealing with half a dozen terrorists.

And what better evidence do we have to support this contention of ours than the fact that to date the Government of Uganda has not released a 75-year-old lady, Mrs. Dora Bloch, who was on her way to the marriage of her son in this country when the plane was hijacked? Moreover the refusal of the Government of Uganda to release the Air France plane immediately after the hijackers were eliminated tends only to confirm the fact of complicity.

What other reason should there be for the Government of Uganda to refuse to return the plane to the French Government, in violation of the Hague Convention of 1970, of which Uganda is a signatory?

If the Government of Uganda is not implicated in this crime, why was a 75-year-old lady, Mrs. Bloch, not released immediately after the hijackers were eliminated? Why was she held in custody under guard in hospital in Kampala?

Why was she not released to the British Consul when he called on her on Sunday, 4 July, after the rescue operation? Why have we suddenly been notified ominously that the Ugandan authorities, four of whose employees reportedly dragged her screaming from the hospital, are unaware of her whereabouts?

Either the Government of Uganda exercises national

sovereignty, in which case it knows where she is, or it does not.

I ask my colleagues, Africans and others here, who are joined to condemn Israel for exercising its inherent right of self-defence, do you or do you not condone the horrifying behaviour which is reflected in this act of "chivalry" on the part of President Amin against Mrs. Dora Bloch, aged 75?

For once, have the courage of your convictions and speak out, or be damned by your own silence.

Here you have a plain, simple case which has no answer and cannot have any answer for decent people wherever they may be.

Here you have the unbelievable, macabre spectacle of a State waging a war against a 75-year-old lady, and supported, presumably, by those who would associate themselves with this despicable and cowardly behaviour. If the Government of Uganda is not implicated, let it now and forthwith produce Mrs. Bloch.

Does this Council propose to remain silent on the fate of Mrs. Bloch?

The disappearance of this old lady and the by now all-too-familiar picture of the terrifying happenings in Amin's Uganda provide ample justification in themselves for the premonition which prompted the action taken by the Government of Israel.

This type of action, which in principle is not unprecedented, is dealt with at considerable length in international law, and there is no doubt whatsoever but that the weight of international law and precedent lies fully in Israel's favour. However, the Israeli action at Entebbe came to remind us that the law we find in statute books is not the only law of mankind. There is also a moral law, and by all that is moral on this earth Israel had the right to do what it did. Indeed, it had also the duty to do so.

Uganda violated a basic tenet of international law in failing to protect foreign nationals on its territory. Furthermore, it behaved in a manner which constituted a gross violation of the 1970 Hague Convention on the Suppression or Unlawful Seizure of Aircraft. This Convention had been ratified by both Israel and Uganda. Article 6 of that Convention maintains that:

"Upon being satisfied that the circumstances so warrant, any Contracting State in the territory of which the offender or the alleged offender is present shall take him into custody and other measures shall be as provided in the law of that State but may only be continued for such time as is necessary to enable any criminal or extradition proceedings to be instituted."

Article 9 states:

"1. When any of the acts mentioned in Article 1 (a) has occurred or is about to occur, Contracting States shall take all appropriate measures to restore control of the aircraft to its lawful commander or to preserve his control of the aircraft.

"2. In the cases contemplated by the preceding paragraph, any Contracting State in which the aircraft or its passengers or crew are present shall facilitate the continuation of the journey of the passengers and crew as soon as practicable and shall without delay return the aircraft and its cargo to the persons lawfully entitled to possession."

The right of a State to take military action to protect its nationals in mortal danger is recognized by all legal authorities in international law. In *Self-Defence in International Law,* Professor Bowett states, on page 87, that

"The right of the State to intervene by the use or threat of force for the protection of its nationals suffering injuries within the territory of another State is generally admitted, both in the writings of jurists and in the practice of States. In the arbitration between Great Britain and Spain in 1925, one of the series known as the Spanish Moroccan claims, Judge Huber, as Rapporteur of the Commission, stated:

" 'However, it cannot be denied that at a certain point the interest of a State in exercising protection over its nationals and their property can take precedence over territorial sovereignty, despite the absence of any conventional provisions. This right of intervention has been claimed by all States. Only its limits are disputed. We now envisage action by the protect-

ing State which involves a *prima facie* violation of the
independence and territorial inviolability of the territorial State. In so far as this action takes effect in
derogation of the sovereignty of the territorial State,
it must necessarily be exceptional in character and
limited to those cases in which no other means of
protection are available. It presupposes the inadequacy
of any other means of protection against some injury,
actual or imminent, to the persons or property of
nationals and, moreover, an injury which results either
from the acts of the territorial State and its authorities
or from the acts of individuals or groups of individuals which the territorial State is unable, or unwilling, to prevent. In the *Law of Nations,* Sixth
Edition, page 627, Brierly states as follows: "Whether
the landing of detachments of troops to save the lives
of nationals under imminent threat of death or serious
injury owing to the breakdown of law and order may
be justifiable is a delicate question. Cases of this form
of intervention have been not infrequent in the past
and, when not attended by suspicion of being a pre-
text for political pressure, have generally been regarded as justified by the sheer necessity of instant
action to save the lives of innocent nationals whom
the local government is unable or unwilling to protect."

He goes on to observe that:

"Every effort must be made to get the United Nations
to act. But, if the United Nations is not in a position
to move in time and the need for instant action is
manifest it would be difficult to deny the legitimacy
of action in defence of nationals which every responsible Government would feel bound to take if it had
the means to do so. This is, of course, on the basis
that the action was strictly limited to securing the safe
removal of the threatened national."

In support of this contention, O'Connell states in *International Law,* Second Edition, page 303:

"Traditional international law has not prohibited
States from protecting their nationals whose lives or

property are imperilled by political conditions in another State, provided the degree of physical presence employed in their protection is proportional to the situation. When the Sixth International Conference of American States at Havana attempted to formulate a legal notion of intervention in 1928, the United States pointed out that intervention would need to be clearly defined, for the United States would not stand by and permit the breakdown of government to endanger the lives and property of American citizens in revolution-ridden countries. Interposition of a temporary character would not, in such circumstances, it was argued, be illegal."

The author continues:

"Article 2 (4) of the United Nations Charter should be interpreted as prohibiting acts of force against the territorial integrity and political independence of nations, and not to prohibit a use of force which is limited in intention and effect to the protection of a State's own integrity and its nationals' vital interests, when the machinery envisaged by the United Nations Charter is ineffective in the situation."

The act of hijacking can well be regarded as one of piracy. Pirates have been *hostis humani generis*—enemies of the human race—since the early days of international law in the Middle Ages. During the war against the slave trade and piracy, certain norms were established in international law which permitted intervention in case of ships engaged in slave trade between Africa and America and against the centres of piracy in North Africa. The principle of national sovereignty was overruled by the higher principles of man's liberty.

In this connexion it is perhaps appropriate to recall here that the United States Marine Corps was established for the purpose of waging war against the pirates. And one cannot fail to note that the Marine anthem refers to "the shores of Tripoli". Apparently, that coast is not new as a haven for terrorists—then for pirates and ships and today for hijackers in airplanes.

Israel's action in Entebbe was very similar to the humanitarian rescue operation which took place in those days. The slave trade then could have claimed that searching the slave ships was in violation of international maritime law. But civilized man defined a higher law, namely, that of human freedom, above which no national sovereignty can claim to be.

Had a Jewish State existed in the thirties, we might well have decided, with the rise of Nazism, to endeavour to undertake an operation to rescue the inmates of the concentration camps. The logic of those who criticize us today would maintain that by so doing we would have been in flagrant violation of the national sovereignty of the Third Reich. What would have been more important: Hitler's sovereignty or rescuing innocent people from a holocaust?

May I recall General Assembly resolution 2645 (XXV) of 1970, the consensus adopted by this Council in document S/10705 on 20 June 1972 on the subject of hijacking, and the 1970 resolution of the Assembly of the Council of Europe condemning acts of hijacking, sabotage, taking of hostages and blackmailing of Governments by Palestinian organizations utilizing the territory of certain Arab States as a refuge, training ground and base for action.

I draw those resolutions and many other relevant resolutions by the United Nations and other international bodies to the Council's attention to remind it that the problem is not new, but that no practical and effective steps have been taken to combat it.

The problem of combating terror has exercised countries throughout the world. Thus the Soviet Union on 3 January 1973 published a new law on criminal liability for the hijacking of aircraft. That law was discussed at length by V. Ivanov in *Izvestiya* on 16 January 1973. Indeed, the mounting of Soviet official concern is evident in Soviet scientific and legal literature and also in a series of official actions.

On 4 December 1970 *Pravda* reported favourably on the International Civil Aviation Organization's Conference at The Hague to draw up a new convention concerning the prevention of hijacking of aircraft. In November 1970 *Pravda* published an article by O. Khlestov praising United Nations General Assembly resolution 2645 (XXV) of 1970. There was a further article in *Izvestiya* on 16 Janu-

ary 1971 by O. Khlestov praising the Hague Convention
of 1970.

Attention is drawn also to an article by P. Yevseyev and
Y. Kolosov entitled "Air Bandits Outlawed", published in
International Affairs in Moscow on 8 November 1971, in
which both United Nations General Assembly resolution
2645 (XXV) and the Hague Convention of 1970 are discussed and—I would remind the Soviet representative—
supported.

The right of self-defence is enshrined in international
law and in the Charter of the United Nations and can be
applied on the basis of the classic formulation, as was done
in the well-known Caroline Case, permitting such action
where there is a

"necessity of self-defence, instant, overwhelming, leaving no choice of means and no moment for delibera-
tion".

That was exactly the situation which faced the Government
of Israel.

In equivalent circumstances other States have acted in
a manner similar to Israel. But a few months ago the
Council discussed actions taken by France in freeing a bus-
load of 30 children held hostage on the Somalia border.
I refer the Council to the remarks of the representative of
France to the Security Council on 18 February 1976.

The representative of France was addressing the Security
Council on an incident which arose out of the holding of
30 French children 6 to 12 years of age in a school bus as
hostages by a group of terrorists in Somalia. The representatives of these terrorists in Somalia made demands on
the French Government and announced that if their demands were not met the terrorists would cut the throats of
the children. The French forces thereupon took action
against the terrorists on the Somali border, killing them;
in the process one of the children was killed by the terrorists and five others were wounded. As the French soldiers
rushed to save the children, fire was directed at them from
the Somali frontier post, seriously wounding a French
lieutenant. The French forces naturally enough returned
fire into Somali territory, causing casualties and damage to
the Somalis. In this case too one hostage was missing, and

the child was found later to be held in Somalia by terrorists. He was happily later returned alive.

The debate is familiar to members of the Council. Suffice it, however, to say that France unequivocally rejected any accusation of aggression in this regard. France on that occasion rightfully exercised its duties under international law in a situation which is similar in many respects to the situation which we had in Entebbe.

In the *Mayaguez* incident last year, in which the United States acted to rescue merchant seamen and their ship, President Ford was quoted as saying:

"The decision to use force was based 100 per cent and entirely on a single consideration, to get the crew and the ship back."

I could continue and present dozens of cases which reveal that international precedent and international law fully justify the Israeli action and show that every country that respects itself would have taken the same action in similar circumstances had it considered such action feasible.

This principle was emphasized by the British Government in the case of British merchant seamen prisoners of war being transported on a German ship, *Altmark,* back to Germany through the territorial waters of Norway in February 1940. The British flotilla led by the destroyer *Cossack* entered the territorial waters of Norway, then a neutral country, which had allowed passage to this German ship. And in 1940 those British prisoners were prisoners of war taken prisoner in accordance with the law of war. Mr. Winston Churchill personally authorized British ships to fire at the Norwegian naval ships in the area should they open fire and thereby endanger the British force. He sent the following order to Captain Vian on the *Cossack* with regard to the Norwegian torpedo boat:

"If she fires upon you . . . you should defend yourself using no more force than is necessary and ceasing fire when she desists".

Sir Winston Churchill in his history of the Second World War enunciates the principle which guided him:

"What mattered at home and in the Cabinet was whether British prisoners were found on board or not ... This was a dominant factor".

What mattered to the Government of Israel in this instance was the lives of the hostages, in danger of their very lives. No consideration other than this humanitarian consideration motivated the Government of Israel.

Israel's rescue operation was not directed against Uganda. Israeli forces were not attacking Uganda—and they were certainly not attacking Africa. They were rescuing their nationals from a band of terrorists and kidnappers who were being aided and abetted by the Ugandan authorities. The means used were the minimum necessary to fulfill that purpose, as is laid down in international law.

Some parallels could be drawn with the right of an individual to use appropriate means to defend himself if he kills someone who is trying to kill him. He is not liable to be found guilty of murder. Judgement takes into account the context and the purpose of the act. The same applies to the use of force in international affairs.

Over the years, Israel in pursuance of its policy of aiding developing countries helped Uganda, as indeed it has co-operated and continues to co-operate with many fellow developing countries throughout the world, including countries in Africa. But there is a limit to the aid which we were prepared to make available to Uganda. In 1972 President Amin came to Israel, produced maps describing his proposed plan to invade Tanzania and asked for Israeli air support in the planned action, including the bombing of Dar Es Salaam. Israel's reply to this preposterous and wicked proposition was such as to bring about a dramatic change in the attitude to Israel on the part of Field Marshal Amin. His frustration with Israel's attitude to his plans for dealing with Tanzania, coupled with the lavish blandishments proferred to him by the ruler of Libya, combined to produce an extreme, violent, anti-Semitic, anti-Israeli attitude on the part of the ruler of Uganda.

The move by the Organization of African Unity to bring this complaint to the Security Council must appear to be completely incongruous were one's senses not completely dulled by the utter incongruity of some of the proceedings of this Organization. The deliberations on this occasion will doubtless be no exception.

Let me recall to my African colleagues the text of a resolution of the Council of Ministers of the Organization of African Unity in 1970.

"The Council of Ministers of the Organization of African Unity, meeting in its fourteenth ordinary session in Addis Ababa, Ethiopia, from 27 February to 6 March 1970.

"Having heard the declaration made by the Foreign Minister of Ethiopia regarding the repeated sabotage and hijacking of civil aircraft thereby endangering the safety of passengers,

"Conscious of the disastrous consequences resulting from such criminal acts of international air travel,

"1. Condemns all attempts and acts of hijacking and sabotaging of civil aircraft;

"2. Calls upon all States to undertake strict measures to protect civilian air travel from being endangered;

"3. Appeals to all States to apprehend and punish such criminals in order to ensure the safety of international air travel."

How do they reconcile their attitude with the text of a resolution on this very issue which they all accepted? Here we are again being selective. Do the member States of the OAU not realize that by condoning acts of piracy and hijacking they are laying themselves open to such acts on their own airlines and in their own countries? Are we to understand that there is to be a selective cataloguing of hijacking, of international murder, of piracy, of brutality and of brigandery according to race, colour or continent to which the murderer or transgressor belongs?

We the Jewish people are only too familiar with this type of selective behaviour and with the awful catastrophe and doom which it brings to those who engage in it.

In this context, may I recall that only last month, in a discussion at this Council table, in reply to remarks made by the representative of the Soviet Union on the issue of terror, I recalled that a distinguished Soviet Foreign Minister, Maxim Litvinov, had once said "Peace is indivisible". I submitted then that terrorism too is indivisible. You cannot be selective about it. The nations of the world will either join hands to destroy this scourge which affects mankind, or they will be destroyed by it.

It is not enough to raise your voice in horror when it affects only you. If terrorism is bad, it is bad for everybody, in every case, on every occasion, by whomever committed, and whoever the victim might be. It must be eliminated.

Summing up the daring and imaginative operation which we are discussing, my Prime Minister stated in the Knesset on 4 July that:

"This rescue operation is an achievement of great importance in the struggle against terrorism. It is Israel's contribution to humanity's struggle against international terror, but it should not be viewed as the final chapter. It will give us encouragement as we continue our efforts, but the struggle is not over; new efforts, new methods and unremitting sophistication will be required. Terrorism will find us neither immobilized nor hidebound by routine."

In many ways, this is a moment of truth for this Organization. If it will seize this opportunity courageously and without flinching to join hands in a war against international terror for the benefit of ordinary men and women throughout this world, then it will be serving the purpose for which it was established. It can yet retrieve, perhaps, in small measure, the prestige and goodwill which it has dissipated by becoming hostage to despots and extremists.

The murder of 11 Israeli athletes in Munich in 1972 moved the Secretary-General to demand of the General Assembly to devise measures for the eradication of the scourge of terrorism off the map of the world. The Arab States and their friends managed to "bury" the subject by means of their "automatic majority". Today the question of international terrorism is before the Security Council, not the General Assembly.

If the Council will fail to seize this opportunity which has been granted it to eliminate the scourge of terrorists, kidnappers, hijackers and blackmailers from our midst, then it will plunge to the lowest depths in the eyes of mankind and will disappear in history as yet another great and tragic lost opportunity in history.

It has fallen to the lot of my small country, embattled as we are, facing the problems which we do, to demonstrate to the world that there is an alternative to surrender to terrorism and blackmail.

It has fallen to our lot to prove to the world that this scourge of international terror can be dealt with. It is now for the nations of the world, regardless of political differences which may divide them, to unite against this common enemy which recognizes no authority, knows no borders, respects no sovereignty, ignores all basic human decencies, and places no limits on human bestiality.

We come with a simple message to the Council: We are proud of what we have done, because we have demonstrated to the world that in a small country, in Israel's circumstances, with which the members of this Council are by now all too familiar, the dignity of man, human life and human freedom constitute the highest values. We are proud not only because we have saved the lives of over 100 innocent people—men, women and children—but because of the significance of our act for the cause of human freedom.

We call on this body to declare war on international terror, to outlaw it and eradicate it wherever it may be. We call on this body, and above all we call on the Member States and countries of the world, to unite in a common effort to place these criminals outside the pale of human society, and with them to place any country which cooperates in any way in their nefarious activities.

In calling this body to action I cannot ignore its limitations, which are daily demonstrated by the fact that this body—this Council—has sat silent through 15 months of the greatest tragedy besetting the world today in the Lebanon, while a nation is torn apart, tens of thousands are killed, tens of thousands more are wounded, and the cup of human suffering overflows daily.

Let me remind you that, when the hijacking took place, this Security Council was debating the report of the so-called Palestine Committee. The Security Council held four meetings on the Palestinian question while an act of terror carried out by Palestinian terrorists was taking place. Yet this Council did not even see fit to raise the question and plead for the release of the innocent civilians.

If this body fails to take action, we call on all freedom-loving countries in the world to come together outside the framework of this body, establish accepted norms of behaviour in relation to terrorists, and declare in no uncertain terms that each and every one of them will have nothing whatsoever to do with any country which violates these norms and which encourages terrorism.

Once hijackers have no country in which to land their planes because receiving such a plane would mean exclusion from the world community, or part of the world community, whether in the field of air transportation, trade, commerce or international relations, there will be no more hijacking.

We are proud to have given the lead in this struggle against international terrorism. This debate is an opportunity for the world to take action on this issue which can affect the lives of every man and woman and child in the world. Those countries which fail to take a clear and unequivocal stand on this issue for reasons of expediency or cowardice will stand damned by all the decent people in this world and despised in history.

There is a time in the affairs of man when even Governments must make difficult decisions guided not by considerations of expediency but by considerations of morality. Israel was guided by these considerations in risking much to save its citizens. May we hope that others will be guided by these principles too?

UGANDA. Mr. Abdalla: I shall not now reply fully to what the representative of Zionist Israel said, but there is one important point in which I wish to reply immediately. I hope to have an opportunity to reply in detail later regarding the unfounded allegations against Uganda and some other friendly countries of Africa.

This world body has been informed of the Israeli invasion of Uganda on 4 July 1976. We are all aware of the efforts made by His Excellency Al-Hajji Field-Marshal

Dr. Idi Amin Dada, V.C., D.S.O., M.C., President of the Republic of Uganda, and the entire people of Uganda to save the lives of all the hostages, numbering 250.

Up to the time of Israel's invasion in the early hours of Sunday, 4 July, President Amin had succeeded in having more than half the hostages released. At the risk of his own life, my President even cut short his stay in Mauritius in order to continue negotiations, thereby saving the lives of the remaining hostages. In his humanitarian efforts my President was concerned not only with the release of all hostages but also about their welfare. In so doing, the basic needs of life—for instance, food and medical services—were provided to all the hostages without discrimination.

It was in this spirit that Mrs. Dora Bloch, who had a piece of food stuck in her throat, was immediately rushed to Uganda's best hospital for medical treatment. When she got better in the evening of Saturday, 3 July, she was returned by the medical authorities to the old Entebbe airport to join the other hostages. In accordance with the understanding given by the Uganda Government to the hijackers, this was done in order not to jeopardize the lives of the hostages who were at that time still at Entebbe airport.

The Israelis committed a naked act of aggression by invading Entebbe airport where the hostages, including Mrs. Dora Bloch, were being held by the hijackers. The Israelis, as the Council has already been informed, used all kinds of weapons, shooting indiscriminately. In the process, many lives, including those of Ugandan soldiers, hijackers, hostages and members of the Israeli invading forces, were lost. The members of the invading force took away all the hostages—dead, injured or otherwise. They also took away all their members of the invading force—again, dead or injured. Therefore, it is for Israel to answer regarding the whereabouts of Mrs. Dora Bloch.

The press reports and diplomatic sources according to which one diplomat saw Mrs. Dora Bloch in hospital on Sunday are false. There is no concrete information about it. Everyone knows about the aggression that was launched against the people of Uganda, which resulted in much loss of life, and my President tried his best to do everything peacefully, but the Israeli aggression would not allow this. So it is Israel that is responsible for answering as to the whereabouts of Mrs. Dora Bloch.

I have done my very best to avoid mentioning Kenya, as it is a sister State and a neighbouring State of Uganda. Unfortunately, the representative of Kenya mentioned Uganda in his statement. I had in mind the Organization of African Unity, and the Minister for Foreign Affairs of Mauritius is here, and not to mention much about Kenya.

So, I should like the Council to follow exactly what are the facts regarding Kenya on this invasion. On 1 July a special Israel military mission was dispatched to Nairobi to communicate the decision on the invasion to the Kenya authorities and, presumably, obtain their clearance and assistance in the operation.

We have irrefutable evidence that that request was readily granted. Besides our own sources of information, I should like to quote from a story on the incident filed from Nairobi by a Mr. James MacManus and published in the London newspaper *The Guardian* of Monday, 5 July 1976. That story reads, in part:

"Although the Kenyan Government has offered no statement on the attack, and is unlikely to do so, officials here have been at pains to minimize the Government's role in the operation. As seen from Nairobi, the sequence of events runs as follows:

"At 9 o'clock local time on Saturday night (7 p.m. British time) a number of eyewitnesses at Kenya's busy international airport reported seeing the arrival of three troop transport planes, allegedly Israeli C-131 military aircraft.

"Shortly afterwards, an airport lounge was turned into a makeshift field hospital complete with operating table, anaesthetic equipment, and oxygen canisters. Kenya Regular Army troops and members of the paramiltary General Service Unit (GSU) had earlier moved in to secure the airport area.

"Around midnight the three aircraft carrying Israeli troops, members of a counter-terrorist unit, took off for the one-hour flight to Entebbe."

From that story it is clear that Israeli invading aircraft not only were allowed to overfly Kenya but were given Kenyan landing and service facilities on their way to raid Uganda and on their way back to Israel.

Another version of the raid is given by another English newspaper, the *Financial Times* of Monday, 5 July 1976. That version states in part:

"According to reports from Nairobi large numbers of Israeli security men arrived in the city during last week and were much in evidence, along with Kenyan security forces, at Embakasi airport as the Israeli aircraft refueled and medical attention was given."

Although in this submission we have shown that a sister member State of the Organization of African Unity connived in the invasion of our country, we wish to state before this Council that Uganda still regards the people of Kenya as their brothers and sisters, and we express the hope that the authorities in Kenya were somehow misled into collaborating in this heinous act.

Accordingly, Uganda does not intend to undertake any retaliatory measures against Kenya for this collaboration.

I should like to mention here my President's statement at the time of the opening of the Organization of African Unity summit in Mauritius. He also gave booklets to all members of the Organization of African Unity proving that he had no ambitions for even an inch of Kenyan soil and that he and the people of Uganda as a whole respect the charter of the Organization of African Unity. Fortunately, the current Chairman of the Organization of African Unity is here. He will say more about the statement by my colleague from Kenya concerning alleged Ugandan claims on Kenyan soil.

ISRAEL. Mr. Herzog: The remarks by the representative of Uganda about Mrs. Dora Bloch give rise to very considerable concern, because what he has said about her is a blatant untruth; it does not accord with the facts that have been published and that are known not only to Israel but also to other countires.

Let me quote from *The New York Times* of today, 9 July 1976:

".. . in the British House of Commons yesterday a Government minister said Mrs. Bloch had been visited in the hospital by a member of the High Commission on the day after the Israeli raid"—

that is, on 4 July 1976.

"The diplomat reported that she was being guarded by two men in plainclothes and that he was denied access to her when he returned an hour later.

"Mulago Hospital sources said their records showed that Mrs. Bloch was admitted last Friday, but listed no details of her treatment or discharge from the hospital." (*The New York Times, 9 July 1976, p. A2*)

Having regard to the veracity of the statement made on this point by the representative of Uganda, I think that we can draw conclusions about the veracity of all the remaining statements he has seen fit to make before this Council. . . .

SOMALIA. Mr. Hussen: We asked to participate in this debate to add our voice to those who preceded us, and to urge the Council to condemn, in the strongest possible terms, the Zionist régime in Tel Aviv for the naked act of aggression which it has committed against the people and Government of the Republic of Uganda. We ask the Council to do so because what is at stake here is the very existence and sovereignty of a member nation. Not only does this act of terrorism and aggression unleashed by the Zionist régime against Uganda on 4 July threaten the aims and principles of the United Nations and its Charter, but it also constitutes a danger to international peace and security.

It is with great indignation that the people and Government of the Somali Democratic Republic view this unprovoked and unlawful act of aggression. This feeling of indignation is aptly summed up in the telegram transmitted by Jaalle Mohamed Siad Barre, President of the Somali Democratic Republic, to His Excellency Idi Amin, President of the Republic of Uganda. In that telegram, the text of which has been circulated as an official document of the Security Council, the President of the Somali Democratic Republic stated:

"I have followed with great shock and dismay the dastardly act of aggression perpetrated by the troops of Zionist Israeli terrorists and imperialist forces at Entebbe Airport on July 4, 1976. This barbarous action is an unprecedented and direct attack on the Republic of Uganda and its Government. It also constitutes an arrogant insult to the dignity of Africa and mankind as a whole and contravenes all norms of international behaviour and conduct. Africa and the international community must draw the necessary conclusion from this shameful act and take the appropriate action so that it may not be repeated, for it may happen to any one of us. It must be therefore vigorously condemned by all men of conscience and the international community as a whole. The wanton killing of many innocent people by the Zionist agents and the destruction of Ugandan property, including its main airport, are but an example of the natures of zionism and its role in the Middle East, a menace and a serious threat to international peace and security. The legitimate struggle of the Arab people of Palestine to regain their homeland and the Arab nation to liberate the Zionist occupied territories shall not be stopped by these acts of terrorism and shall continue until final and complete victory is achieved. The shameful statement made by the Prime Minister of Israel stating that in support of this operation it was Israel's 'contribution to the fight against terrorism, a fight that has not ended' must be a lesson to the Arab nations for the Palestinian fight for liberation cannot be equated with terrorism. In their struggle the Palestinians have always shown a deep respect for human lives and have always spared the lives of the innocent for in this case they could have blown up the aircraft. In conclusion I should like to offer to you, dear Brother, and through you to the Government and people of Uganda, on behalf of the Central Committee of the Socialist Party, people and Government of the Somali Democratic Republic our militant support and solidarity and our deep and sincere condolence for the loss of many Ugandan lives in the shameful episode. Their memory will be a guiding torch for us all. Peace be upon their souls."

The Republic of Uganda is not the first peace-loving country whose sovereignty and territorial integrity have been violated by the arrogant racist Zionist régime. Since its illegal occupation of the Arab land of Palestine 30 years ago, this régime has been engaged in committing unprovoked aggression after aggression against sovereign nations. For an illustration of Israel's habitual transgression and its unbelievable, barefaced inclination to indulge in an unrestrained attitude, we need only look at the surrounding Arab States. We can recall the numerous occasions on which the world came to the brink of an all-engulfing war because of the callous behaviour of the Zionist régime in the Middle East and its utter disregard for international law. The plight of the Palestinian Arab nation is a perfect example of the fiendish mentality of the Israeli régime.

It is too well known a fact that this racist Zionist régime has been engaged, through the years, in wilful violence and subversion in Africa and elsewhere. It is fitting in this regard to quote from *The New York Times* of 10 July 1976. which, in a long article dedicated to the discrediting of the Head of State of a member country of this Organization, touched incidentally upon Israel's open interference in the internal affairs of other Arab and African countries. It stated, *inter alia*:

> "Israel's interest in Uganda was largely motivated by the Sudanese civil war, in which Southern Sudanese . . . had been fighting for 10 years with Northern Sudanese".

Though it is a well-recorded fact, the paper has reconfirmed that throughout this long period Israel continued to supply "arms shipments to the Southern Sudanese". *(Ibid.)* Other countries, including my own, have also been subjected to the same unwarranted interference in a variety of forms. Uganda is only the latest victim of the continuous terror and intimidation perpetrated by Israel.

Numerous hijackings, most of them politically motivated, have taken place over the years. The victims of these acts have been innocent civilian citizens of different nationalities. The international community has consistently demanded the release of these innocent people and their safe conduct to their destinations. Yet, we all know that the safety of such victims, important and legitimate as it is, cannot be a justification for a blatant act of aggression against the sovereignty and territorial integrity of a State and the wanton killing of its innocent citizens. Such a despicable act could only be committed by Israel which, assured of the full support of a powerful country and always shamefully anxious to display its arrogance, has made it a major principle of its governmental policies to espouse State terrorism. Such an attitude is not the least surprising, for Israel is itself a product of terrorism.

It also made it a habit that it is customarily expected for its delegations at international fora to remind us, as it did before this Council on 9 July, of the Nazi holocaust in Europe in order to enlist sympathy and support. Israel should realize that, if the world had condemned Hitler and his Nazi philosophy based on racial purity, it is only logical that it must expect the same from the world community as Israel practices policies similar to, if not identical with, those of Hitler yesterday and those of Pretoria's white minority régime today.

The Zionist régime claims that it was alone in planning and executing its latest atrocity in Uganda. The Government and people of the Somali Democratic Republic find it very hard to believe that Israel did not get a helping hand from its customary supporters in conducting this sordid affair, as has been the case in all its past military adventures. We feel strongly that the conspiracy is larger than has been admitted to, that the truth will come out in time, and that whoever took part in this shameful act will ultimately be uncovered.

The representative of Israel tried to convince us—especially the members of the Council—that even my country, Somalia, was involved in the hijacking of the French airbus. He tried to make the participation of the Somali Ambassador in the negotiations for the safety of the hostages look as if the Government of Somalia was linked to the venture. This sinister allegation is unfounded and slanderous, to say the least. The reason why the Somali Ambassador accepted the plea to participate in the negotiations, apart from his natural sympathy, compassion and concern for human life, was that he was the dean of the

Arab Ambassadors accredited to Uganda. In that capacity, as has been explained by President Idi Amin in his communication contained in document S/12124, the Somali Ambassador agreed to participate in the negotiations along with his French counterpart. It is difficult to believe that the Israeli representative would have the insolence to distort the facts and to attempt to discredit the compassionate action undertaken by the Somali Ambassador. Had the Somali Ambassador done otherwise and refused to lend his requested services to the cause of saving the hostages, it would, in our opinion, have been an unforgivable act on his part. For this reason there is no room for the Israeli allegation. However, this is merely another demonstration of the desperate and cynical attitude which the Zionist régime has for anything that smacks of humanitarianism.

Throughout his statement, the Israeli representative continuously endeavoured to drive a wedge between the Arab States and African States by acting as the self-appointed devil's advocate. It is not, of course, new to us that he should do so, because we know the history of Israel and the fact that it thrives on sowing seeds of trouble and subversion. We know, too, that the Tel Aviv régime derives its inspiration, strangely enough, from discord and violence.

In his fruitless groping for previous examples of what I can describe as "justifiable violence", the Israeli representative once again attempted to feed us another distorted version of the unfortunate incident at Loyada, a small village on the border of the Somali Democratic Republic with the so-called French Somaliland. If the Zionist representative had any desire for the truth, he would not have blinded himself to the facts of that incident. If it were not for his deviousness, he would have recalled—for it is there in the records of this Council—that, first of all, the vehicle in which the children were held was in a territory under French rule, and not in the Somali Republic's territory, as he would have us believe. The Zionist representative, in his desperate effort to grope for an elusive justification for his régime's shameful and unprecedented action, assembled examples of other activities involving violence which had been committed by other Powers. He cited incidents such as Mayaguez, Loyada and Entebbe—all of which are incidents of aggression by those States whose arrogance of power has made them oblivious to respect for the principles of international law and for equality and sovereignty among nations, large and small, the very principles for which this Organization was created to safeguard and to uphold. We believe that it is the duty of the Council to reject such a contention, which, if passed unchallenged, might undermine the very reason for the existence of this world body. This idea is nothing but a suggestion to return to the law of the jungle, where only the strong should survive.

Even the Organization of African Unity was not spared indiscriminate harassment on the part of the Tel Aviv representative. He felt no shame in offending an organization of 48 independent States. Allow me to refer to what he said in this respect:

"The move by the Organization of African Unity to bring this complaint to the Security Council must appear to be completely incongruous were one's senses not completely dulled by the utter incongruity of . . . the proceedings of this Organization. The deliberations on this occasion will doubtless be no exception". (1939th meeting, p. 61)

Such an insolence on the part of a régime that fully shares with Pretoria's minority régime the belief that they are superior races and that other races are inferior to them is preposterous and utterly unacceptable. Africa makes no compromise on the rejection and denunciation of such an absurd notion.

In conclusion, I should like, on behalf of my delegation, to emphasize once again that my delegation urges the Council to take adequate and prompt measures against the Israeli régime and to condemn it for its unlawful act of aggression against the Republic of Uganda.

ISRAEL. Mr. Herzog: The weight of evidence to prove Ugandan complicity has been growing by the day as the detailed statements of the hostages are analysed and new evidence becomes available. We now know from the debriefing of the passengers that the map in the hands of the leader of the hijacking group, Wilfred Böse, which he produced immediately after the plane took off from Athens, was already clearly marked with the route Athens–Benghazi–Entebbe. We know, too, as has indeed been published, that before the arrival of the plane at Entebbe, Idi Amin dispatched his personal plane to Somalia in order to pick up and bring to Entebbe the leader of the terrorists, who took control of the plane after it landed at Entebbe.

Furthermore, the members of the Council are fully aware by now that four terrorists hijacked the plane at Athens. The evidence which I have produced, and which other representatives have confirmed, shows that the plane was met at Entebbe Airport by reinforcements of terrorists, some five in number. Four terrorists hijacked the plane. Seven terrorists were accorded a State funeral with full military honours by the Government of Uganda. In other words, by all accounts—including, impliedly, by Ugandan accounts—terrorist reinforcements appeared on the scene in Entebbe. In fact, we know that they were driven onto the scene in two official Ugandan cars, one driven by a soldier in uniform.

It is interesting to note that, despite the overwhelming body of evidence which confirms the fact that the hijackers were reinforced in Kampala, there is no reference to it directly in either President Amin's message contained in document S/12124 or the two statements made by his Foreign Minister here on Friday, 9 July.

I listened carefully to the statement made by the Foreign Minister of Mauritius, and nowhere was there any reference to the reinforcement of terrorists awaiting the hijackers in Entebbe. So far as the Foreign Minister of Mauritius is concerned, they did not exist. The eloquence of the Foreign Minister of Mauritius in speech was equalled only by his eloquent silence.

Shortly after 101 hostages were released on 1 July, the following dispatch was sent from the Associated Press in Paris:

"Hostages newly released by hijackers of an Air France jetliner arrived here early today and said three or four heavily armed men, apparently Arabs, were waiting to reinforce four original hijackers when the plane commandeered over Greece landed in Entebbe, Uganda."

After the Israeli rescue operation, the French Newspaper *Le Monde* gave full details of this aerial piracy in its issue of 5 July, which included the following: (*Spoke in French*)

"On their arrival at Kampala, they were joined on the field, immediately after landing, by a group of four or five Palestinians armed with sub-machine-guns."

(*Continued in English*)
Similar reports appeared in many other newspapers, magazines and on many radio and television stations. All reports were based on information given by released hostages and Government officials. There is not the slightest doubt in anyone's mind that in fact the hijackers were reinforced in Uganda. Careful reading of President Amin's message to the President of the Security Council and the statement by his Foreign Minister reveal an inadvertent, indirect admission of the fact that the hijackers were indeed reinforced by other terrorists in Kampala. In President Amin's message, he states that:

"The Israeli invaders quickly mounted an attack on the hijackers, killing seven of them." (*S/12124, annex, p. 1*)

A similar reference to seven hijackers killed also appears in the Ugandan Foreign Minister's statement on page 17 of document S/PV.1939. President Amin's reference to "seven of them" implies that there were more than seven. However, as we all recall, only four commandeered the Air France plane after it departed from Athens Airport. Thus in fact, both President Amin and his Foreign Minister have implicitly admitted that the original hijackers were reinforced by more terrorists at Entebbe Airport in Uganda. What better proof of Uganda's complicity in this crime does one need than the fact that Uganda allowed a reinforcement of four to five Arab armed terrorists to join the hijackers?

Furthermore, the important role played by the terrorists who joined the hijackers at Kampala adds further proof that the Entebbe part of the hijacking was a carefully planned operation which could not have been carried out without the complicity of the Government of Uganda. *The New York Times,* which was correctly referred to by the Foreign Minister of Mauritius as a highly respected newspapers, interviewed one of the released hostages, Mr. Michel Cojot, and the following was reported on 6 July:

"Although the West German man was clearly in charge on the plane, Mr. Cojot said, he added that it was equally clear that the four hijackers were simply the soldiers in the plot and did not have authority to negotiate for the hostages or to make any decisions beyond capturing them and keeping them calm.

" 'It was the three Arabs who joined them on the ground at Entebbe who were in charge of the further decisions,' he said. 'The orders were coming from somewhere else. One of them spoke Spanish.' "

In other words, the hijacking operation of the Popular Front for the Liberation of Palestine could not have been carried out as planned unless the hijacked plane arrived at its predetermined destination, Uganda, where the leader of the operation was waiting.

If Uganda was not implicated how did it happen that these reinforcements were allowed to drive up? Why have those representatives, who have identified themselves in so moving a manner out of a feeling of common interest with Idi Amin's Uganda and with the cause of international terror, not addressed themselves to this rather strange development, which in itself proves their thesis to be false?

Furthermore, if there was no connivance, where are the other terrorists? What has happened to the two or three survivors of the rescue operation at Entebbe Airport? Why have they not been apprehended and produced in accordance with The Hague Convention of 1970?

Since the press was quoted at length in our proceedings, let me do my share, too. Another detailed account of Ugandan collusion appeared on 5 July in *The New York Times.* Allow me to quote part of the article, for it summarizes numerous reports which confirm that the Ugan-

dan authorities worked hand in glove with the terrorists. The report from Paris states:

"Officials and released hostages said here today
that they had substantial evidence that President Idi
Amin had been in collusion with the hijackers of an
Air France airbus in the seizure of the plane as well as
after it landed in Uganda. . . .

"A highly placed French source said that President Amin had refused to allow Pierre Renard, the
French Ambassador to Uganda, or a special French
envoy to deal with the hijackers directly. . . .

"They also noted that during the first 24 hours
after the aircraft reached Entebbe, the hijackers with-
drew to rest and Ugandans guarded the hostages.

"Other evidence pointing to the Ugandan President's involvement with the terrorists was included in
comments by French diplomats and the reports of
hostages freed earlier by the terrorists. . . .

"Among the passengers released last week were
Michel Cojot and his 12-year-old son, Oliver. Mr.
Cojot, a French management consultant, served as
interpreter for the hostages, and negotiated on their
behalf for small conveniences during the ordeal.

"Mr. Cojot said that he had 'not a shadow of a
doubt' that Uganda knew of the hijack plan in advance and had prepared for action. . . .

"Mr. Cojot said that after landing at Entebbe,
Kampala's international airport, everyone remained
on the plane for several hours.

" 'The terrorists packed up their grenades and put
them back in the sacks they had carried aboard. They
put the 7.65 Czech automatic pistols, which had
never left their hands for a second during the flight,
into their belts and sat down together in the front of
the plane,' he said. 'Until then there had always been
at least one in front and one in back to cover us.'

"Mr. Cojot said that at that point he managed to
talk with one of the crew members and suggested that
it would be possible to overcome the four hijackers,
who were grouped together without weapons in their

hands, and for someone to ship out of the exit and summon help.

" 'We agreed, though, that the hijackers were acting as though they felt completely at home. The sudden relaxation of their previously thorough discipline showed they considered themselves on friendly ground'. . . .

" '. . . The whole time we felt we were being guarded by both the hijackers and the Ugandans.'

"Friends of the hijackers who joined them at the airport appeared to be Palestinians, Mr. Cojot said. 'They came and went freely in a Datsun with local license plates and a diplomatic plate, carrying weapons,' he added.

"The Ugandan civilian manager at the airport had food and drink ready for the hostages not longer after their arrival. 'But nonetheless I had to talk to him,' Mr. Cojot said, 'because there weren't enough plates at one time and then not enough glasses. I was joking and said, "Well, it must be hard to look after 263 unexpected guests" '.

" 'The manager replied, "Oh, but I was expecting you," ' Mr. Cojot said."

The Washington Post of 5 July similarly carried a detailed indictment of President Amin:

"The accounts of the 148 non-Jewish hostages released earlier in the week supported the Israelis' view.

"The freed hostages spoke of Amin's embracing the leader of the hijack gang and of the four hijackers then leaving the hostages to be guarded by Ugandan troops for 24 hours.

"Afterward, the two Arabs and two Germans who hijacked the Air France plane over Greece returned, looking refreshed after a night's sleep and a bath.

"The four hijackers were later joined by at least three Palestinians, and the gang was supplied with additional automatic weapons, according to French and Greek hostages.

"A Greek ship mechanic, Christos Sarantis, speaking for the seven Greeks freed earlier in the week, said, 'We were guarded by black soldiers and by about a hundred persons in civilian dress, who had excellent relations and co-operated with the hijackers. There was full co-operation between Amin, his men and the hijackers.' "

I am fully aware of the statement made by Captain Bacos, as reported in *The New York Times* of 6 July and quoted here by the Foreign Minister of Mauritius. However, the overwhelming body of evidence corroborated by the majority of the hostages that were released—as was, indeed, reported many times in the press—proves that indeed Ugandan troops participated together with the terrorists in guard duty over the 260-odd innocent passengers and crew. I regret that the Foreign Minister of Mauritius chose to ignore the extensive evidence available, which proves Uganda's collusion with the terrorists.

I have already, in my statement of Friday last, referred to the fact that the terrorists, always aided by the Ugandans, interrogated some Israelis, at times using force and even threats of death. *The New York Times* of Sunday, 11 July, carried a vivid description of one such interrogation conducted by both the terrorists and the Ugandans:

"During one period of questioning by the terrorists about what he really knew about Israel, Mr. Dahan was slapped in the face, punched in the back and his fingers were twisted backwards. He was told to write long reports about Israel and he proceeded to turn in documents dealing with kibbutz life and how he picked grapefruit.

"After one of these exercises, a Ugandan tore the paper out of his hand and threw it on the floor, saying:

" 'This is not what we want. . . . We want to know about the army. We want to know where the bases are. We want the name of your general.'

"A tall Palestinian carrying a gun and another called 'George' joined four Ugandan officers in the questioning. At one point, George put a gun to Mr. Dahan's chest."

In view of the overwhelming body of evidence corroborated by most of the 260 passengers and crew of the hijacked plane, I am left with no other choice but to call the two statements of the Foreign Minister of Uganda nothing but the most formidable collection of distortions, half-truths, deliberate omissions and outright falsehoods this Council has heard in a long time.

I shall not tire the Council by listing each and every distortion. They are too numerous to count, and it would prove very time consuming. However, there is one abominable lie which my country cannot pass over in silence, and it is incumbent upon me to show the true faces of the President of Uganda and his Foreign Minister for what they are.

The Foreign Minister of Uganda has stated before this Security Council that

"When she"—Mrs. Bloch—"got better in the evening of Saturday, 3 July, she was returned by the medical authorities to the old Entebbe airport to join the other hostages. . . .

"The Israelis committed a naked act of aggression by invading Entebbe airport where the hostages, including Mrs. Dora Bloch, were being held by the hijackers. . . . The members of the invading force took away all the hostages—dead, injured or otherwise. . . .

"The press reports and diplomatic sources according to which one diplomat saw Mrs. Dora Bloch in hospital on Sunday are false. There is no concrete information about it." (1939th meeting, p. 112)

So much for the statement of the Foreign Minister of Uganda before this Council.

I repeat that that is a damnable lie. Mrs. Bloch was visited in the hospital by a British diplomat on Sunday, 4 July, after Israel's rescue operation at Entebbe Airport, as was clearly stated to this Council by the representative of the United Kingdom. The diplomat reported that she was being guarded by two men, and when he returned an hour later he was not allowed to see her. That diplomat, we were informed yesterday by the representative of the United Kingdom, is to be expelled from Uganda today.

And we now have the ominous news that the Government of Uganda is applying the threat of blackmail to foreign nationals in Uganda in connexion with the current proceedings in the Security Council. In other words, for the first time in history, a direct attempt is being made by threats of blackmail of the most ominous character to influence the proceedings in this Council.

How can this Council pass over this in silence? How can it ignore a blatant attempt to influence this body? How can the members of this Council ignore this flagrant attempt to interfere with their national sovereignty? This whole sordid affair condemns not only the Government of Uganda but all the countries which have spoken out against the Israeli rescue mission during this debate. They have ignored the basic cause of this issue, namely the hijacking of the plane, and, for reasons of political expediency, they have not even had the good grace to say one word about the fate of an old lady of 75 dragged out of the hospital, in all probability to the horrible fate that has been meted out to tens of thousands of Ugandans, a fate the nature of which has been described by the Foreign Minister of Kenya in the letter he addressed to you today, Mr. President.

With all due respect to the Foreign Minister of Mauritius and to other members who have joined him in condemning Israel, the fact that they did not see fit even to mention in passing the fate of Mrs. Bloch and did not see fit to address an appeal to the Ugandan authorities in respect to her whereabouts removes from them the moral right to any standing in this debate.

The case of Mrs. Bloch only emphasizes in a most tragic manner the scope of the complicity of the Ugandans. And let me quote from a statement by Mr. Yigal Allon, our Foreign Minister, in the Knesset yesterday:

"The disappearance of Mrs. Bloch constitutes an inseparable part of the whole hijacking incident. The fate which befell her gives vivid substance to the awful danger which threatened the lives of all the hijacked passengers at Entebbe until they were freed in the magnificent rescue operation conducted by the Israel defence forces. It also proves once and forever

how empty and devoid of contempt, human, moral
and legal alike, were those voices which rushed to
condemn Israel in the international arena for carrying out the elementary duty towards its citizens
and saving them from this awful danger."

Again I wish to draw the attention of this Council to a
fact conveniently ignored—namely, that to date, 10 days
after the release of the hostages, the French Air France
plant has not yet been released. Again, this is a significant factor, though perhaps a minor one against the
background of the bloodshed, terror, human misery and
suffering which that operation has entailed.

I do not wish to refute many of the speeches made at
this table, because in certain circumstances they have
been made by countries whose régimes have so much in
common with the régime in Uganda that there is no
point in addressing myself to their remarks on a legal or
moral basis. One of those countries is Somalia, which, as
I have mentioned before, has become a centre for terrorist operations and a threat to its neighbouring State.
The representative of Somalia furthermore went out of
his way to misquote some of my remarks, a fact which
does not surprise me. However, I should like to refer to
some of the statements that have been made.

As for the Mexican letter, document S/12135, of 9
July 1976, addressed to you, Mr. President, we have always followed with understanding the very active campaign that Mexico is conducting against the terrorism
which affects it. We are therefore all the more surprised
that Mexico is unable to reveal a similar measure of
understanding when action is taken designed to combat
terror in cases where the victims are not Mexicans. It is
utterly incredible and beyond the realm of comprehen-
sion that political expediency should dictate to the Government of Mexico and lead it to attack a small State
defending itself against a common enemy of Mexico and
Israel, namely international terror.

I cannot hide my amazement at the fact that the representative of Yugoslavia saw fit this time too, as in cases
in the past, to intervene in a debate on the side of those
condemning Israel, in his anxious desire to demonstrate

his loyal alignment with the remarks of the so-called non-aligned countries. If any country in the world should be interested today in a move against terror, if any country in the world should have had a word of condolence to say for the victims of the hijacking and terror, then it should have been Yugoslavia. The Yugoslav delegate, let it be noted, had words of condolence for Uganda. Innocent Israeli hostages were killed too in this operation. Why had Yugoslavia not one word to say for them? It is sad indeed to see the Yugoslav Government, on each occasion in this forum, rushing to the head of the line in order to condemn Israel, regardless of the issue, blinded apparently by an extreme anti-Israel attitude and by an espousal of the cause of the new anti-Semitism in the world today. Yugoslavia, like many other countries which spoke at this debate, does not realize that international terrorism—from which it suffers no less than do others—will yet make them eat the words expressed by their representative on this occasion at this Council table.

Frankly, I regret perhaps more than many of the other interventions that of the representative of Tanzania. I regret it because of the personal high regard in which I hold him and because of the very great respect in which I, together with many others in Israel, regard his great mu'allim, teacher, the President of Tanzania, whose guest I have had the honour to be. In his legal arguments he conveniently forgets that the legal authorities which he quotes do justify, in international law, such actions as we are discussing, on the grounds of individual self-defence or collective self-defence, as I believe I pointed out when quoting at great length from authorities on international law in my speech last Friday. He and others quoted Article 2, paragraph 4 of the United Nations Charter, obligating countries to settle their disputes by peaceful means. Let me again quote O'Connell in *International Law,* second edition, page 303:

"Article 2 (4) of the United Nations Charter should be interpreted as prohibiting acts of force against the territorial integrity and political independence of nations, and not to prohibit a use of force which is lim-

ited in intention and effect to the protection of a
state's own integrity and its nationals' vital interests,
when the machinery envisaged by the United Nations Charter is ineffective in the situation."

One's mind tends to be dulled and one's memory to be
hazy as the debate goes on in this Council. Let me remind the Council that we are talking about a decision by
the Government of Israel to protect its citizens, hostages
threatened with their very lives, over 100 men, women and
children held at gun point by terrorists who had hijacked
them, who recognize no sovereignty, know no law, and
who have proved in the past that there are no limits to
their bestiality.

These are the selfsame people who shot diplomats,
bound hand and foot; who murdered sportsmen at the
Olympic games, bound hand and foot and who, in the
past, have held children hostage and were ready to slaughter them. These people were being aided and abetted by a
Government headed by a racist murderer who had applauded the slaughter of Israeli sportsmen, bound hand
and foot by the same terrorists; who had called for the
extinction of Israel in this United Nations, and who had
not only praised Hitler for the murder of six million Jews
but had proposed building a monument to Hitler—a move
which prompted even the Soviet Ambassador in Kampala to suggest to President Amin that he was going too
far.

This was the problem that faced the Government of
Israel: over 100 men, women and children, innocent hostages with terrorist guns pointed at them and with no
doubt whatsoever in anybody's mind as to the intention of
these terrorists to carry out their wicked plan and slaughter innocent people as they had done in the past. This is
the picture which must be in the mind's eye of representatives as they discuss this problem.

I regret many of the remarks made by the representative of Tanzania because I suspect they do not reflect his
true feelings or the true feelings of the Government of
Tanzania.

I reject out of hand his ridiculous attempt to equate

with an attack on Africa this Israeli rescue operation to
save its passengers. How can the representative of Tanzania make such a remark?

Would Africa have looked better if Palestinian terrorists,
in connivance with President Amin, had slaughtered
over 100 men, women and children?

Would Africa have looked better with the blood of
those innocent victims bespattering the soil of Africa?

Who has besmirched Africa? Israel, for exercising its
right to save its citizens in accordance with international
law? Or that racist régime in Uganda, waging a heroic
war against a defenceless old lady of 75 years?

Who is threatening Africa? Israel which has done so
much to help so many African countries, including many
today, in the fields of agriculture, of technology, of
health? Or the country which has dispatched this week 30
fighter-planes as reinforcements to Uganda, namely the
Government of Libya? Against whom are these planes directed and by whom are they flown? You know as well
as I do that they are directed against Kenya and Tanzania,
which have been threatened and continue to be threatened
openly in statements by the President of Uganda, and that
the planes are flown by, amongst others, PLO pilots.

Who is threatening Africa and the Africans?

Israel, whose refusal to be associated in any way with
President Amin's proposal to invade and bomb Tanzania
in 1972 brought about Uganda's break with Israel, or the
Head of State who produced in Israel and in other coun-
tries incidentally maps describing his plans to invade
Tanzania?

Who has treated Africa with contempt if not the President of Uganda, who has labelled the President of Tanzania, a man of international stature and standing, in
words which are despicable and disgusting and which I
do not wish to repeat because of the high regard which I
and my people have for the President of Tanzania.

The representative of Tanzania says he "would have
preferred principles to be given priority over expediency".

What principles are you talking about? The principles
of Uganda which are reflected in the grim recital of murder, kidnapping and banditry in the document dis-
tributed today by the Foreign Minister of Kenya? Have

you said one word here against these Ugandan principles? Is it principle or expediency which brought you, the distinguished representative of a very distinguished country, to be a co-sponsor of this resolution with Libya, the paymaster and centre of world terrorism and the country which is supplying fighter aircraft to Uganda? You know as well as I do that those planes will not be used by Uganda against Israel.

If you, my dear friend, wish to discuss principles and expediency, by all means let us do so. But let us spell them out too. Let us not be selective about principles and expediency, just as we should not be selective about terror and rescue operations.

I can only reiterate what I said on Friday: let us stop being selective. If terror is bad, it is bad everywhere, for everybody and on every occasion. It is bad whatever the colour, race, creed or nationality of the terrorist. It is bad whatever the colour, race, creed or nationality of the victim.

That is the issue before us. That is the issue with which the United Nations has failed to deal. That is the issue which will plague the whole world until we deal with it.

I listened to the remarks of the representative of Pakistan. Frankly, I would have accorded them more respect if they had not come from the representative of a régime which has locked up its entire political opposition in gaol. Here was the miserable apparition of the representative of a State whose own people were brutally driven out of Uganda by the racist régime of Idi Amin falling over himself to ingratiate himself with the oppressors of his own kith and kin. How despicable can one be?

The representative of the Soviet Union asked me why we did not quote the documents of the United Nations banning aggression in international relations. The representative of the Soviet Union must be aware that the definition of aggression adopted by the General Assembly on 15 December 1974 has been widely criticized in all legal circles. It is not a binding statement of international law and does not, incidentally, rule out an act like that carried out by Israel.

When the representative of the Soviet Union asked why Israel did not file a complaint to the Security Council, I did not know whether he was naive or he assumed that I was naive. Let me assure him that at least in this respect I cannot be characterized as such, and I have no doubt that he is anything but naive.

I ask the representative of the Soviet Union: Had we submitted a complaint, would the Soviet Union have supported us? Why was there no Soviet statement when the plane was hijacked? Why have they not condemned the terrorist acts of the PLO on many occasions in the past? Why did they not issue a statement or an appeal when the innocent hostages were being held in Entebbe? Why did not the representative of the Soviet Union have even one word to say about the fate of Mrs. Dora Bloch? Or one word of appeal directly to the representative of Uganda in this respect? After all, you have influence in Uganda.

Is the representative of the Soviet Union not aware that since 1954 the Soviet Union has blocked every attempt on the part of Israel to bring its case to the Security Council? For 22 years we have had no remedy in this Council because of the Soviet veto. We are used to cynicism in this body but the cynical question of the representative of the Soviet Union—"Why did we not complain to this Council"—when he knows in advance that, without regard to the substance of the claim, he would have vetoed it, is, I submit, the height of cynicism.

I note the Soviet representative's concern for the inviolability of African territory, and I sincerely trust that his touching concern will be reflected in Soviet Union policies and actions.

The representative of the Soviet Union talked about aggression and the inviolability of territorial integrity and national sovereignty. On these subjects I defer to him, having regard to the Soviet Union's very considerable record in these respects in Hungary, in Czechoslovakia and in other countries in Eastern Europe. My colleague from China could doubtless elaborate on this subject.

Let me assure the representative of the Soviet Union that the people of Hungary in 1956 and of Czechoslovakia in 1968 would have been only too delighted if the Soviet intervention had been to save 100 hostages and had been of a duration not exceeding 53 minutes, as was the case at Entebbe. At that time the Soviet Union went to great pains to explain its position. Sergei Kovalev, in *Sovereignity and the International Duties of Socialist Countries*, published in *Pravda* on 26 September 1968, explained the Soviet Union's justifications of such actions as follows:

"Those who talk about the 'illegal' actions of the allied socialist countries in Czechoslovakia forget that in a class society there is not and there cannot be law that is independent of class."

In a civilized society there is not and cannot be law that is independent of the loftiest principles of man, namely, freedom and dignity of man. That, my colleague from the Soviet Union, was the principle that Israel was defending at Entebbe.

Perhaps the more indicative of all in attitudes of Governments was the document from Algeria circulated to this Council, which was welcomed yesterday by the representative of the Soviet Union.

It is indeed appropriate that Algeria should speak out for the terrorists and hijackers, having regard to the fact that it was Algeria to which the first hijacked plane in operations against Israel in 1968 was directed. Algeria was directly involved in that operation and blazed the way for future terrorist exploits. One could hardly expect Algeria, which has played such a prominent part in the history of air hijacking, international kidnapping and the use of diplomatic immunity for terrorist purposes, to forfeit its place in the "hall of fame" of international terrorism. They had to get into the act. After all, what Amin did two weeks ago, they did in 1968.

In the course of all these discussions some delegations have tended to ignore the group which organized this hijacking, namely, the PLO. The PLO has issued a statement disassociating itself from this operation. This is a lie. The PFLP, to which the hijackers belonged, is a constituent member of the PLO. Members will recall that in the past the PLO denied any knowledge of the Black September organization, although Yassir Arafat's second-in-command actually commanded it. They were the group which, according to the President of the Sudan, Yassir Arafat personally instructed to execute the American and

Belgian diplomats in the Saudi Arabian Embassy in Khartoum in 1973.

The PLO's policy is a matter of record. It is one based on the most brutal terrorism, in the course of which attacks have been made upon innocent people, including unsuspecting women and children. These gangs have cut down pregnant women in cold blood in Kiryat Shmona, have shot Olympic athletes bound hand and foot, have hijacked planes, have engaged in open assassination, have held small school children hostage in Ma'alot causing the death of over 20 children and over 60 wounded. These are the same individuals who tried to impose a reign of terror on the Palestinian Arabs in the West Bank and Gaza, killing cold-bloodedly those suspected of not agreeing with them. These are the same individuals who planned the assassination of the Heads of five Arab States at Rabat in 1974. Fourteen members of the PLO were then arrested by Morocco. These are members of the same organization which executed in the most cowardly manner Wasfi Tal, the Prime Minister of Jordan, during a visit to Cairo. One of the assassins, not content with shooting the Prime Minister in the back, felt obliged to drink his blood publicly on the steps of the Sheraton Hotel in Cairo.

These are the same people who on 31 January 1974 sabotaged the oil installations in Singapore.

These are the same people who gained control of the Egyptian Embassy in Madrid and held three members of the staff, including the ambassador, as hostages.

These are the same people who murdered American and Belgian diplomats in Khartoum in 1973. These are the people who have been instrumental in destroying the Lebanese State, tearing it apart while this Council remains silent, killing tens of thousands and wounding thousands of others. These are the terrorists who kidnapped and held as hostages the ministers attending the OPEC Conference in Vienna and were then released by the Government of Algeria in an act which constituted a blatant condoning of the criminal terror acts of that group. From there they proceeded to Libya, where they were greeted and embraced by Prime Minister Jalloud of Libya, the same terrorists who had shot one of Libya's citizens a day before in Vienna.

These are the people who have brought misery, murder and assassination to the area of the Middle East and who have introduced terrorism as a form of international idiom —terrorism which affects innocent people wherever they may be.

I note too, as I am already discussing Arab compliance in terrorism, that the Government of Egypt has co-sponsored the decision of the Organization of African Unity to bring this matter before the Council. Let me remind the Council that the Government of Egypt released the cowardly assassins who shot Prime Minister Wasfi Tal of Jordan on the steps of the Sheraton Hotel in Cairo and then drank his blood. In 1970 the Government of Egypt released the terrorists from the Black September organization who had landed the hijacked Pan-American jumbo plane at Cairo airport and had blown it up at that airport.

I listened carefully to the long-drawn-out point of order made yesterday by the representative of Libya, and I must admit that I quite appreciate his concern—which he expressed again today. Who but the representative of Libya, a country which has been the paymaster and haven of international terrorism, would want to avoid a discussion in this Council on the evil: international terrorism? Libya's role in supporting international terrorism financially, militarily and politically and its involvement in attempts at the assassination of foreign leaders, including Arab Heads of State, is known to all of us, and I need not repeat it here.

However, the motivation behind the timing of the point of order is quite clear in view of information revealed over the weekend by the President of Egypt. In an interview with the Egyptian newspaper *Akhbar El Yom*, as reported by the *Middle East News Agency* on 10 July, President Sadat, who only last week expelled the Libyan Ambassador for complicity in acts of terror, discussed publicly and on the record Libya's criminal involvement in international terror.

It is apparent that Libya is the haven and refuge for the most wanted international terrorists, whose colleagues were among those who carried out the hijacking of an Air France plane to Uganda.

Indeed, while the deliberations in this Council were proceeding, forces financed and backed by Libya were actively continuing subversive operations in the Sudan against the Government of Sudan.

What further evidence is necessary to prove that Libya has forfeited its right to vote on this question and indeed is disqualified to be a member of the Security Council, a body charged with the duty to promote international peace and security?

In conclusion, may I express my appreciation to those representatives who have had the courage to take a stand clearly and unequivocally on the side of human decency and human freedom and against the scourge of international terror and those countries that support it, whether by commission or by omission.

The eloquent and moving statement by the representative of the United States of America, Mr. Scranton, and the call of all the other delegations that urged this body to take action, must evoke an echo throughout the world, regardless of political differences. I urge those countries that have already expressed their views on this issue at this table to join together to take action against hijackers and international terrorism.

I am sure that many will follow their lead. This series of meetings will decide in more ways than one whether the United Nations will continue its downward path in the grip of despots or will reassume its rightful role on behalf of humanity and international peace.

UGANDA. Mr. Abdalla: The allegations made by the Israeli delegation are not true. In the first place, on the question of complicity, the Israeli representative has referred to Mr. Cojot's words, but Cojot is just one of the people who have said something on the Entebbe incident. On the other hand, some accounts have been given by other members of the crew which are favourable to my President. For example, the plane's mechanical engineer and captain gave accounts that may be found in *Le Monde*.

As regards Mrs. Bloch, I have nothing to add to what I told the Council on Friday. As I said then, the Israeli invading forces took away with them all the hostages remaining at Entebbe, including Mrs. Bloch.

Let us not digress. We have come here to condemn the Israeli aggression and nothing else. On behalf of the Ugandan delegation I therefore totally rejecting all the allegations levelled against my country by the representative of Zionist Israel. Most of what he has said is nothing but a pack of lies.

This debate is dragging us nowhere but to a pack of lies and confusion, and, Mr. President, it is your responsibility to guide this Council so that we can arrive at a concrete condemnation of Israel.

Israel, of course, has the right to boast here of the killing of Ugandan officers and men and the destruction of property, and those so-called super-Powers try to cover up for Israel.

Perhaps it will not take a long time; it will, perhaps, be by the will of God. But those who say they are super-Powers today will be buried.

We are not children, although we are small countries. We are not to be toyed with.

The representative of Israel condemns Uganda, all the African States and the third world for what they have done. Because we are small, we cannot fight the United States, the United Kingdom and Israel. We have no arms. We have nothing to bring them to their knees. But I am telling you that one day history will tell us.

TRANSCRIPT OF THREE TELEPHONE CONVERSATIONS BETWEEN COLONEL BARUCH BAR-LEV AND PRESIDENT IDI AMIN

Wednesday, June 30, 2:00 p.m.

Bar-Lev: The president?

Amin: Who's speaking?

Bar-Lev: Colonel Bar-Lev.

Amin: How are you, my friend?

Bar-Lev: How are you feeling, sir?

Amin: I'm very pleased to hear your voice today.

Bar-Lev: I'm speaking from my home. I heard what has happened. May I ask something of you?

Amin: I agree, because you are my good friend.

Bar-Lev: I know, sir . . . My friend, you have a great opportunity to go down in history as a great peacemaker. Many people abroad, in England, in America, in Europe, are writing bad things about you, and now you have an opportunity to show them that you are a great peacemaker, if you free those people, you'll go down in history as a very great man and that will be against those who speak against you. I have been thinking about it all morning, since I heard about those things on the radio.

Amin: I have spoken satisfactorily with the Popular Front for the Liberation of Palestine. They have freed 47 of the hostages. Now they have 145 Israelis and Jews together, and other hostages, 250 altogether . . . I've just released 47 hostages and passed them to the French ambassador. It is important that you listen to Radio Uganda at 5:00 p.m.

Bar-Lev: What about the Israeli hostages?

Amin: The PFLP have now completely surrounded the remaining hostages . . . They say that if the government of Israel doesn't give in to their demands, they'll blow up the French plane and all the hostages, tomorrow at 12:00 noon Greenwich Mean Time. So I advise you, my friend, report to Rabin, General Rabin, the prime minister, I know him, he's my friend, and to General Dayan,

I know that he's my friend even though he's not in the government, that your government must do everything possible to free the hostages immediately, that's the Palestinian demand.

I'm doing the best I can, I'm giving them mattresses, blankets, medical attention. There's someone receiving medical care in hospital and on doctor's advice will be flown to Paris, when the doctor approves. I want you to do everything possible. I've just spoken to the Israelis, and they're very happy. What they said has been recorded on television. They asked me to pass this message to your government, immediately.

Bar-Lev: Mr. President, you are the ruler in your country. I think that you have the power to free these people. You will go down in history as a great man.

Amin: I want you to know that you're my friend for all time . . . I told the American journalists that Colonel Bar-Lev is my friend. I shall be pleased to see you, because I know you well. I'm prepared to make peace between the Israelis and the Arabs. I want you to tell this to your government. Anything you want from me, tell me. Report to your government that they convey this declaration through the French, that I want to accept the Palestinians' demands to save the lives of the Israelis.

Bar-Lev: Can you do something to stop them from killing?

Amin: I can do something if your government accepts their demands immediately . . . They're calling me now. At 5:00 they'll publish their final decision, and so things must be settled quickly, before tomorrow at noon. If not, they'll blow up the plane and kill all the hostages. Your government must do everything possible.

Bar-Lev: Mr. President . . . do you remember your mother, who said to you before she died that you should help the Israelis in the Holy Land? If you want to be a great and holy man, and to go down in history, and perhaps even receive the Nobel prize, you must free these people . . . It's a great opportunity. It's been given to you by God, to show everyone that you are great and good.

Amin: How are you, my friend, and your wife?

Bar-Lev: They are all fine. Do you want me to come to you?

Amin: I'll be pleased to see you.

Bar-Lev: Can you stop them killing until I arrive?

Amin: Can you appeal to your government quickly, so that I can get an answer?

Bar-Lev: Very well, sir. I'll call you back later.

Amin: You can call me whenever you like. I'm waiting . . . I'm speaking from the airport. I haven't slept for three days. I want to save these people.

Wednesday, June 30, 11:05 p.m.

Bar-Lev: I've passed on your advice to the government through a friend. They said they accept your advice and will act on it, through the French government, as you proposed. Now I'm trying to find a way to visit you . . .

Amin: If you come, you'll be at home . . . because you're my good friend. No one will harm you.

Bar-Lev: I can trust in you and in God. No one else.

Amin: My daughter [son?] Sharon sends her [his?] regards.

Bar-Lev: Thank you, Your Excellency. Until I find a way of coming to visit you, can you take every possible step to make sure that nothing happens to the hostages?

Amin: . . . Now I'm with the leader of the PFLP. He's only just arrived. The man I negotiated with previously was their number two. Now the right man has arrived. Forty minutes ago he told me that he won't change his decision, if he doesn't receive a reply by tomorrow at 10:00 a.m., Uganda time . . .

Bar-Lev: Your Excellency, I'm doing everything I can to come to see you. Perhaps I can be useful to you . . . when I heard the news on the radio, I said: Now my friend Idi Amin Dada has a great opportunity, a chance to do something really great. Everyone will talk about him. Please, stop the bloodshed. I'll try to come and find another solution.

Amin: But they've moved 145 Jews together, and they said they will surround them with high explosives, so there must be an immediate answer.

Bar-Lev: I'm only a private individual . . . Remember, I always gave you good advice and never gave you bad advice. It's your country and you're the president and you have the power. If something happens you'll be blamed. And if you save them, you'll be a holy man. What is the situation, Your Excellency?

Amin: They have refused. They have surrounded them and they say they can blow up all the hostages and the Ugandan army around them.

Bar-Lev: I understand. I don't think they have that much explosive. How could they come by plane with so much explosive? Your Excellency, I want you to understand that they want to free murderers, who committed many murders. They killed women and children. I don't believe that if someone tried to kill you, you would allow him to go. It's not easy to persuade people here to release murderers. You must understand. I am speaking to you as a soldier. You would never give up and free a murderer. It's not an easy thing to do. I am certain that you, as president of a state, won't let anyone else decide what to do in your country.

Amin: I absolutely agree with what you say. But the situation is very complicated now, because these people brought complete charges of TNT even on their bodies, and it's very complicated.

Bar-Lev: Sir, it will take me another day or two till I can reach you and be of help to you. Can you keep them quiet for a couple of days?

Amin: They refused and said that the deadline is tomorrow noon. They won't wait for me, they said they will commit suicide with the hostages. They've already prepared everything to press the button, to blow up everything with themselves.

Bar-Lev: Where are the people, in the hotel or the plane? Where are they sleeping?

Amin: In the old terminal of Entebbe, we built a modern terminal . . . The old one is just a building, and that's where they're holding all the hostages. There's no plane there. They asked us to remove all the planes. All air force personnel are now out of Entebbe . . . They've put high explosives around everything . . . Two lines of high explosives, outside and inside. They came with high explosives in the plane, in boxes. I think that certain people, perhaps in Athens, received something not to check the boxes . . .

Bar-Lev: Where is the French plane?

Amin: Close to me. They have some people in it with high explosives, and they're prepared to blow it up . . . If you can persuade your government to release those people,

the ones you call criminals . . . It's better to save the
lives of 200 people . . . They said they are going to kill
them all. They'll start by blowing up the plane, then
they'll kill everybody with high explosives. They said
that if any plane comes to Uganda, they'll automatically
blow up everything. They want to negotiate through
France. I told them that I have some friends in Israel,
like you, General Dayan, even the prime minister, that
I can negotiate with them, but they said they want only
the French government.

Bar-Lev: Remember, sir, you have a great opportunity,
given to you by God.

Amin: Tell your government they must put pressure on the
Kenyan government to release the prisoners they caught.
Otherwise something terrible will happen to Kenya. The
leader of the Palestinians told me that if I can get in
touch with you, I must tell you about Kenya . . . If not,
Kenya will be terribly punished.

Bar-Lev: Good, sir. I'll do the best I can, but I'm a private
person. I saw a great opportunity for you to go down
in history as a great man, a holy man . . . I'll try to do
what you asked.

Amin: Tell your government, I'd like to see you in a very
important position.

Bar-Lev: Thank you very much and good night, sir.

Thursday, July 1, after 10:00 a.m. (shortly before expiration of ultimatum)

Amin: Inform your government officially that the PFLP
will make an announcement at 11:00 a.m. [2:00 p.m.
East Africa time], that's the only answer I can give you.
Those are the instructions I received from the front.
OK? We had very difficult talks till now. It's best that
you wait for the announcement.

Bar-Lev: Can you tell what's happening? What are the
main points?

Amin: You know that what I'm saying isn't secret, because my voice is recorded on the Voice of America.

Bar-Lev: Can you prevent them from doing anything before I arrive? I'm coming with some very interesting
proposals.

Amin: Call me after you hear the announcement.

Bar-Lev: Sir, how did it happen that additional PFLP people reached Uganda? There were only 6 in the plane, and now there are more than 6 . . . 20 or more . . . How did they enter?

Amin: They were in the plane. There weren't only 6, there were about 30 from all over the world. Nobody came by another plane to Uganda. For your information, I tried to put the hostages in a bus and to drive them in a different direction, but the hijackers wanted all of them to be brought to the old air terminal. It's very difficult for me, I did the best I could, but I think that your government is responsible for the fate of the Israelis and the passengers with dual nationality, and the rest of the hostages.

Bar-Lev: My government is trying to help by sending me to you with some new ideas . . . Once again I say to you, you have an opportunity given you by God to do a great deed that will go down in history . . . Don't be influenced by these PFLP people just because they are sitting next to you and telling you all kinds of stories . . .

Amin: I'm not influenced by the PFLP. I make my own decisions, and I am doing everything I can to save the lives of the Israelis and the other passengers. So what you said about wanting to come to Uganda, it isn't necessary that you should come. If you have something extremely important to tell me, listen to the announcement, phone me, and I'll tell you what to do. I want to tell you again that had I not done everything I could, all the hostages including the crew wouldn't be alive now . . . You must consider my position, you mustn't insult me as you just did when you said that I am collaborating with the hijackers, who are not innocent people. But my position is extremely difficult and you must realize it. The whole world must realize it.

Bar-Lev: I know three things about you: that you are a great soldier, a Ugandan, and a man who trusts only in God, so I think that you can prevent a massacre and bloodshed. Nobody can give you instructions. You can do what is good for the people of your country and as commanded by God. The people from the PFLP have no right to do this within the territory of your country.

Amin: They surounded the hostages with high explosives

and they moved my soldiers away. The lives of the hostages are in their hands. What can I do now?

Bar-Lev: You can tell them that they are your guests and that they are placing your country in a difficult position ... If such a thing were to happen in Israel, and it did happen, we managed to free hostages. The front has never succeeded in doing what they want in Israel, even when they had high explosives, because we didn't permit them to. The world will never accept the claim that you and your great army couldn't overpower 6 to 10 people. How will the world believe that the PFLP can do what it likes in Uganda, and the entire Ugandan army cannot overpower them?

Amin: I know that you are saying that they never succeeded in your country and that I can kill the terrorists.

Bar-Lev: You are granting them protection. They are living in Uganda as if they were in a hotel. You are a good friend of the Palestinians and the Arabs, so they shouldn't place you in a difficult situation and harm you. They mustn't say and think that they are operating in Uganda and they don't care what happens in Uganda. They must consider your problem, not just you consider theirs. You are a good friend of theirs and they must think about you too. I think that they won't do anything if Field Marshal General Idi Amin asks them to do nothing and delay operations for a day until I can arrive.

Amin: I want to tell you that they are not living like guests in a hotel. They are together with the hostages and if we take any action we are endangering the lives of the hostages, they even [?] together. They are not my guests. I agree that I am their good friend. I want peace in Palestine. It is the responsibility of your government. You must not continue with this Zionist policy and activity.

Sunday, July 4, 1:00 a.m. (after Israeli army raid. Amin did not yet know about the raid)

Bar-Lev: Sir, I want to thank you for your cooperation and I thank you very much.

Amin: You know I did not succeed.

Bar-Lev: Thank you very much for your cooperation. What? The cooperation didn't succeed? Why?

Amin: Have I done anything at all?

Bar-Lev: I just want to thank you, sir, for the cooperation.

Amin: Have I done anything?

Bar-Lev: I did exactly what you wanted.

Amin: Wh—— Wh—— What happened?

Bar-Lev: What happened?

Amin: Yes?

Bar-Lev: I don't know.

Amin: Can't you tell me?

Bar-Lev: No. I don't know. I have been requested to thank you for your cooperation.

Amin: Can you tell me about the suggestion you mentioned?

Bar-Lev: I have been requested by a friend with good connections in the government to thank you for the cooperation. I don't know what was meant by it, but I think you do know.

Amin: I don't know because I've only now returned hurriedly from Mauritius.

Bar-Lev: Ah . . .

Amin: . . . In order to solve the problem before the ultimatum expires tomorrow morning.

Bar-Lev: I understand very well, sir . . . Thank you for the cooperation. Perhaps I'll call you again tomorrow morning. Do you want me to call you again tomorrow morning?

Amin: Yes.

Bar-Lev: Very well, thank you sir. Goodbye.